APOSTATE

TITLES FROM KEVIN SWANSON

Family Bible Study Guides

Genesis: A Family Bible Study Guide
Psalms I: A Family Bible Study Guide
Psalms II: A Family Bible Study Guide
Psalms III/IV: A Family Bible Study Guide
Proverbs I: A Family Bible Study Guide
Proverbs II: A Family Bible Study Guide
Proverbs III: A Family Bible Study Guide
Matthew: A Family Bible Study Guide

Christian Curriculum Project

Christian Classics Study Guide - Volume I
Great Christian Classics: Five Great Narratives of the Faith
Christian Classics Study Guide - Junior Level
What Does the Bible Say About That?
Proverbs: A Companion Lesson Book for Children

The Second Mayflower
Upgrade: 10 Secrets to the Best Education for Your Child

Audio/Media Resources

Vision for Generations (MP3)
Vision for Generations (CD)
Vision for Generations (DVD)
Reforming the Church in the 21st Century (CD)
Family Economics Audio Series (MP3)
Family Economics Audio Series (CD)
Family Economics Video Series (DVD)
The Best Of Generations Radio, Vol. 1 (MP3)

APOSTATE

An Exposé of the Men Who Dismantled the Christian West

Kevin Swanson

ISBN: 978-0-9853651-5-8

Scripture taken from the King James Version.

Published by
Generations with Vision
10461 South Parker Road
Parker, Colorado, 80134
www.generationswithvision.com

Editors: Ann Sechrist, Susan Malone, Carol Swanson, Julianna Dotten
Production Management: Joshua Schwisow
Layout: Winslow Robbins
Graphic Design: Ray Suzuki, Winslow Robbins

For more information on this and
other titles from Generations with Vision,
visit www.generationswithvision.com or call 1-888-839-6132.

CONTENTS

PREFACE

J ohn Locke. Jean-Jacques Rousseau. John Stuart Mill. John-Paul Sartre. John Dewey. John Lennon. John Steinbeck.

Each of these should be familiar names. They were all "men of renown," the greatest men of the age. They were men of towering importance in the unfolding, or rather unraveling of Western civilization; and together they defined the modern world. John Locke and Jean-Jacques Rousseau set the trajectory for modern political philosophy. John-Paul Sartre influenced culture and entertainment, and John Dewey was the father of modern, secular education. John Lennon and his band sold more albums than any other musical group in the history of mass media. However, of more significance for the present treatise is their given name. Each of them inherited 1500 years of Christian thinking and culture. They were born in Christian families in Europe or America, and their parents named them John after the Apostle who wrote the fourth Gospel.

Many years ago, the West had a rich Christian heritage. That is why many parents named their sons John. Between 400 AD and 1400 AD, the Christian Gospel penetrated the entire Western world. But after the 15th century another religion or faith commitment called "Humanism" worked its way into the consciousness of the West. It was highly organized, complete with sacraments, institutions, buildings, ethical systems, social theories, and cultural emanations. To this day, the early Christian influence is recognizable: Christianity has made an indelible impact on language, art, architecture, music, education, hospitals and healthcare, charity, science, political freedoms, the treatment of women, respect for human life, names given to children, and the elimination of pagan practices like widow-burning, child-sacrifice, and chattel slavery.

For over a thousand years, Christian burials replaced cremation, and it would have been hard to find the pagan practices of cannibalism, homosexuality, body mutilation, and tattoos (all of which were almost completely absent from Christian societies). Then at the break of the 20th century, everything changed.

Because history often seems to play out in slow motion, it is not difficult to trace the macro trends. Within one hundred years, the powerful ideas of the philosophers began to shape the minds of the most brilliant writers, educators, musicians and artists. In succeeding generations, these ideas formed the course content for the liberal arts universities. Finally, after another hundred years or so, these ideas filtered into the mass culture. It is a three step process, and this is how the West was lost.

First, the intellectual philosophers developed revolutionary humanist ideas which they incorporated into their own lives. These ideas will be thoroughly reviewed in the first section of this book.

Next, the great literary masters and artists incarnated these philosophical ideas in literary and art forms, which were then taught in the liberal arts universities and high schools. There is no better way to infiltrate nations with new ideas than through the educational systems. How else would one overturn all of Western civilization without corrupting each successive generation of pastors, priests, political leaders, and teachers by way of the universities and seminaries? This is how we have gone from the New England Primer's first lesson, "In Adam's fall, We sinned all" to *Heather Has Two Daddies* (pro-homosexual curriculum for first grade children used in public schools in the later 20th century). Profound cultural changes take a civilization from Johann Sebastian Bach's chorales in 1700 to Eminem's popular "rape rap" in 2000. If ideas shape the culture, then these powerful forces replace Puritan leaders like John Winthrop and Oliver Cromwell with secular humanist leaders like Barrack Obama and Josef Stalin. It was the liberal arts education and humanist trends in "literature" that reshaped everything else including seminaries, pastors, and churches. For the purposes of this historical survey, we will look at four prominent works of literature which contributed greatly to the apostasy, the rise in humanist thinking, and the decline of Western civilization.

Finally, the philosophies of the 19th century penetrated the mass culture through mass media in the 20th and 21st centuries. At least 95%

of present day perspectives and attitudes, culture, media, family life, and education are rooted in the destructive ideology of the 18th and 19th century philosophers. It is vitally important that the reader be able to discern those ideas. The incarnation of these philosophies in mass culture will be explained in the final section of the book.

The first phase of the fall of Western civilization took place between 1700 and 1850. The second phase played out between 1820 and 1920, and the final stage is happening right now through mass media. None of this would have materialized without the centralization of power in both universities and mass media outlets that could impose a uniform world and life view on the Western world.

Nevertheless, there is always hope for new civilizations and cultures in the future. The monolith of Western civilization is no more. It is hard to reassemble a deconstructed civilization. Perhaps the best historical comparison available to the present day is the Fall of Rome in 475 A.D. After centralization comes decentralization until equilibrium is achieved in Christian society based on the Trinitarian law-order (that can effectively balance unity and diversity). We are on the cusp of the decentralization of information and media sources, while simultaneously we are witnessing the gradual collapse of the brick-and-mortar university monopoly over Western thought and economics. The time has come to reform and rebuild the ideas and educational systems that make up the Western world.

BY THEIR FRUITS YE SHALL KNOW THEM

As we trace the plight of Western civilization, we shall examine both the ideas and the lives of the great civilization changers of the last three hundred years. Generally, the philosophies are difficult to understand for the layman. However, Jesus Christ provided a useful test for identifying false teachers, one that may be employed by even the more obtuse of His followers: "By their fruits ye shall know them," He said. This is helpful, because most people reading the "great" philosophers find it hard to follow the thread of their ideas. Sometimes they will say one thing, and then contradict themselves more or less in the next paragraph. They will purposefully obscure their true presuppositional framework and only hint at their real agenda (so as to be missed by some and caught only by other apostatizing souls). In the end, the truth is obscured and lost in their pseudo-intellectualism, convoluted argumentation, and academic hubris. Thus, according to Jesus Christ it is quite appropriate for the average Christian to analyze a man's philosophies by the fruit of his life and his work: "By their fruits ye shall know them!"

This is why it is important to know that Marx's daughters committed suicide, that Rousseau abandoned his five children on the steps of an orphanage, and that Ernest Hemingway wished to kill his father and then took his own life. For those who may not have the time to study the confusing labyrinth of these men's twisted minds, it is sometimes more helpful to examine the "fruits" and draw a quick conclusion as to the nature of the "tree." Even if the student fails to pick up on the trajectory of the ideas laid out in the writings of this book, at the least he should know something about the lives of the men who served as the intellectual leaders of the fall of the Western world.

If the major academic institutions in this nation led the apostasy from the Christian faith, it is important to assess the content of their educational programs. From the beginning, colleges such as Harvard, Yale, Princeton, Bowdoin, and William and Mary incorporated a thoroughly Greek and Roman education. It should be understood that this was not a distinctively Christian education. At first, there were men like Increase Mather (the last of the Puritans and an early President of Harvard College) who fought hard to establish a Christian education at Harvard. In 1685, Mather complained that the pastors trained at the college knew more of Cicero and Aristotle than they did of Paul, Moses, and David. He did what he could to purge Aristotle's Ethics from the school and replace it with biblical ethics—but to no avail. Harvard College was under complete control of the Latitudinarians by 1705.[1]

It wasn't as much the Greeks and the Romans that set the course for the Western world as it was the philosophers who attended those universities. In the end, it was Christian apostates like Jean-Jacques Rousseau, Jeremy Bentham, John Stuart Mill, Karl Marx, Ralph Waldo Emerson, Charles Darwin, and John Dewey who made the difference. At first, they may have drunk deeply of the humanist wells of the old Greek and Roman writers, then later developed their own version of humanism for the Christianized west. Whereas Christian thought overwhelmed

---

1. Michael G. Hall, *The Last American Puritan - The Life of Increase Mather* (Middletown: Wesleyan University Press, 1988), 199, 321.

pagan thinking from 475 A.D. through 1200 A.D., it was humanist ideologies that would overcome Christian thought in the West during the subsequent eight hundred years (from 1200 A.D. through 2000 A.D.).

The literary giants took their queues from the philosophical giants and weaned the American liberal arts curriculum away from Christian thinking entirely. It was a gradual process, but by the end of the 19th century John Calvin and John Bunyan were far less important in America's high school literature curriculum than the great Transcendentalists and humanists such as Ralph Waldo Emerson, Walt Whitman, William Shakespeare, Nathaniel Hawthorne, and Mark Twain.

If American secular high schools of the 20th century were self-consciously humanist in their trajectory, it would be helpful for Christians to consider the lists of core books which made up the liberal arts curriculum. A critical worldview analysis of these books is certainly in order for anybody who cares about the demise of the Christian faith in the West. This is the gist of the second section of the book. Typically the books assigned include classics such as William Shakespeare's *Macbeth*, Nathaniel Hawthorne's *Scarlet Letter*, Stephen Crane's *Red Badge of Courage*, Mark Twain's *Huckleberry Finn*, Ernest Hemingway's *Old Man and the Sea*, John Steinbeck's *Of Mice and Men*, or J.D. Salinger's *Catcher in the Rye*.[2]

For those who didn't pay attention in their high school liberal arts classes, there was always college. The university provided even more opportunities for total immersion in the humanist ideas of the philosophers and the liberal arts masters.

Most high schools and colleges in the latter 19th and 20th centuries never used Augustine's *Confessions* or John Bunyan's *Pilgrim's Progress* in the literature class. In the vast majority of the schools, they selected the books written by Unitarians, Transcendentalists, Latitudinarians, Atheists, Deists, and Greeks first. For most students, the writings of Nathaniel Hawthorne and Mark Twain were far more important than the Sunday School stories. After all, *these were the "great" books and the "great" authors, and they shaped the thinking of hundreds of millions of American school children for the last five to six generations.*

This is no time for naiveté for the Christian student. Educational

2. Reference http://nylusmilk.wordpress.com/2008/11/28/top-10-most-taught-books-in-high-school/, and http://www.goodreads.com/shelf/show/high-school-literature

method and content are both important. If we have learned anything from the last two hundred years, it is that ideas can be extremely dangerous. Schools can be intellectually and spiritually fatal for the unwary student. Should a family set their children at the feet of the wrong teachers, they will destroy the faith within a generation or two.

In this book, we will first proceed with the seminal thinkers: the philosophers who dismantled the Christian faith in the Western world and replaced it with humanist ideas and institutions. As always happens to empires built on man-centered ideas, these humanist empires will soon collapse. The Christian foundations of Western civilization were sound before the humanist empires came along. But when their philosophies introduced dryrot into the foundations that were originally Christian, they planted the seeds of their own destruction. By the end of this book, I hope the reader will fully understand how this happened.

THE WAR OF IDEAS

Why then spend any time grappling with the philosophies of these great thinkers who led the Western world to its present state? The answer should be obvious because it is contained within the question. If these ideas are widely incorporated into modern life, certainly we ought to understand something about the ideas upon which our system operates today. However, we are also called to battle. Not all ideas contain equal truth value, and some ideas can bring about unimaginable destruction! For the Christian to refuse to fight in the war of ideas is to capitulate and to lose the war against the world, the flesh, and the devil. Paul delivers these marching orders in 2 Corinthians 10:4-5. It is our duty to "cast down imaginations and every high thing that exalts itself above the knowledge of God in Christ." It is not for us to fear evil. It is for us to fear God, and reprove the unfruitful works of darkness.

For the love of our families and our fellow man, we need to be aware of the influence of the exceedingly powerful humanist philosophers, and the real and present danger that attends the outworking of their ideas. Dr. Benjamin Wiker, in his book *Ten Books That Screwed up the World and Five Others That Didn't Help*, tells the story of the Scottish essayist, Thomas Carlyle. He "was once scolded at a dinner party for endlessly chattering about books: 'Ideas, Mr. Carlyle, ideas, nothing but ideas!' To which he replied, 'There once was a man called Rousseau who wrote a book containing nothing but ideas. The second edition was bound in the skins of those who laughed at the first.'" Of course, Carlyle speaks of the bloody nightmare of the French Revolution that formed out of the ideas of Rousseau.

The battle of ideas is harrowing and difficult, so as a father, I am hesitant to have my young children engage it by themselves. The great thinkers can be dangerous men, and they are very accomplished at what they do. Our young men and women may have a hard time comprehending the writings of the philosophers, let alone understanding the harmful character of the ideas expressed. On first pass, they will not catch all of the nuances, the double entendres, and the worldview perspectives conveyed in the writings. I want to bring them into the battle of ideas, but I know they will not be able to wage war at the level of these literary masters.

I would freely admit that the battle is not for everybody. It is neither for the faint of heart, nor the faithless, nor for the immature student. But the reader must understand that liberal arts education at the high school and college levels, in secular schools, Christian schools, classical schools, and home schools have generally failed to properly address the antithesis. The source of much of Western apostasy is found in the liberal arts classroom. *An uncritical consideration of the "Great" Literature programs is perilous and corrupting.* I place the word "great" between quotations for a reason. Aristotle was *not* great, and Thomas Aquinas was *not* great.[3] Karl Marx and Mark Twain were *not* great thinkers or writers. They may have been skilled at wielding the sword of the pen, but they used it for the wrong ends. These men openly opposed a biblical theory of truth and ethics. For some reason, even Christian academics are very reticent to

---

3. The Reformers understood these issues clearly. John Knox's dying words included the warning, *"Beware of the universities!*

Also, the great German Reformer, Martin Luther warned of Aristotelian thinking that had crept into the church: *"My soul longs for nothing so ardently as to expose and publicly shame that Greek buffoon, who like a spectre has befooled the Church. If Aristotle had not lived in the flesh I should not hesitate to call him a devil."*

Luther continued, *"The schoolmen had forced the contents of divine revelation into the thought forms of the Aristotelian philosophy. In course of time they had borrowed from him not only the dialectical forms, but also his definitions and principles. Aristotle had behaved himself as the proverbial camel. At first the schoolmen had allowed him to protrude his nose into the tent of Christian theology. He had ended by forcing his way in completely. Philosophy at first had acted as the handmaid of theology, but finally became its mistress. Hagar had usurped Sarah's place. The teaching of the Church had been corrupted by a rationalism, in which Aristotle had been permitted to sit in judgment on Christ and the Apostles. . .The greatest part of my cross is to be forced to see brothers with brilliant minds, born for useful studies, compelled to spend their lives and waste their labor in these follies."*

criticize the major humanist thinkers who destroyed the Christian West. *Incredibly, one philosophy professor from a Christian college even attempts a soft sell on Karl Marx,* claiming that, "Marx, at least philosophically, must be credited with good intentions, but his ideas have been applied badly. Any great idea can be perverted."[4] This analysis of Karl Marx is at best blindness. At worst, the professor renders complicit aid to a madman whose evil ideas resulted in the deaths of hundreds of millions of people! All of Marx's "great" ideas stand in stark opposition to a biblical metaphysic, a biblical epistemology, a biblical theory of history, a biblical ethic, a biblical social theory, a biblical political theory, and a biblical economic theory. How could any Christian ever approve of this man's "great" ideas?

Another liberal arts professor at a well-known Christian college goes to great lengths to defend Hawthorne's "hell-fired" tale, *The Scarlet Letter* as a "Christian classic" that in this man's words, portrays "the heart of the Christian gospel."[5] Clearly, Nathaniel Hawthorne would have disagreed with the good professor. Many, if not most Christian liberal arts professors hesitate to criticize the philosophical method, the metaphysical construct, the meta-ethical theory, the political theory, the social theory, or the economic theory of the "Great" thinkers, because they themselves lack a well-defined biblical epistemology and ethic. The Bible for them is a collection of stories that bears no distinctive worldview. They cannot see that the Bible provides a law-order for life, and the only basis for truth. They prefer natural law or Aristotelian law or Jeremy Bentham's utilitarianism to biblical law. For this reason, these "Christian" intellectuals render themselves powerless in the battle of ideas, and they only give aid to the enemy.

Some of those who read the great Humanist (or Apostate) writers wish to separate the content of their writings from their method. But can one really enjoy the *experience* of the story while rejecting the *meaning* of the story? The American author, Flannery O'Connor would never separate the story itself from the meaning of the story: "The whole story is the meaning, because it is an experience, not an abstraction."[6] Would Paul have appreciated the artistry of the idol sculptors of Athens, while

---

4. John Mark Reynolds, ed., *The Great Books Reader* (Minneapolis: Bethany House, 2011), 513.
5. Leland Ryken, *Realms of Gold* (Wheaton: Harold Shaw, 1991), 153.
6. Flannery O'Connor, *Mystery and Manners*, ed. Sally and Robert Fitzgerald (New York: Farrar, Straus & Giroux, 1961), 73.

APOSTATE

at the same time condemning the idolatry of it? Or would he forget to condemn the idolatry in his fixation on the method? This business of remaining "unspotted from the world" (James 1:27) is not easy to achieve. As Christians sidle up to the artistry of the idolatrous and the banquet tables of the idols in Athens, they run the risk of imbibing deeply of the idolatry itself. They may wish to borrow the "turn of a phrase" from humanist authors or they may admire their use of satire. But it is far too tempting for the serious Christian liberal arts student to take on the academic pride of the Greeks, the high-handed skepticism and cynicism of Mark Twain, and the tortured, doubting mind of Nathaniel Hawthorne. How can one approve of a humanist classic (written by the Greeks or the Christian apostates) for its story and method, while rejecting the ideas contained in it?

This is not to say that one can never borrow anything from the pagans. They brush their teeth and trim their nails too. When analyzing their stories and writings, one must cut ever so carefully between the contours of truth and error. I recommend a thin scalpel. This is especially true when the writers themselves are the product of one thousand years of Christian heritage, while at the same time they are nurturing a slow and steady apostasy that will work its way out over three hundred years. When they are in the midst of the war of ideas, Christians must be extremely careful not to synthesize the ideas of the enemy. Regrettably, this is the sad legacy of Christian seminaries, colleges, and schools for the last 800 years of history. One would think that the last few believers remaining in the Western world have learned this lesson by now.

Of course Christians belong in the battle, but they must *do more battle*. Liberal arts instruction in most Christian colleges and secular colleges is more toxic to the Christian faith than any other teaching coming out of these schools.[7] Because the Christian liberal arts schools fail to engage the antithesis in the battle of ideas, they are responsible for the failure of the faith in the Western world. This is why practically every Christian college and seminary has rejected all semblance of the biblical faith over the last 800 years (since Thomas Aquinas). All the while, these Christian institutions are preparing the future pastors, educational

---

7. Unbelievably, nearly twice as many Religion Department Heads in Christian Colleges hold to evolutionary naturalism in origins than Science Department Heads; and it is not because the Religion Department heads are better trained in science! The liberal arts students and professors are almost always more likely to compromise with humanism than others. Source: Ken Ham, *Already Compromised*.

leaders, and political leaders to lead our nations towards more man-centered humanism or liberalism. The liberal arts colleges usually tell their students to "join in the great conversation with the great thinkers and writers in Western civilization."[8] We say instead, *Welcome to the Great Confrontation!*

8. Reynolds, *Great Books Reader*, 12.

APOSTATE

Part I

THE NEPHILIM

One

APOSTASY

Western civilization is over. Everybody knows it. There may be a few remnants from the old order that wish it were not so. Here and there, reformers are still working to salvage small pieces of it. But the 21st century Westerner knows full well that the old order is over. And, at present, there is no new order to take its place.

It should go without saying that cultural Christianity has faded in both Europe and North America. This means that the majority of people in these lands have given up on both the Christian faith and the culture that must always accompany faith. Culture is religion externalized, so a loss of Christian faith means a loss of Christian culture. People always live out their fundamental beliefs. They may *say* they believe one thing while their lives reflect some other creed. In a world of a thousand hypocrisies and lies, there is only one way to determine the true creed of a man. Observe his life and culture.

The Western world has lost any meaningful faith in the resurrection of

Jesus Christ. This is evident in its dress, music, politics, and economics. There are millions of possible examples to which we might refer in order to prove this point, including the abandonment of Christian burial (in favor of cremation), the neglect of Sunday worship services, the pattern of birth implosions, the widespread acceptance of witchcraft and cannibalism (vampirism),[1] and body mutilation, as well as the wholesale acceptance of homosexuality in the schools, university, and media. Now, more people celebrate the Day of the Dead (Halloween) than the Resurrection of Christ (Easter).[2] The most popular children's book series of the 20th Century concerns a fictional hero named Harry Potter who is immersed in witchcraft and trained by a homosexual.[3] As the novels were made into motion pictures, the franchise netted the highest box office receipt totals of any movie franchise in the history of film ($2.4 billion), handily exceeding the Star Wars franchise.[4] All of the above are obvious examples of a macro-cultural shift away from the Christian faith, and much of this has taken place within just the last thirty years!

Consensus on the definition of Western civilization is elusive, to say the least. Yet most historians would agree that this conglomerate of Europe and North America still retains something Christian in its worldview foundation, language, culture, music, government, law, and science. Throughout the centuries, the Christian worldview formed some degree of synthesis with Greek Humanism (during the Constantinian era, the Renaissance, and the Enlightenment). Now whatever is left of that synthesis is dying. The objective of this book is to identify the cause of the decline and fall of Western civilization. The blame cannot rest on the Christian faith, because there is scarcely anything left of the Christian worldview in the foundations of this civilization. It would be hard to find a country that would identify itself as "Christian." As shall be demonstrated in this book, the materialist worldview has assumed control of the major institutions in the Western world. For the post-modernist, this secular humanist vision is quickly passing from high utopian expectations to dystopian disappointment. It will prove to be

1. http://www.time.com/time/arts/article/0,8599,1942086,00.html
2. Retail Survey Shows Record Halloween Participation, http://www.wicz.com/news2005/viewar-ticle.asp?a=25152
3. http://en.wikipedia.org/wiki/List_of_best-selling_books
http://today.msnbc.msn.com/id/21407911/ns/today-books/t/dumbledores-outing-gives-text-new-meaning/
4. http://www.boxofficemojo.com/franchises/?view=Franchise&sort=sumgross&order=-DESC&p=.htm

a failure. Already, sociologists and political leaders are questioning the future state of the Western nations that face a significant birth implosion and immigration from both the South and Middle-East.[5] Will Islam content itself with a pluralist, secular state?[6] Will the existentialist-driven decline in the Western birthrates create a similar problem for the Islamists enough to reduce their influence in Europe? These are serious questions facing the social architects and political leaders of our day.

Meanwhile, the Christian faith is more dispersed than ever before, as the diaspora pushes Christian believers into the nooks and crannies of countries all over the world. Whatever remains of Western civilization is fading. How did we get to this point? That is the question at hand.

THE NEPHILIM

The Christian influence in the West has dissipated, and my mission in this book is to chronicle *how it happened*. It is always helpful to study history both to better understand the present and to better prepare for the future. As the old saying goes, there are those who make things happen, those who watch things happen, and those who wonder what happened. For lack of knowledge, people do perish (Hosea 4:6). I take this to be a bad thing, and would like to do what I can to prevent it from happening.

I should make it clear to my readers from the outset that I am a Christian. I believe in the historical death and resurrection of a man named Jesus Christ. I believe that Jesus Christ is the Son of God, and retains both a human and divine nature. I believe that He sits at the right hand of the Father, and maintains sovereign control over all of history. This is the orthodox Christian faith which was taught by men like the Apostle Paul, Augustine of Hippo, and Patrick of Ireland, and this is what I believe.

I do not believe the Christian faith will ever disappear from the earth. I believe that the kingdom of Jesus Christ will outlast every kingdom that has ever attempted to rule the world, including the Roman Empire, the Spanish Empire, the French Empire, the English Empire, the American Empire, the Soviet Union, and the growing Islamic empire. Most of these kingdoms have already disappeared. Always, history serves as a formidable

5. http://books.google.com/books/about/The_Death_of_the_West.html?id=MTrg__Jyf0kC
6. As of 2013, nations like Egypt and Iraq are moving away from the "secular" state ideal towards the Islamic state, and France and Germany may soon follow.

apologetic for the Christian faith.

Nevertheless, there appears to be a winnowing occurring in this century and *it is pervasive*. Those of us who are still hanging on to the faith are disappointed to see it happen. It is unprecedented in its extent and rapidity, as far as I can tell from my read of history.

How does this happen? What are the ultimate causes at work in these gigantic cultural and religious seismic shifts? From the perspective of a Christian worldview, the doctrine of God's sovereignty over reality is fundamental. "Man proposes, but God disposes." Christians automatically reject the idea that the devil has taken complete control of things, or that man frustrates God's purposes. At the same time, man is responsible for his apostasies and rebellion. This is the plain teaching of the Old Testament prophets in relation to the apostasy of Judah and Israel. The fault for the failure of faith lies with men who failed to "disciple the nations" generation by generation (Matt. 28:18-20). If the faith faltered somewhere between 1620 and 2020, it is fair to say that Christians "dropped the ball." Somebody must have "turned back in the day of battle," and refused to walk in God's laws, and neglected to pass the heritage on to their children. (Psalm 78:5-11).

The time is right for this book, because apostasy is in full force in America. A recent poll conducted by the Barna organization found that only 0.5% of American young people (ages 18-25) hold a Christian worldview as compared to 14% in the previous generation.[7] This indicates that an astounding 97% of children raised in homes where parents still retain a Christian view of God (as an Absolute) are turning away from the faith in a single generation! Some polls indicate lower apostasy rates as judged by church attendance and similar indicators. Whatever the case, the vast majority of successive generations no longer embrace primary Christian beliefs that have formed the Western worldview for 1500 years! *Apostasy is now.*

My goal is to salvage something of the Christian faith in English-speaking, Western nations during the fall of Western civilization. I want to establish the Christian faith in my own family, specifically in my children's and grandchildren's generations. But it is more than the faith that is fading. Our civilization, our social systems, and our economic

---

7. http://www.barna.org/barna-update/article/21-transformation/252-barna-survey-examines-changes-in-worldview-among-christians-over-the-past-13-years

systems are failing too. Rudyard Kipling foretold this predicament when he associated those two vital elements for human civilization: "The women had no more children, and the men lost reason and faith."[8] Both are happening simultaneously. As men become increasingly conscious of their humanist and relativist worldviews, they lose the will to carry on their civilizations. Birth rates implode as men lose a sense of purpose and meaning. Their purely existentialist and materialist worldviews are incapable of sustaining a civilization.

It is important that every person in Europe and North America realizes that this is a time of apostasy. Sadly, so few people recognize the symptoms of a dying social system and a dying culture. They don't concern themselves with articles emblazoning the covers of mainstream magazines like *Newsweek* or *Time*, headlined "The End of Christian America."[9] Many churches can hardly be bothered by the fact that the last twenty years of ministry have produced a 97% apostasy rate among the twenty-somethings!

If the faith will be saved and Christian civilization re-established in the years to come, it would be advantageous to trace the roots, and discern the methods and doctrines of the leaders of the present apostasy. Wherever nations have been touched by the corrosive Western apostasies and destructive worldviews, individual families with a commitment to the Christian faith should be aware of these forces. If fathers and mothers, and grandfathers and grandmothers are at all concerned, I hope they will read this book. In so doing, perhaps they will retain a vision for preserving the faith for generations to come.

Throughout this book, I will refer to the leaders of the apostasy as "The Nephilim." This title adds something to the drama of what has taken place. It brings to mind the dreadful tribe of pre-diluvian men who arose out of the ungodly synthesis between the sons of God and the daughters of men. Some say this was an unholy marriage of angels and the fallen daughters of men. I do not take this view, but suffice it to say that it was a devastating mixture of bloodlines. This synthesis brought about unimaginable terror and violence, according to the pre-flood account found in Genesis 6:1-5. The Hebrew word "Nephilim" may be translated "giant" or "tyrant." These were men with tremendous character, but with

8. Rudyard Kipling, *The Gods of the Copybook Headings*
9. http://www.thedailybeast.com/newsweek/2009/04/03/the-end-of-christian-america.html

an evil twist. The strength of a godly heritage was used for foul ends. By their remarkable ability to influence men and control large empires, they multiplied the impact of their evil intentions on the earth. Evidently, the threat was so great that God "pulled the plug" on the entire operation. He initiated a gigantic cataclysm that is still remembered in various forms by different cultures around the world as "The Worldwide Flood." May we never forget that it was the dreadful Nephilim that precipitated the horrific displays of violence, leading to the destruction of the prediluvian world!

What I want to capture in this book is the incredible destructive force leveled by a handful of men upon the entire world. They were all men who maintained something of their Christian past, while assimilating the dangerous ideas of humanism. Over time, they became increasingly "epistemologically self-conscious" of their atheism and autonomy. The sheer magnitude of their influence over the last few centuries is truly remarkable. That such a small number of men should have such powerful effects on billions of people around the world over many centuries, should be sobering to even the most disinterested bystander in this historical drama.

APOSTASY

Apostasies are not new. Adam's firstborn, Cain may have been the first apostate when he refused to bring God the proper sacrifice (Gen. 4:3-9). From that time forward, Moses and the prophets, and Jesus and the Apostles all dealt with the problem of apostasy. It is a major theme in the Bible. Within weeks after leaving Egypt, Moses faced the problem of apostasy with the children of Israel. The problem did not abate during the period of the Judges, or during the period of the Kings, or during the life of Christ. How much of the ministry of John the Baptist and Jesus Christ was taken up with warnings concerning apostasy and impending judgment? Whether apostasy occurs on a national or ethnic scale, or on an individual scale (as in the case of Demas, Alexander the Coppersmith, Ananias and Saphira, and others), this seems to be an ever-present reality in the community of God's people.

Considering what has happened over the last two centuries in Europe and America, it must be the Gentiles' turn now! We are soon to emerge out of the most significant Christian apostasy of all time. As measured by sheer numbers, there is no other apostasy so extensive in recorded history. Perhaps the Apostle Paul's warning in Romans 11:20-22 applies to this sad state of affairs. After considering the struggles with apostasy and faithlessness on the part of the Jews, Paul warns the Gentiles against boasting, and for good reason. With church attendance in England declining from 60% to 6% in 150 years, it's hard not to interpret this as a bit of pruning! Following centuries of pride, schism, compromise, synthesis with humanism, and general hard-heartedness, God may be withdrawing His grace from the Western nations—at least for the time being. Nevertheless, there is always mercy for those who seek it and those who are humbled before almighty God (Rom. 11:20).

THE APOSTATES

The position taken by this author is neither controversial nor tenuous, and the facts are not obscure or debatable. *A few men armed with powerful ideas changed the world.* Generally, most humanists and Christians agree that the world is very different today than it was in the 17th century. Both sides agree that the Western world has abandoned Christian foundations. There may be a little disagreement on the list of names of those who led the apostasy, as there are both "First-Tier" Nephilim and "Second-Tier" Nephilim. However there is no doubt that the primary philosophical and cultural leaders were apostates; both the autobiographies and the biographers generally agree on this point. Nevertheless, the humanists will never agree with the conclusions I have drawn concerning the work of these "great" men. That is because, from a Christian perspective, these principal apostates were extraordinarily dangerous men. Their fruit was bad and it will rot. If professing Christians disagree with me on this point, I wonder if they have joined the other side, or if perhaps they are too fearful to recognize the true magnitude of the social and cultural problems that confront the modern world.

After studying this major Western apostasy for many years, I would offer several notable observations.

THE PAINFUL PROCESS OF APOSTASY

Apostasy. The word itself is ugly, even frightening perhaps. While the postmodern relativist couldn't be bothered with meaningless concepts like truth and error, almost everybody agrees that apostasy is a reality.

People shift their perspectives and commitments, and a great many people abandon the Christian faith. In some cases, the forsaking of the faith occurs rapidly and at other times it works its way out through generations. Nevertheless, it is a slippery theological word, and various schools of theology offer differing explanations. Even within the subset of evangelicalism there are varying positions on whether one can "lose" his salvation.[10] Biblically speaking, apostasy is real. It is variously described as: "cast forth, withered branches" (John 15:6), "stony" or "thorny ground" hearers (Matt. 13:5-7), those in "the gall of bitterness, and the bond of iniquity" (Acts 8:23), "candlesticks" removed (Rev. 2:5), "branches" snapped off (Rom. 11:19), or "enlightened partakers of the Holy Ghost" that produce thorns (Heb. 6:4,8). These apostasies may include individuals, local churches, large denominations, or segments of peoples, since various people groups of faith are often presented in Scripture as trees, plants, and vines. Also multiple generations of faith (including grandparents, parents, and children) are typically represented in Scripture using organic, agricultural terms.

These biblical analogies paint a picture of an apostate who is somehow connected in an external way to Christian culture and church, while there is no substantial, life-sustaining connection on the inside. Essentially, they are dry branches incapable of yielding fruit. These John helpfully describes as those who *"went out from us, but they were not of us; for if they had been of us, they would no doubt have continued with us: but they went out, that they might be made manifest that they were not all of us"* (1 John 2:19).

This doesn't answer all of the questions raised concerning apostasy, however. In the case of a generational apostasy, we may ask, was there any genuine faith at all in the lives of previous generations? As apostasy worked slowly from the orthodox faith to John Locke's Latitudinarianism to William Emerson's Unitarianism to (his son), Ralph Waldo Emerson's Transcendentalism, where does the branch die? How many propositions must one believe to still be counted part of the body of the Christian faith? For the purposes of this book, I'm not interested in answering these questions. My major interest is the trajectory of the lives of these men and of the generations that followed them.

---

10. This is a larger theological discussion that is best resolved in a covenantal understanding of soteriology. It is not my purpose to explain these complex doctrinal matters in this particular book. I would encourage my reader to include Phil. 1:6, 1 Pet. 1:5-10, and John 10:28 in the consideration of these things.

What we will find in this eye-opening account of prominent apostasies is a slowly progressing, generational development over many years. It was excruciatingly difficult for men like Jean-Paul Sartre. He described the process with painful and disturbing detail in his autobiography *The Words*. However, in the present day, faith roots are shallow and generational continuity in the faith is rare. It seems that apostasy comes much more rapidly than it did in previous centuries. And, there are an endless number of heterodoxies, cults, and denominations that will accommodate the apostasy of the day.

CROSS-DENOMINATIONAL APOSTASY

Perhaps the most surprising element of the great apostasy in the West is its cross-denominational representation. The line-up of great minds covered in this book are commonly accepted as the true "greats." While there may be a little debate on one or two names, all of them were seminal thinkers and powerful influencers. Collect twenty lists of the top twenty most important writers and thinkers of the last millennium and these selections will appear on all of the lists. We simply ask, who were the men who influenced the developing Western trends in philosophy, education, science, morality, politics, and culture? Who framed the zeitgeist (the "spirit of the age") in the Western states? These men have received affirmation and condemnation from hundreds of great political leaders, social scientists, theologians, educators, and authors over the centuries.

One thing that may be said about the men who appear on this list, they come from just about every major sect of orthodox (Trinitarian) Christianity.

René Descartes - Roman Catholic
John Locke - Puritan, Protestant
Jean-Jacques Rousseau - Calvinist, Protestant
Jeremy Bentham - Anglican, Protestant
Ralph Waldo Emerson - Congregationalist, Protestant
Charles Darwin - Anglican, Protestant
Friedrich Nietzsche - Lutheran, Protestant
Karl Marx - Lutheran, Protestant
John Dewey - Congregationalist, Protestant
Jean-Paul Sartre - Roman Catholic and Protestant

Nathaniel Hawthorne - Congregationalist, Protestant
Mark Twain - Presbyterian, Protestant
Ernest Hemingway - Baptist, Protestant

This Western regression of faith has continued steadily since the days of the Protestant Reformation and the Humanist Renaissance, and has included both Protestants and Roman Catholics. In the 18th and 19th centuries, the Trinitarian faith devolved into Unitarian and Deist commitments. In some cases, men who attended a Christian church earlier in their lives would profess agnosticism and atheism before they were middle-aged (Karl Marx and Ernest Hemingway); casting off their Christian heritage in a single generation. Others like Jeremy Bentham, John Stuart Mill, Ralph Waldo Emerson, and Charles Darwin would play a role in a multigenerational apostasy that would take three to four generations to arrive at a full-fledged atheism. But each of them would gradually desert the Trinitarian faith, which has always been seen as irrational to the autonomous mind of the modern who relies heavily on human reason and "what seems to make sense to me."

Although the Reformation preserved something of the faith in the Western world and stimulated a missionary movement, it was incapable of stemming the tide towards apostasy. Many Protestants were as enthusiastic with their support of the humanist universities as the Catholics. Tremendous movements towards apostasy developed out of Protestantism—especially in the mainline denominations. To this day, attempts at conserving the faith by denominational fracturing prove to be ineffectual. Inevitably, these halfway house reformations tend to slide back into humanism, universalism, deism, and antinomianism.

Virtually all of the mainline Christian denominations have contributed their share of apostates to the task of breaking down the Christian faith in the West. This does not imply that all denominations and doctrinal perspectives should be accepted as equally true to the historical, biblical faith. Certainly, there are some churches and pastors that steward God's kingdom resources better than others. If there is anything we have learned from the last five-hundred years, it is that the seeds of apostasy lie everywhere, and all would do well to take heed, lest they fall!

SOMETHING WICKED THIS WAY COMES

As Christians who still hold to a supernatural reality, we would be negligent to ignore the spiritual elements of this apostasy. Although the self-conscious materialist rejects any notion of a supernatural or spiritual world, it is surprising how many of the apostates were afflicted by spiritual forces, *and actually gave credence to them in their writings.*

Judging from the radical changes in the spiritual condition of the West, the social collapse of the family, and the disintegration of Western morals, it is safe to say that something strange happened in the 18th century. If the breakdown of morals and family life, and the rise of tyrannical governments and the slaughter of the innocents are deemed evil conditions, then all of this must have something to do with unseen, spiritual forces. Somehow, Harvard College moved from Trinitarianism and Reformed Puritanism to Unitarianism and Transcendentalism, more rooted in the Bhagavad-Gita than the Christian Bible! Also, the first of the bloody humanist revolutions in France were inspired by the first of the humanist, intellectual apostates - Rousseau and Voltaire. Surely, man must take responsibility for his own sins; but there is also a devil. When there is no obvious explanation for the powerful conspiracies, the reign of terror, mass murders, genocides, homosexuality, apostasy, and the like, we can be sure that the devil is involved. This tsunami of apostasy that rolled over Europe and America in the 19th and 20th centuries can only be the result of spiritual powers greater than man himself.

In God's providence, a powerful force from the pit of hell was unleashed upon the modern world. If wickedness is defined as a rejection of God's truth and God's law, then it was wickedness that captured the Western world between 1780 and the present day. Interestingly, this spiritual presence is confirmed by the authors of this apostasy, themselves. Upon Hawthorne's release of his magnum opus, *The Scarlet Letter*, his friend Herman Melville suggested that Hawthorne had written by the inspiration of the same demon that had possessed him. Hawthorne himself admitted it to be a "hell-fired tale." His virulent hatred for his own ancestors and their opposition to witchcraft was one of the major threads found in his important works. His fundamental allegiances are obvious when we discover that he participated in séances and witchcraft himself.

Letters from the Earth, by Mark Twain, is one of the oddest pieces of literature ever written - it is evil incarnate. Published posthumously in

1962, Mark Twain takes on the persona of Satan himself in this work, recording 30,000 words of pure blasphemy in the form of letters written by the devil to the archangels Gabriel and Michael. These "Letters from Hell" provide interesting insight into the innermost thoughts of the arch demon himself.

Under the influence of Satan, Karl Marx wrote a number of poems and plays, some of which are referred to in this book. It should come as no surprise to anyone, that this man who was responsible for more mass murders than anyone else in history was possessed —at least for a time—by Satan himself.

For over 300 years, a number of these great minds including Shakespeare, Bentham, Emerson, and Whitman, toyed with ultimate rebellion against the Creator and His social order in the form of homosexuality. For hundreds of years, these men fiddled with the lock on this cage of demons. It took several centuries before the corrupting scourge of sodomy was unleashed in full force upon our world. By the end of the 20th Century, stories of men attempting the ancient Greek manifestations of pedophilia were almost commonplace among sports coaches, Roman Catholic priests, Evangelical pastors, and even parents. To those with a spiritual sense for what is going on in the world, they cannot but conclude that, *something wicked this way comes.*

Two

THE CONTOURS OF THE BATTLE

The crux of the worldview battle of the last half millennium is centered on the matter of *who will be God.* It is a battle between God and man over the question of whether man will be God or whether God will be God. Do we assume that man is God and then build a world and life view upon that presupposition? Or do we assume that God is God and build a world and life view on *that* presupposition? What we mean by "God" is obviously critical to the discussion, since we must be clear about what we are fighting over. We need to know, *what is it to be "God" or to be "a god?"* Simply stated, to be a god is to be in a position of high authority over some persons or realm. That authority assumes the power to rule and control a realm, the power to require obedience, and the right to be heard and believed.

Polytheistic worldviews maintain competing gods and values; atheists refuse to divulge the name of their god (usually man is their god), and monotheists hold to one ultimate authority. That ultimate authority must be "an authority greater than does not exist," applying Anselm's definition. If there is a God, He must be the final authority in truth, reality and ethics. Because He is the Source of all wisdom, power and right, there is no higher court of appeal above Him. There is no other source of wisdom, no other reservoir of power, and no standard of justice or judicial power above Him. That is what makes God, God.

A worldview is defined as a set of fundamental beliefs which address metaphysics, epistemology and ethics. For better or for worse, every person retains some basic perspective concerning reality, truth, and ethics. We believe that certain things are real, certain things are true, and certain things are right or wrong, based upon criteria that may or may not be completely rational or internally consistent. Every worldview engages at this point. How does God relate to man's truth, reality and ethics? Briefly, the following summarizes a Christian worldview.

EPISTEMOLOGY - A THEORY OF TRUTH

"For since I learned of You, I have not forgotten You. Where I found truth, there I found my God, the Truth itself."[1]

Epistemology is the study of what is true and how one determines what is true. When any philosopher of epistemology wants to develop a theory of knowledge, he must seek an ultimate authority, since there must be some final standard by which all claims of truth may be tested. For the humanist, the final standard is man himself. For the Christian, the standard is God. The God of Christianity is nothing less than the God above all gods, that authority above all authorities. That being the case, there can be no authority that speaks with more authority than does this God. By virtue of His very nature and position in relation to reality, God establishes what is true.

> *"For the LORD is a great God, and a great King above all gods"* (Psalm 95:3).

The Christian recognizes that this is God's world, planned and implemented by the mind of God. Therefore, God's truth is the only possible standard for truth. As far as man will adopt God's truth or stay

---

1. Augustine, *Confessions, Book 10*

connected to that standard, he will find truth. However, should he cut himself loose from the tether of the truth of God and His revelation, he will wander aimlessly in the blinding snowstorm of relativism and eventually be reduced to brute paganism and ignorance.

In the worldview conflict of the centuries, the humanist stepped forward to question the authority of anybody outside of himself who would claim to be ultimate. If God were attempting to cash a check at the supermarket, the humanist would unabashedly ask for His driver's license. Of course, he neglects to check the agency that issued the driver's license, and he doesn't realize that he is unqualified to perform the inspection. The humanist refuses to accept a God who speaks as only God could speak, with an ultimate, unquestionable authority. Rather, he turns to himself as the ultimate source of truth, usurping—in his own imagination—the authority of the living and true God.

But what if men refused to trust God's revelatory truth? What if they began to test His Word, all of it or part of it, by the scrutiny of scientific minds? What if they were to reduce His revelation to just one potential source of truth among many, and presume that God was simply incapable of communicating by an objective Word? What if they were to question the historicity of the Bible, the resurrection, the miracles, the virgin birth, and anything else that threatened a purely naturalist worldview? What if they were to look to the mind of man as the arbiter of all propositional statements? What if they were to demand that God's Word conform to certain standards for truth as preconceived in their own minds? What if they repudiated all certainty and conviction concerning God's revelation? What if they were more instructed by personal anecdotes, dreams, prophecies, revelations, and entertainment than by the authoritative words of Christ? What if the church itself splintered into a thousand denominations with a thousand novel interpretations of what they hoped Scripture said? If they did all of these things, we would have to conclude that man had made himself the final measure of truth. Whatever God communicated by special revelation would be questioned, misinterpreted, mistranslated, misapplied and misused in order to accommodate the autonomous minds of men. None of this should be unfamiliar to the average churchgoer in the West. Inch by inch, year by year, denomination by denomination, Christian churches have worked steadily and consistently to remove God as the Source of truth from the consciousness of modern man.

> *"O the depth of the riches both of the wisdom and knowledge of God! How unsearchable are his judgments, and his ways past finding out! For who hath known the mind of the Lord? Or who hath been his counselor? Or who hath first given to him, and it shall be recompensed unto him again? For of him, and through him, and to him, are all things: to whom be glory for ever. Amen" (Romans 11:32-36).*

ETHICS

> *"For as among the government of men, the great authority is obeyed in preference to the lesser, so God must be obeyed above all."[2]*

Ethics is the consideration of what is good and right. What establishes the criterion for what is good and right? Who or what authority has the right to command a certain behavior from men? These questions are easily answered in terms of a biblical worldview: God establishes what is good and right. The glory of God is the highest good, and all other causes are subservient to God's glory (Rom. 11:36). God also establishes what is right in terms of His revealed law. There is nobody besides God who could ever know what would constitute the highest good, let alone what would *produce* the highest good. It should make perfect sense that if man is a personal, self-consciously moral creature, and if a personal creature is made by a personal Creator, then the personal Creator must have a personal interest in the personal creatures He made.

The Christian faith teaches that God is God and He tells us what to do. He is the supreme Lawgiver and Judge and He will punish those who reject Him as Lawgiver and Savior.

> *"And I will punish the world for their evil, and the wicked for their iniquity; and I will cause the arrogancy of the proud to cease, and will lay low the haughtiness of the terrible" (Is. 13:11).*

The humanist revolts against the notion that God would tell him what to do. He seeks to be a law to himself, and he will fight every inch of the way for the right to determine his own ethics. As my reader will quickly

---

2. Augustine, *Confessions Book III*

realize, the last three hundred years have presented one prolonged, bitter revolt against a Christian moral order in the Western world. As early as the 17th century, seminaries rejected biblical law and quickly turned to Aristotelian ethics or natural law. By the end of the 18th century, much of the Christian church had abandoned God's Old and New Testament laws.

It should be obvious that a sovereign authority has the right to tell people what to do. However, the rejection of God as Lawgiver was an incremental process, working its way out by surreptitious compromise over the centuries. What if men would simply ignore the law of God? What if they were to invent theological systems that would undermine the relevance and importance of God's revealed law in church, family, and state? Or what if they reduced God's law to a nebulous definition of love, such that God's will could be interpreted in a thousand ways by a thousand different people? What if they removed the Ten Commandments from the school walls? What if they were to remove any mention of them from evangelism? What if they were to remove them from church liturgy and teaching? What if their churches were afraid to correct societal sins like homosexuality, abortion, or cannibalism? What if their schools and cultural systems began to call evil "good," and good "evil?" What if they began to curtail the authority of God's law over the civil magistrate? What if the majority of the community came to view God's laws found in the Bible as old-fashioned, ignorant, and even unjust? What if the populace would sooner trust the ethics of Sigmund Freud, Karl Marx, John Maynard Keynes, and Margaret Sanger than Moses, Solomon, and Paul? If God chose to reveal something of His holy character and His revealed will, what can we say about those who ignore, dismiss, or even ridicule that revelation? There has been an all-out, frontal attack on the "God-ness" of God in the Western world. If humanists were to undermine the Christian faith, minimize the importance of the atonement of Christ, attack the righteous rule of Christ, and obliterate the Christian God from the consciousness of modern man, they had to eliminate God as the source of ethics. This has happened, and the Christian faith has been dealt a serious blow since the 1700s in the war of the worldviews.

METAPHYSICS

"Who else calls us back from the death of all errors, except the Life which

cannot die and the Wisdom which, needing no light, enlightens the minds that need it, and by which the universe is directed, down to the whirling leaves of trees?"[3]

Metaphysics considers the nature of reality from existence to causality. What is real? Where did this world come from? Is everything that happens in life the product of indeterminate chance or is it part of a determined plan? How is God related to this reality? Christianity has always held that God is the Creator of all reality. God is ultimate existence, eternal existence, and underived existence. Therefore, our existence must be derived from that ultimate existence. Our existence is certain only because God's existence is unquestionably certain.

A majority of Americans still accept God as Creator. It is only when it is suggested that man's continuing reality or existence is dependent on God that many will choke. However, the Bible teaches an intensive and ultimate divine relationship with man's world, man's existence, and man's life. God created the world, but He also creates each moment. He takes an intimate interest in every detail and everything happening there. In an explicitly Christian worldview, the hand of God is very real and most ultimate. But since 1800, even Christian theology has chipped away at this doctrine of Divine Providence. Theologians have been busy, scurrying about to find some area of the universe or some area of man's life that is beyond God's purview. But God's Word as revealed in Old and New Testaments stands firm. God establishes the original reality by creation, and He establishes the continuing reality of that creation by His providential hand over all things (Prov. 16:33, Dan. 2:20-21, Prov. 20:21, Ezra 7:6, Acts 2:23).

The humanist dispenses with God's involvement in creation insisting that the universe is self-existent and not created. Evolution, atheism, and agnosticism remove any notion of God as Creator. The deist removed God from any and all immediate control of the universe. By the 1920s, John Dewey's *Humanist Manifesto* announced that "man alone is responsible for achieving the world of his dreams," and God is nothing but a "faded piece of metaphysical goods."

Clearly, the doctrine of Providence is neither understood nor assumed in the mind of today's average Christian as it was previously in

---

3. Augustine, *Confessions Books VII*

our history. It is rare to find a Christian as committed to the idea that God providentially directs the affairs of men as they did at the founding of this nation in 1776. It would be refreshing to hear pastors refer to the Providence of God as deists like Benjamin Franklin so testified at the Constitutional Convention! Humanism has taught us to reject a God who is so connected to reality. If he were honest, the humanist must admit that man makes for a poor god, yet he is offended at the notion that there might be someone who is God. Nevertheless, he applies himself enthusiastically to the task of predestinating his own future as well as the destiny of the whole world - but he just pretends.[4] The humanist utterly rejects the notion that there is a God who has any control over man and His world. But what kind of ultimate authority does not have ultimate authority over the reality he creates?

The sovereignty of God has been dying a slow death of a thousand qualifications. Theologically, the teachers in the church fabricate a logical contradiction between man's free will and God's sovereignty; they insist that man's will must somehow trump God's will. The masses are led to believe that they alone are responsible for the "realization of the world of their dreams," and they have the power within themselves to achieve whatever they conceive. Then, what happens when the "sovereign" individual turns his own "sovereignty" over to the democratic state? What if men attempt to replace God with the sovereign state? What happens if they construct a police state, complete with concentration camps, fascist regulation of private business, hundreds of thousands of social planners, and video cameras on every street corner? What will happen if the churches refuse to recognize God's sovereignty? What if they ignore it, dismiss it, minimize its importance, or even teach against it? This is what the humanist apostasy looks like in its most raw form.

This worldview rages on a third front, called metaphysics. If God cannot control the world and the many events that take place within it, then His other perfections—once commonly recognized by most of the Western world—begin to crumble: His foreknowledge and omniscience, omnipotence, justice, and His sovereign mercy.

If God is the ultimate authority in man's knowledge, ethics, and reality, then He must be the central focus of life. He should permeate the

---

4. None betray more desperation in attempts to retain some level of optimism despite holding to a pessimistic worldview, as the existentialist, Jean-Paul Sartre. He encourages his followers to live the authentic life, acting freely as if independent of all constraints.

thoughts, the motives, the academic teaching, the counseling, the family life, and the worship of the Christian. The glory of God becomes his chief end (1 Cor. 10:31). But what if we were to seek our own needs first, in the church? What if we were to speak and write for men more than for God? What if we were to center worship around the needs of men, rather than on God? No doubt God would slip out of the central focus of the life and worship of the Christian. Sadly, this scenario is all too common in a day where man-centric humanism runs rampant through the media, literature, education, politics, and the church.

THE PROBLEM WITH MAN AS GOD

"I have described two cities. . . the heavenly and earthly, intermingled as they have been from the beginning and are to be until the end of time. The earthly one has made for herself, according to her heart's desire, false gods out of any source at all, even out of human beings, that she might adore them with sacrifices. The heavenly one... is made by the true God that she may herself be a true sacrifice to Him."[5]

If God has lost the authority to be sovereign over reality, if He has lost the authority to provide objective law, and if He has lost the authority to reveal absolute truth, then in the eyes of men, He has lost the right to be God. He has been stripped of his "God-ness," or the very attributes which make Him God. At the same time, man is never content to be godless. He must have a god. Somebody or something must provide that authority. Thus, modern man gladly assumes that position, and humanist man becomes his own ultimate authority.

The problem with man as God is that he makes a terrible god. Humanist man makes his own laws and then proceeds to break them (Rom. 2:14,15). His sole ethic is to attain happiness, but he struggles to define it and he is quickly forced to admit he doesn't have a clue as to what would produce it. He pretends to be sovereign, but he finds that he cannot even control his own wife. He wants to be the center of life and worship, but finds that nobody else worships him. He speaks with a voice of commanding authority, and the next day he is proven wrong by his two-year-old son. In his waning years, he runs out of money to provide for his own needs. Man makes a very poor god indeed! Therefore

5. Augustine, *City of God* (Garden City: Image Books, 1958), 425.

man must turn outside of himself to find another god more qualified for the position. That is where he will turn to corporate man or to the state to fill the role. This too will prove a disappointment. After several generations of debt-based economics, socialism, welfare, dumbed-down public education, and soaring illegitimacy rates, the state will prove itself to be a very inadequate god indeed - a total failure.

Man turns within himself, seeking to fill the "God-shaped" vacuum. However he is always disappointed with the results. In the end, he is more hopeless and suicidal than the pagan who still seeks for some kind of god outside of himself. Thus pure, undiluted humanism cannot last for long. Either societies must awaken to the true faith or sink into the chaos of paganism. After five or six generations of apostasy, humanist societies turn to deconstructed language, pluralism, relativism, polytheism, and competing truth systems.

For our purposes, the larger concern is not so much the decline of the culture, as the condition of the Christian faith. If we want there to be some faith extant in the year 2060, we must direct ourselves to the near total synthesis of the Christian church with the thought patterns of the anti-Christian worldview. To the degree that the organized Christian faith has absorbed the doctrines of humanism, it fails to act as the salt preservative for our societies. Instead of leading the culture, the church growth proponents have worked diligently to remain "relevant" and attractive to those who have already apostatized! What they fail to realize is that our civilizations cannot continue for much longer on compromised foundations. The church will either lead the culture or lose itself with the dying culture. Our own civilization is already dissolving into paganism, polytheism, relativism, and nihilism. The synthesized church therefore finds itself under the unhappy curse of being both compromised and irrelevant. It is only when the church defines itself as distinctly Christian by the Word of God that the blessing of God and the relevance of the Word in the culture will be apparent.

THE CRUX OF THE WORLDVIEW CONFLICT

The crux of the worldview conflict which has ravaged the culture and entered the foyer of the Christian church in the third millennium A.D. is the denial of God's right to be God, and the usurpation of that right by man. In a word, it is a life or death struggle over *sovereignty*. Who will be sovereign - man or God? Noah Webster defined sovereignty as, "the possession of the highest power, or of uncontrollable power."[6] Thus, God must possess the highest and ultimate authority and power. He is beyond all control of man or of any other being or authority.

If the direction of a civilization is determined by the dominant ideas inculcated by that society, then it is important to define those ideas which displaced the old order. As we review the story of the plight of Western civilization, it is impossible to miss the vigorous conflict of antithetical ideas set forth. This book itself intends to set the battle in array against the humanist battalions that occupy our world. There is no sense in feigning neutrality. The war of ideas is a high stakes game, and the battle lines are important. Nor is it prudent to get hung up on the minor skirmishes. If we could accurately define the major contours of the battle, then perhaps the "good guys" could find a basis for unity and salvage something of the faith. Then we might properly assess the damage inflicted by the enemy and the extent of corruption found in the church and the wider culture.

There is a great antithesis between the statements about God contained in the Bible and those which are taught by modern man. It is a fundamental disagreement in the war of worldviews. At the most basic level of human thought, we disagree on the basic presuppositions which make up our understanding of truth and the universe. What follows is a summary of these differences:

We believe in the ultimacy or sovereignty of God:

> God is the ultimate authority in truth.
> God is the ultimate authority in reality.
> God is the ultimate authority in law.
> God is the ultimate source of man's salvation.
> God must be the center of man's life and worship.

Humanism counters with its own basic presuppositions, asserting the sovereignty of man:

> Man is the ultimate authority in truth.
> Man is the ultimate authority in reality.

---

6. Noah Webster, *American Dictionary of the English Language* (1828; repr., Foundation for American Christian Education, 1967)

Man is the ultimate authority in law.
Man is the ultimate source of man's salvation.
Man must be the center of man's life and worship.

Either God will be God in these real and concrete ways, or man will be god. This is the point at which the humanist worldview and the Christian worldview must clash in the mind of every Christian. This is the point at which the humanist, with his materialism, socialism, egalitarianism, utilitarianism, abortion advocacy, deviant sexuality, and evolution, violently conflicts with Christianity. All other diverging points at which Christianity opposes humanism are simply side skirmishes in the war of the worldviews. This is the Gettysburg of the worldview war of the 21st century.

FOLLOWING THE APOSTASY

Faced with a worldview claiming the centrality of God in the face of man's existence, the modern humanist reacts, "But I don't want God to control my truth! I don't want God controlling my ethical behavior! I don't want God in control of my reality!" But in the ultimate sense, it doesn't matter whether the humanist wants God to be God or not. If God really is sovereign Lord and Judge, then man cannot divest Him of His sovereignty by denying it. Effectively, it is only in the minds of men that God has been stripped of His God-ness. The end result of denying the God-ness of God is a defective worldview which will inevitably produce a defective life and culture.

Hundreds of millions of Westerners may continue to worship a god on Sundays, and church attendance remains about the same as ever in the United States. They may speak of one named "Jesus," and take an hour or two in "praise and worship." But who is this god whom they worship? Is He the sovereign God of the Bible, or has He died the death of a thousand qualifications in the mind of the postmodern? In some church communities and families, the reality of the true and living God has largely faded over the generations. This is the direct result of a five-hundred year, full-orbed frontal attack on the Christian worldview. When Christianity abandons the centrality of God, it loses a critical, distinctive element of the Christian worldview. Entire church communities and family lines slowly turn into "non-Christians," following the trajectory of humanist apostasy. There can be no question that in this monumental war of worldviews, Christianity itself has taken a significant hit in the hull. Repairs are in order.

This issue is significant because it touches the very heart of the Christian faith. A god that is not sovereign in metaphysics, epistemology, and ethics, is a god unworthy of our life's devotion. A Christian cannot worship a god like this without his religion being shallow, ineffective, and weak.

The Bible-honoring Christian understands that God speaks with a voice of irreducible authority, a voice that creates the original reality of the universe and controls all things therein. He speaks to men with words that will be used to judge them at the final day (John 12:48). That alone should be awe-inspiring. The Christian understands that God is behind every miniscule event of his life, providing ultimate significance and meaning to everything that happens in this world. The Christian also knows that God has set out the normative principles by which he should act. This should command a daily reverence in the heart of the Christian, as well as heart-driven obedience. The Christian understands that God is everywhere. God is behind every action and reaction, and God is underneath everything that we can and will know. God has ethical and judicial interest in our every thought, word, and action. We cannot know anything without Him. We cannot escape His purposes all around us and through us. We cannot act outside of His fatherly discipline or judicial scrutiny. In Him we truly live, move, and have our being.

This is a God who is extensively and intensively real. The person who is absorbed in a Christian worldview simply cannot escape the pervasive reality, authority, relevance, and ultimacy of God. He is the Source of all knowing and being. He is ultimately worthy of our attention, reverence, obedience, and worship. It is just because He is ultimate in truth, reality, and ethics that He is to be heard, revered, trusted, obeyed, and worshipped. It is because He is the source of truth, law, and reality, that He is worthy to be trusted for our salvation. When we realize His very personal ultimacy in truth, reality, and ethics in relation to us, we are pressed towards heartfelt reverence, obedience and worship.

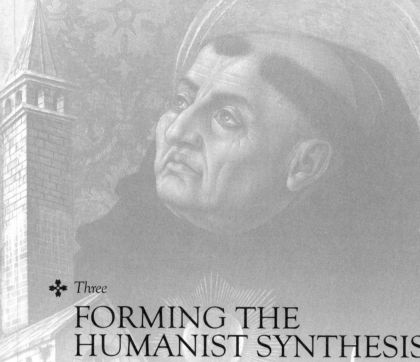

Three

FORMING THE HUMANIST SYNTHESIS

THOMAS AQUINAS | 1225-1274 A.D.

A s we consider the causes and processes that brought about the slow and steady 800-year erosion of the Christian faith in Italy, Germany, France, England, Scotland, and America, we must start with the first universities - where the great humanist incursion began. The University of Bologna commenced its work in 1088. By the 1270s, there were universities at Paris, Orleans, Toulouse, Montpellier, Cambridge, Oxford, Padua, Bologna, Naples, Salerno, Salamanca, Coimbra, and Lisbon. These academic institutions were established on humanist ideas that served as the foundation for the humanist renaissance. For a thousand years previous, the church had generally followed the education model propounded by Christ. It was the old, humble "University of Jesus from Nazareth" - more sandals and walking sticks than pin-striped suits and airy lecture halls. It was more love of the brethren than love of books. It was more kingdom of God than empires of men. It was more Old Testament law than Aristotelian ethics. It was more prayer and parables than podiums and prose. It was more discipleship than education. It was no mere coincidence that these universities formed in concert with the development of the Holy Roman Empire; there was an unholy alliance between an increasingly power-oriented church and a power-consumed state. Eventually, the humanist state would overpower the church. In the 12th century, the universities revived the humanist thinking of the Greeks and Romans creating the new synthesis of humanist thought and Christian thought. Initially, a strong element of the Christian church resisted this movement, and that is where Thomas Aquinas comes into play.

Immediately, some will take offense at the inclusion of Aquinas in a book on apostates. He is still regarded as a great hero to many Catholics and Protestants alike. Even those who consider themselves Reformed out of respect for the Protestant Reformation are enthusiastic about Aquinas' work. But before this whole treatise is dismissed out of hand, I need to make several important qualifications. First, we have very little information about Aquinas's personal life, and for this reason I am hesitant to call him an "apostate." Also, the famous statement he made to his friend Reginald of Piperno shortly before he died is highly significant: Thomas said, "All that I have written seems like straw to me *(mihi videtur ut palea)."* There is no record of the Apostles commenting on their own work in this manner; nor did Augustine, Justin Martyr, Clement, Iraneaus, John Calvin, Martin Luther, and hundreds of other important contributors to the church of Christ over the centuries speak of their work in this way. Some may pass Aquinas's comment off as self-effacing humility, but I believe that it was more than that. Aquinas himself must have identified something of an "Achille's heel" in his work, and he felt it important to warn others about it. Whatever the case, thousands of institutions and billions of people did not consider Aquinas's philosophy to be the straw he declared it to be. Quite the contrary, they proceeded to develop their universities, seminaries, philosophies, and apologetic methods upon his epistemological framework.

I trust that God showed mercy to this man in his humility. Who among us has not included a little error here and there in his work? Without question, Thomas wrote many good things. He defended the orthodox Trinitarian faith and retained a strong God-centeredness in his metaphysics. Yet, Aquinas's work was deeply flawed. If we compared his teachings to a skyscraper with a hundred floors, then much of the building may have been in pretty good shape. In fact, all one hundred floors may have been fairly well built. The problem however, is discovered within the foundations. In fact, one of the most important footers in his worldview - his theory of knowledge, was fundamentally defective, as I shall demonstrate in this chapter. If the foundation was compromised, the building was doomed from the start. That is why we must begin with Thomas Aquinas in our consideration of the philosophers who have formed the mind of the Western world (between 1300 and 2000 A.D.).

Thomas Aquinas, was the intermediary link between the old Christian Europe and the increasingly secularized, humanist Western world. During Thomas's life, there was great tension between the conservative faction of the church and the new humanism that was creeping into the medieval church. As a Dominican priest, Thomas took it upon himself to counteract the growing fear of the Aristotelian ideologies, to resolve the tension developing between the secular university and the church. Gifted with a tremendous mind, Thomas set out to create a comfortable synthesis between humanist philosophy and God-sourced revelatory truth. Between 1270 and 1272, he produced a series of disputations to address this, including *De virtutibus in communi* (*On Virtues in General*), *De virtutibus cardinalibus* (*On Cardinal Virtues*), and *De spe* (*On Hope*).

INFLUENCE

Thomas Aquinas had an extraordinary influence on the Western church. Even though it has been over 750 years since his death, most Christian academic leaders speak of him in glowing terms. One evangelical college professor writes, "Thomas Aquinas is a phenomenal gift to the entire church... here is a mind that was Catholic enough to embrace any good idea from wherever it came."[1] Another says, "I am totally convinced that Saint Thomas Aquinas was the greatest, wisest, most intelligent merely human theologian who ever lived."[2] Remarkable testimonies indeed, if the list of "mere human theologians" included men like the Apostle Paul, John Calvin, and Augustine!

The Roman Catholics share a similar view of Aquinas as those evangelical, protestant doctors of philosophy quoted above. "Since the

1. John Mark Reynolds, ed., *The Great Books Reader* (Minneapolis: Bethany House, 2011), 145.
2. Peter Kreeft, "The Truth of Saint Thomas Aquinas" in *The Great Books Reader*, 163.

days of Aristotle, probably no one man has exercised such a powerful influence on the thinking world as did St. Thomas... An attempt to give names of Catholic writers who have expressed their appreciation of St. Thomas and of his influence would be an impossible undertaking; for the list would include nearly all who have written on philosophy or theology since the thirteenth century, as well as hundreds of writers on other subjects."[3] What finer complements have ever been used for mere men? The epistemological work of Aquinas and his systematization of the doctrines of merit, venial and mortal sins, etc. greatly influenced the future canons of the Roman church. The Catholic Encyclopedia maintains that, "The principles of St. Thomas on the relations between faith and reason were solemnly proclaimed in the Vatican Council."[4] The Roman Pontiff Innocent VI offered this commendation for Aquinas: "His teaching above that of others, the canons alone excepted, enjoys such an elegance of phraseology, a method of statement, a truth of proposition, that those who hold it are never found swerving from the path of truth, and he who dare assail it will always be suspected of error."[5]

PHILOSOPHY

Aquinas' magnum opus is *The Summa Theologiae*, a highly systematized theology. Again, much of his teaching may be helpful for the defense of an orthodox, Trinitiarian faith. It is just that the first article was terribly flawed.

> "Now Scripture, inspired by God, is no part of philosophical science [knowledge], which has been built up by human reason. Therefore it is useful that besides philosophical science, there should be other knowledge, i.e. inspired of God. I answer that, it was necessary for man's salvation that there should be a knowledge revealed by God besides philosophical science [knowledge] built up by human reason... Hence theology included in sacred doctrine differs in kind from that theology which is part of philosophy."[6]

Thus, Aquinas proposed two systems of knowledge: the one sacred

---

3. "St. Thomas Aquinas" in *Catholic Encyclopedia*, http://www.newadvent.org/cathen/14663b.html
4. Ibid.
5. Ibid.
6. Thomas Aquinas, *Summa Theologiae*, Q1, A1

APOSTATE

and the other secular (or philosophical). This broke away from the old Augustinian view of knowledge, summed up in the Latin phrase "*Credo ut intelligam,*" or, "Believe in order to understand."[7] Augustine would not separate his Christian faith from understanding. In his *Confessions,* Augustine wrote, "The mind needs to be enlightened by light from outside itself, so that it can participate in truth, because it is not itself the nature of truth. You will light my lamp, Lord."[8] Aquinas broke from this view when he proposed a second form of knowledge "different in kind" from that obtained in Scripture. The secular universities were now free to build their systems of knowledge entirely without the divine revelation of Scripture.

Importantly, Thomas Aquinas really believed that natural man in his fallen state could build a reliable system of philosophical knowledge on "human reason." He did not believe that man's reason was seriously tainted by the fall into sin. How does this comport with the Apostle Paul's warning for the Christians up in Greece about the "vain and deceptive philosophies" taught by the Greeks (Col. 2:8)? It's hard to believe that the Apostle Paul was as gaga over Aristotle as was this "great" teacher of the 13th century. In an attempt to reconcile the Scriptures with the rising humanist university, Aquinas turned into the great apologist for this Greek who took his best shot at building his philosophy on defective human reason.

This lends too much credence to man's natural capacity to determine truth apart from God's special revelation. From the beginning, man has always relied upon God's verbal revelation for his ethical behavior. Immediately upon creating Adam, God spoke to him concerning His ethical requirements (Genesis 2:16-19). Then man's fall into sin darkened his mind (Rom. 1:21), and he could not receive the things of God (1 Cor. 2:14). From then on, the natural man's reason has been clouded by layers upon layers of demonic deception (2 Cor. 4:4), and he is incapable of providing a solid basis for truth and ethics by his own reasoning capabilities. While he remains unaided by God's divine revelation and God's Spirit, in a fundamental sense he will think wrongly about everything. Man's need for God's direct and special revelation is even more vital after the fall.

7. Augustine, *Tractate on Gospel of John,* 29.6
8. Augustine, *Confessions,* Book 4.15

However, it is nigh impossible to completely expunge all Christian ideas from an unbeliever's thought processes because he operates in a world saturated in 2,000 years of Christian culture, calendars, law, and teaching. Therefore, he may still borrow some truthful presuppositions linked to divine revelation that originated with Noah or Moses or Christ. But his essential worldview is permanently skewed—short of the grace of God illuminating his mind by the Spirit and by the Word.

Despite Aquinas' invitation to separate philosophical science from a biblical world and life view, many early Christians did not do so. Most—if not all—of the men who formed modern science (Isaac Newton, Robert Boyle, Louis Pasteur, Michael Faraday, etc.), were professing Christians who strongly held to a basically biblical metaphysic and ethic.

Contrary to what Aquinas taught, the Bible does not present two different kinds of thinking or knowledge (Proverbs 2:1-6, Col. 2:1-3). There is only one source and one fountain of learning, and this is the Lord Jesus Christ. However, the Bible does present *two forms of revelation* in Psalm 19 and in Romans 1:18-22, but *not two different kinds of thinking, philosophy, or knowledge*. It is true that "the invisible things of God from the creation of the world are clearly seen being understood by the things that are made, even His eternal power and Godhead." These two forms of revelation are vital for faith and life. Though men are given a law of sorts written on their hearts, Paul reminds us that they deceive themselves and suppress the truth in unrighteousness (Rom. 1:18, 21, 22); they become vain in their imaginations, and their foolish heart is darkened. Moreover, the source of knowledge that comes by way of this natural revelation is *not* human reason. For *God* has shown it unto them according to verse 19, so it is clear that God is the source of this knowledge as well. Therefore, the Bible would never commend a philosophy that was not rooted in divine revelation but rather assembled purely by man's reason, as Aquinas proposes! There may be various forms of revelation, but the source of all knowledge is God Himself.

In the first few paragraphs of *The Summa*, Thomas Aquinas dealt a heavy blow to the Christian faith in the Western world. For the ensuing 800 years, Christians would disconnect mathematics, music, culture, and science from the worldview framework revealed in Holy Scripture. It wasn't long before the domain of "sacred" knowledge became smaller and smaller, and the field referred to as "philosophical" knowledge expanded to gargantuan proportions. When secular philosophy took ownership of epistemology, metaphysics, ethics, law, social theory, political theory, etc., it wasn't long before sacred doctrine was left with... well, almost nothing. In time, rational "Christians" would reject the orthodox doctrine of the Trinity as unreasonable, since this doctrine didn't make sense to the modern philosopher. Seminaries amalgamated into secular universities by borrowing their ideas and teaching methodologies, thus assuring the destruction of the Christian church. In effect, when Christians adopt a worldview built upon a foundation of human reason, at some point Scripture is incapable of speaking with ultimate authority on any matter whatsoever. This was the end result of Aquinas' innovation, some 800 years later.

The Man of Straw, Thomas Aquinas provided the epistemological juggernaut that paved the way for humanism and the ruin of the faith in Western society.

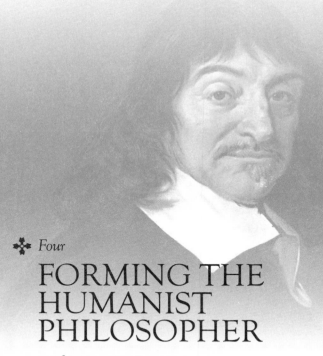

❖ *Four*

FORMING THE HUMANIST PHILOSOPHER

RENÉ DESCARTES | 1596-1650 A.D.

I n the 13th century, Thomas Aquinas proposed two distinct systems of knowledge: one which is revealed through sacred doctrine and one which is built upon human reason. Four centuries later, the philosopher René Descartes accepted the proposition, dedicating his life to the search for the first principles that would form the building blocks for a humanist (man-centered) worldview apart from the use of Scripture. Technically, he never apostatized from the Roman Catholic Church. But he did set a hard and fast separation between his religious life and his philosophical life. He kept his "faith" neatly compartmentalized so that never the twain should meet. This happens constantly in our day when, for example political leaders most acceptant of anti-Christian policies like abortion and homosexuality are members in good standing of Catholic or Protestant churches.

By definition, the term "apostasy" requires a previous allegiance to a church that commits to some ultimate authority. If the Christian faith would be abandoned in the West, it could not happen by the leadership of some born-and-bred atheist! An apostasy of this magnitude could only begin with a churchman. But it also had to address epistemological foundations, and this was Descartes' area of focus. What could possibly bring down the towering influence of the Christian faith in the Western world, but an attack on the foundations? It would take a distinctively humanist worldview approach to the theory of knowledge itself.

Unquestionably, René Descartes was a giant in the development of modern philosophy, a true original source of humanist thinking for the West. He lived in the Netherlands for most of his adult life, though he did not accept the biblical, Reformation thinking that defined 17th-century Holland. In fact, Blaise Pascal, a contemporary mathematician and thinker, said of him, *"I cannot forgive Descartes; in all his philosophy, Descartes did his best to dispense with God. But Descartes could not avoid prodding God to set the world in motion with a snap of [H]is lordly fingers; after that, he had no more use for God."*[1]

Descartes' mother died when he was only one year old. His father encouraged him to study law, but he rejected this advice in pursuit of a "higher calling." He embarked on a journey to reinvent knowledge. In his *Discourse on Method*, he wrote, "I entirely abandoned the study of letters. Resolving to seek no knowledge other than that of which could be found in myself or else in the great book of the world, I spent the rest of my youth traveling, visiting courts and armies, mixing with people of diverse temperaments and ranks, gathering various experiences, testing myself in the situations which fortune offered me, and at all times reflecting upon whatever came my way so as to derive some profit from it."

MORAL CHARACTER

In 1634, at 38 years of age, René Descartes committed fornication with a servant girl named Helena Jans van der Strom, while he lodged with his friend Thomas Sargeant in Amsterdam. He did not marry the girl, though he did take care of their illegitimate daughter who was born as a result. Descartes' lifestyle of fornication was extremely unusual for the 17th century. Records obtained from parishes in Protestant countries from that period indicate that illegitimacy rates were only

1. Blaise Pascal, *Pensees, Book 2*

0.69%.[2] Incredible though it seems, these conditions could only exist before humanists destroyed both morality and the family in the Western world, which boosted illegitimacy rates above 60% in some nations. The Bible takes the sin of fornication very seriously, but it is not certain that Descartes took it seriously, as we can find no indication of remorse concerning his behavior in his writings.

> *"But the fearful, and unbelieving, and the abominable, and murderers, and whoremongers, and sorcerers, and idolaters, and all liars, shall have their part in the lake which burneth with fire and brimstone: which is the second death" Revelation 21:8.*

It is truly remarkable that the great father of modern philosophy lacked such moral integrity. What would we say about influential Christian writers such as John Calvin, Thomas A'Kempis, Martin Luther, John Bunyan, and Jonathan Edwards if their ministries had been interrupted by a similar tragic incident of moral failure? Granted, there are godly men who fail, but their repentance is undeniably present in their writings. This was not true of Descartes, who as a humanist considered moral integrity unimportant. The fact that men fornicate with women and produce more orphans in the world is of little importance. To him, what really matters is that the new ideas formulated are radical, human-centered, innovative, and autonomous - that is what makes a genius. In the centuries following, far more people followed the humanist epistemology of Descartes than, for example, the God-centered epistemology found in the first chapter of John Calvin's *Institutes of the Christian Religion.* *"By their fruits ye shall know them."*

INFLUENCE

The modern humanist is very much indebted to the work of Descartes. The writer of the online encyclopedia article on this great philosopher puts it succinctly:

> *Descartes has been often dubbed as the father of modern Western philosophy, the philosopher that with his skeptic approach has profoundly*

---

2. Richard W. Price, "Bastardy or Illegitimacy in England," in *Ancestral Trails*, (original edition and Tate's *The Parish Chest*), http://pricegen.com/resources/illegitimacy.htm

changed the course of Western philosophy and set the basis for modernity. The first two of his Meditations on First Philosophy, those that formulate the famous methodic doubt are the portion of Descartes' writings that most influenced modern thinking. It has been argued that Descartes himself didn't realize the extent of his revolutionary gesture. In shifting the debate from 'what is true' to 'of what can I be certain?,' **Descartes shifted the authoritative guarantor of truth from God to Man."** *(Italics added.)*[3]

Descartes is arguably one of the first deists who began to envision a sharp separation between the created order and the spiritual reality of God. Although later empiricists like John Locke rejected the rationalism of René Descartes, Locke interacted with Descartes a great deal in his writings since each of them applied the same fundamental methodology in their thinking. Descartes can rightly be considered the pioneer in this form of humanism.

DESCARTES' PHILOSOPHY

In the autobiographical note above, we observe that Descartes' quest for knowledge does not include the great book of Scripture containing God's revealed truth. He resolves to seek *"no other knowledge"* than that found in himself and the "great book of the world." The words "no other knowledge" are important; they are the fundamental credo of the humanist, since his quest for knowledge is a self-contained search. The humanist believes that man is sufficient of himself to determine truth. But the Christian worldview takes leave from Descartes at this point. To judge any proposition from a philosopher or magician who peeps and mutters, the believer must always return "to the law and to the testimony" to determine whether there is any light in the proposition (Is. 8:20). Only in God's light, can we see light (Ps. 36:9). The source of truth is always Christ, the Son of God, who reveals the Father to man. Only Christ is the way, the truth, and the life (John 14:6). There is no other fount of knowledge except Christ (Col. 2:3). So why doesn't Descartes consider Christ in his search for knowledge? That would be the simple question which Christian men like Augustine, A'Kempis, Calvin, and Paul would have liked to pose this eminent philosopher.

3. "René Descartes," http://en.wikipedia.org/wiki/Ren%C3%A9_Descartes

Instead of beginning with Christ as the source of all knowledge, René Descartes accepts Thomas Aquinas's challenge to build his "philosophical knowledge" (as opposed to "sacred knowledge") upon human reason. There are usually two ways that this can be attempted. On the one hand, men may seek ultimate knowledge or first propositions within themselves, or they may try to find some truth outside of themselves and process the information in complete reliance on their own intellect. Descartes takes the first approach, attempting to find some incontrovertible truth within himself. *Independent of any and all revelation from God, while suspending all belief in God's existence, Descartes pretends that he can produce the first and most basic truths required to understand the world.*

His magnum opus begins with the "fact" that he doubts. Then after months of cogitating, he finally moves from "I doubt" to "I think, therefore I am."[4] But Descartes is not entirely honest in his reasoning. First, he assumes his own existence when he uses the word "I" in his first premise: "I doubt." He still continues to assume his existence before he gets to the business of doubting his own existence. Then he goes on to use the fact that he doubts, to prove his own existence. As he moves along in *The Discourse*, he attempts to "prove" the existence of his own physical body, and then on to "proving" the existence of God. Surely, God must have been relieved that Descartes has proved His existence. But the important thing to understand in *this* discussion is that Descartes' first and most fundamental truth is simply *his own thinking*. His second fundamental truth is his own existence. Then finally he concludes that God exists.

Christians build their system of knowledge on much different foundations. We know that we cannot begin with the proposition of our own existence (or our own thinking, or our own doubting, for that matter), because "the beginning of knowledge is the fear of the LORD" (Proverbs 1:7). We cannot begin to know anything with certainty without first assuming God's existence and fearing Him. It would be nothing less than cosmic treachery and ultimate intellectual rebellion to pretend that God did not exist while we go about proving our own existence (or anything else for that matter), for nothing could exist if God did not exist (Acts 17:28). What would Descartes or Aquinas say to this reasoning? Naturally, they would wholeheartedly agree that Proverbs 1:7 applies to the area of sacred doctrine, but not to philosophical knowledge built on human

4. Rene' Descartes, *Discourse on Method*, Chapter 4.

reason. What we have then is an irreconcilable difference between the teaching of the Bible and the reasoning of Descartes. According to the Bible, the most fundamental truth is God's existence, and any knowledge of God must be attended by the fear of God. The Christian understands that the first and most believable propositions are not those that "occur to us." The first and most believable proposition is that which God speaks. "Thy Word is truth" says Christ (John 17:17). However, according to Descartes, his own existence and his own doubting are more fundamental truths. He knows that he exists, however he is not so sure about God's existence yet. *At this very fine point of reasoning, the apostasy begins.*

Incredibly, Descartes begins with doubting or uncertainty as his fundamental belief, and then moves to certainty. Later, philosophers like John Dewey returns to doubt and uncertainty, rooting their humanist worldview upon quicksand. How one can get to certainty from doubt is hard to fathom!

As Descartes builds up his philosophical knowledge on human reason, he can not help but place the existence of God in the mix. If sacred doctrine constitutes a knowledge "different in kind" to that of philosophical knowledge, you would think that human reason would avoid this "existence-of-God business." But human reason is enthroned in Descartes epistemology and man's intellect must become the great judge concerning what is "believable" and "reasonable." The same humanist mindset that found the existence of God to be "reasonable" in the 17th century, would find the same thing "unreasonable" a century or two later. This is why Descartes' *Discourse on Method* was so dangerous! He was supposed to be working with *philosophical science*, not sacred doctrine. This philosophical science, according to Aquinas, "proceeds from self-evident principles." No doubt Aquinas would have been glad to see Descartes' attempt to create his philosophical science by his self-evident principles.

How does a person come to the knowledge of God, from the Christian worldview perspective? According to Scripture, it has nothing to do with Descartes establishing his own existence in his own mind. Knowing the Father has everything to do with the Son revealing the Father to men - "All things are delivered unto Me of My Father: and no man knoweth the Son, but the Father; neither knoweth any man the Father, save the

Son, and he to whomsoever the Son will reveal Him" (Matt. 11:27). This is the basis of knowledge for Christians, a far cry from that which Rene Descartes proposed.

Five

FORMING THE HUMANIST THEOLOGIAN

JOHN LOCKE | 1632-1704 A.D.

J ohn Locke was the son of Puritan parents, born at the zenith of the Protestant Reformation in England where both the government and church were cast into a state of turmoil. The English Reformation was a fragile tenuous ordeal, and the church was quickly fracturing into different sects representing varying flavors of orthodoxy - the good, the bad, and the ugly. At this point, the major threat to the orthodox faith was not Roman Catholicism, but the rising tsunami wave of humanism in the universities. He was baptized into the parish of Wrington in Somerset by the minister, Dr. Samuel Crook - an exemplary Puritan preacher by all accounts. This man was known to have preached as many as three sermons every day, hoping to see the conversion of each member of his congregation, including young John Locke.[1]

However, for many years of his life (1652-1674) John Locke studied and tutored at Oxford University. There he drank deeply from the wells

1. Maurice Cranston, *John Locke: A Biography* (London: Longman, 1959), 1-2.

of humanism which had originated in the Renaissance of Greek and Roman philosophies. It was during Locke's lifetime that the universities in the West moved towards a fundamentally man-centered view of knowledge, truth, and ethics.

The humanist philosophy stood in stark contrast with what John Locke received from the Puritan pastors in his early years. These godly men were known for their commitment to the Scriptures and to the Reformed doctrines summarized in the *Westminster Confession of Faith*. This confession strongly asserted the biblical doctrines of the authority and inspiration of Scripture, the Trinity, the sovereignty of God in salvation, justification by faith alone, the eternal nature of hell, and original sin. However, John Locke completely rejected his Puritan roots. By 1668 he was attending one of the most liberal churches in London, pastored by Benjamin Whichcote,[2] and he was also a confirmed Latitudinarian (a term used for those who were softening on key biblical doctrines). Both Unitarianism and Latitudinarianism were apostate movements that quickly developed out of the "liberal" Protestants in 17th century England. The Unitarians insisted that God was a single person, and that Jesus Christ was not God. Hoping to serve as a moderate voice of religious apostasy, the Latitudinarians tried to avoid both the dogmatism of the Unitarians and the Trinitarians. After the smoke has settled on the burned-out Christian world in England, it is hard to figure which group was worse—the Unitarians or the Latitudinarians.

If we were to compare the apostasy of John Locke with that of Descartes, Locke's rejection of the Christian faith was more pronounced. Wherever there was a softening on biblical orthodoxy and the Reformed faith, John Locke was all for it. Over his lifetime he retreated from the long-standing orthodox principles that had constituted the Christian faith in the West for 1500 years. He rejected outright the doctrine of original sin. He strongly eschewed biblical Old Testament ethics, and advocated the abandonment of biblical epistemology. By 1685, he openly confessed doubts about the verbal inspiration of the Bible. Writing to a Dutch friend of the humanist "Remonstrant" movement, he stated, "If everything in the Holy Scriptures is to be indiscriminately accepted by us as divinely inspired, a great opportunity will be given to philosophers

2. Ibid. 126.

for doubting our faith and sincerity."[3] His words were prophetic, for that became the fundamental starting point for every liberal in the church, from the higher critics of the 18th century to the Neo-orthodox thinkers of the 20th century. John Locke could see that philosophical knowledge built upon human reason would eventually consume practically every proposition of sacred doctrine found in Holy Scripture in future years. And he led the way.

Many accuse John Locke of Unitarian or Socinian leanings.[4] One biographer refers to Locke's book, *The Reasonableness of Christianity*, as "a Unitarian or Socinian book in everything but name."[5] However, it was not Locke's intention to defend either position in the book. The point he was trying to make was that *it didn't matter*. In other words, for Locke there would be no real difference between a Jehovah's Witness and an Athanasian Christian. He boldly attacked the Athanasian creed and other "tri-theistic" accretions in favor of the "simple," "reasonable" interpretations he drew from Scripture. Evidently, Locke's pride could not tolerate the mysteries and incomprehensibility of the Godhead. By this time, human reason was king, and any apparent paradoxes were made to fit with "what seems right to us."

While his opponents were sure of his anti-Trinitarian views, others were ambivalent. Towards the end of his life, even a close friend, Edward Stillingfleet, Bishop of Worcester, referred to him as a Socinian and in a series of published letters, gently called for his repentance. Curiously, John Locke did not deny the charge directly. Instead, he shifted the focus to tertiary issues in his response, attempting to find common ground on some less fundamental doctrine. A careful reading of the books and letters of John Locke will identify the contours of the story of Christian apostasy in the 17th century.

In the end, John Locke attempted to separate faith from knowledge entirely. While he still held that knowledge could achieve certainty, he believed that faith could not. "When it is brought to certainty, faith is destroyed," Locke wrote.[6] But his attempt to separate faith and knowledge could never succeed, since knowledge is defined as a *justified,*

---

3. Ibid. 255.
4. The Socinian sect originated in Italy during the latter part of the 16th century. They rejected the doctrines of the Trinity and the deity of Christ.
5. Ibid. 390.
6. John Locke, *Reply to the Bishop of Worcester's Answer to his Letter.*

true belief. What then is belief, but the faith that something is true? By the time Locke had come to the conclusion that there was no connection between faith and knowledge, all that was left of Aquinas' sacred knowledge and the certainty of divine revelation had eroded. Clearly Locke's faithlessness was quickly losing certainty. The Apostles would have contended strongly with him.

> *"For I know whom I have believed, and am persuaded that he is able to keep that which I have committed unto him against that day." 2 Tim. 1:12*

> *"These things have I written unto you that believe on the name of the Son of God; that ye may know that ye have eternal life, and that ye may believe on the name of the Son of God." 1 John 5:13.*

There is no absolute agreement among scholars on the *degree* of compromise in John Locke's Christian orthodoxy. However, we can be certain that Locke was not a Reformed, orthodox Puritan by the end of his life. This man set a bad direction for himself and for the Western world. If he had been a Christian, would there have been any doubt concerning his commitment to the fundamental Christian doctrines, such as the deity of Christ and the Trinity?

INFLUENCE

In the 18th century, humanist rationalism progressively trumped the teachings of Scripture, and John Locke was an indispensable link in the chain of apostasy in Europe and America. By his powerful ideas and influence, John Locke weakened core Christian commitments that had reigned in the Western world for almost 1500 years.

Some dramatic changes came about in our world between 1630 and 1730. The radical ideas that were overtaking the universities in England began seeping into America. Established as the training ground for most of America's pastors, Harvard University quickly succumbed to the Latitudinarians and then moved towards Unitarianism in the 19th century. The Western apostasy was in full swing. In response to the liberalization of Harvard, conservative churchmen opened Yale College in 1701 and the College of New Jersey (Princeton College) in 1748. Many have wondered how America could have moved so quickly from solid, Reformed, Trinitarian theology to a weakened Unitarian theology by the 1770s. What happened between 1632 and 1704 that brought about the weakening of the Christian faith at Harvard Seminary? During John Locke's life span (1632 to 1704), Harvard was founded and succumbed to Latitudinarianism. John Locke and his fellow academics provided the intellectual ammunition needed for the breakdown of the Christian faith at the university level. According to one source, "Locke's religious trajectory began in Calvinist Trinitarianism, but by the time of the *Reflections* (1695), Locke was advocating not just Socinian views on tolerance but also Socinian Christology; with veiled denial of the pre-existence of Christ."[7]

John Locke's influence on the Western world is truly remarkable. Historians Charles Taylor and Jerrold Seigal claim that Locke's "Essay Concerning Human Understanding" marked "the beginning of the modern Western conception of the self."[8] The French revolutionary and left-wing enlightenment philosopher Voltaire referred to him as "le sage Locke." Thomas Jefferson included a verbatim quote from Locke in the *Declaration of Independence.* According to *USHistory.org*, "the single most important influence that shaped the founding of the United States comes from John Locke." Even Christian organizations that trace the roots of our nation find John Locke to be the seminal thinker behind the formation of the Republic. *Wallbuilders.com* comments, "It is not an exaggeration to say that without [John Locke's] substantial influence on American thinking, there might well be no United States of America today."[9]

There is little debate concerning John Locke's significant influence on modern democracy. However, it is perhaps more instructive to identify the type of influence Locke had on the formation of the American Republic. Whereas previous state charters had self-consciously included references to God in their compacts, John Locke regarded compacts as civil contracts made *between men.*[10] In this regard, Locke's theory of government was not that much different than that of Jean-Jacques

7. "John Locke," http://en.wikipedia.org/wiki/John_Locke
8. Ibid.
9. David Barton, "John Locke, A Philosophical Founder of America," http://www.wallbuilders.com/libissuesarticles.asp?id=99156
10. John Locke, *First Treatise on Civil Government*, 8.1

Rousseau (who represented the left-wing enlightenment later in the 18th century). It was this thinking that shifted America's civil compacts from the words "In the Name of God, Amen" to "We the People of the United States." The Mayflower Pilgrims had explicitly included God in the very first words of their compact laid down in 1620. But by 1788, the United States Constitution was carefully worded to avoid this important reference. *It was John Locke who set the trajectory towards the secular democracies and republics.*

Putting all that aside, it was more John Locke's philosophical approach that yielded the most devastating assault on the Christian worldview in the West. Consider the following quote from a modern scholar:

Locke's attack on innate ideas was part and parcel of his anti-authoritarianism and his emphasis on the importance of free and autonomous inquiry... Bishop Stillingfleet, the most prominent of Locke's early critics, claimed that Locke's new way of ideas would lead to skepticism and that his account of substance undermined the doctrine of the trinity. Locke denied this, but given that we have good reason to hold that Locke was an anti-trinitarian, we have some reason to doubt that this denial is sincere. Locke's epistemological views and his advocacy of rational religion were taken up by early eighteenth century deists such as John Toland and Anthony Collins who drew conclusions about religion that outraged the orthodox. The age of rational religion was coming to a close by the middle of the eighteenth century.[11]

Of highest importance is a man's epistemological system, because it is so fundamental to his religion and poitics. If the foundations are compromised, then the super-struture will suffer the consequences. Undoubtably, it was his confidence in human reason that led him to doubt the doctrine of the Trinity.

"For many deceivers are entered into the world, who confess not that Jesus Christ is come in the flesh. This is a deceiver and an antichrist. Look to yourselves, that we lose not those things which we have wrought, but that we receive a full reward. Whosoever transgresseth, and abideth

11. "The Influence of John Locke's Works," *Stanford Encyclopedia of Philosophy*, http://plato.stanford.edu/entries/locke/influence.html

APOSTATE

not in the doctrine of Christ, hath not God. He that abideth in the doctrine of Christ, he hath both the Father and the Son." (2 John 7-9).

LOCKE'S PHILOSOPHY

John Locke introduces his *Essay Concerning Human Understanding* with these familiar words that describe his philosophical empiricism:

> Let us then suppose the mind to be, as we say, white paper, void of all characters, without any ideas: —How comes it to be furnished? Whence comes it by that vast store which the busy and boundless fancy of man has painted on it with an almost endless variety? To this I answer, in one word, from experience. In that all our knowledge is founded; and from that it ultimately derives itself. Our observation employed either, about external sensible objects or about the internal operations of our minds perceived and reflected on by ourselves, is that which supplies our understandings with all the materials of thinking. These two are the fountains of knowledge, from whence all the ideas we have, or can naturally have, do spring.[12]

When Locke's philosophical system comes to address knowledge, God is completely out of the picture. Right away, the Christian is alerted to the sounds of epistemological heterodoxy, for the Bible presents God, and more specifically, Jesus Christ, as the fount of all knowledge and wisdom (Col. 2:3, John 14:6). How can the autonomous human mind, apart from God and His revelation, derive any certain knowledge from mere experience? If the mind starts with nothing, how does it process the first data that enters it? How can the mind be sure that the first network of presuppositions that is presented to it has any validity and is well suited to process new data? Eventually, even the well-known philosophical skeptic David Hume rejected this theory of knowledge outright.

This autonomous human reasoning is foolishness to the mind of the believer who understands that the source of all knowledge must be God Who reveals it to man by His natural and special revelation (Psalm 19, Rom. 1:19-22). However, the mind of the unbeliever rejects both natural and special revelation as God's communicated truth. Because his foolish mind is darkened, he will mishandle that knowledge and contort his

12. John Locke, *An Essay Concerning Human Understanding*, vol.1.

worldview. Over time, he will find himself processing information badly, resulting in a breakdown of knowledge. Eventually, this will lead to a disintegration of his social systems, economics, education, and scientific endeavors. True knowledge can only come from God, whether by oral or written form, by natural or special revelation. As the knowledge of Christ's Word spread throughout the world, this knowledge became more accessible to the masses. Much of the world has emerged from the darkness of paganism over 2,000 years only because they have had some access to a Western, biblical worldview - although it is now fading in the West.

If we are entirely dependent upon our senses and the internal operations of our minds to know that a certain proposition is true, then the Word of God is hardly necessary to "equip the man of God for every good work" (2 Tim. 3:16, 17). According to Locke, one's own mind is sufficient to discern truth apart from divine revelation. Thus, we may gain a right perspective concerning the most fundamental truths, as well as ethics and civil government, without the authoritative instruction of God's Word. Locke does not see a need for God's revelation to frame his thoughts in any form before processing information in his mind.

LOCKE'S THEOLOGICAL MEANDERINGS

Since John Locke considers the human mind as the ultimate measure of what might be termed "reasonable," he subjects the Christian faith and the Bible to this test in *The Reasonableness of Christianity*. In an attempt to reduce the faith to one simple statement, he writes; "Whoever takes Jesus the Messiah for his King, with a resolution to live by His laws, and does sincerely repent, as often as he transgresses any of them, is His subject; all such are Christians."[13] While many Christians would not disagree with Locke's creed thus far, still he rejects doctrines like the Trinity, the Sovereignty of God, the Atonement of Christ, and the Resurrection of Christ as essential to the Christian faith. Apparently, according to Locke, there is some man named Christ who is King and we are supposed to obey His laws, but this applies only to certain laws that Locke finds acceptable. This philosophy becomes the dominant religion in 18th century England and America.

Later in the same paragraph from *Reasonableness*, Locke writes, "Since

13. John Locke, *The Reasonableness of Christianity*

APOSTATE

it is impossible explicitly to believe any proposition of the Christian doctrine, but what we understand, or in any other sense, than we understand it to have been delivered in; an explicit belief is or can be required in no man, of more than what he understands of that doctrine." This is an example of Latitudinarian rationalism at its best. John Locke would have nothing to do with mysteries, even though the Bible is filled with them. In Scripture, one of the qualifications for church leaders is that they are able to hold the "mysteries of the faith in a pure conscience" (1 Tim. 3:12). John Locke argues here that these mysterious doctrines (like the Trinity) are not essential to the faith. He also finds the Old Testament too irrational, unethical, and unrealistic to the civilized, rational mind of the 17th century humanist. All in all, he places far too high a trust in human reason. To say that there is one God in three persons, all of the same essence, does not "make sense" to human reason. Moreover, Locke fails to distinguish between the words "understand" and "comprehend." While we may not fully comprehend the mysterious Trinitarian nature of God, it should not be difficult to understand what the Bible says about the Trinity. We may not be able to resolve the apparent paradox of the one and the three. But Locke wants to allow "latitude" for the rational mind of the Anti-Trinitarian. If he cannot fully explain the doctrine and resolve the mysteries of it, he has the right to reject it. Whereas Locke does not want to deny the doctrine of the Trinity publicly, he certainly allows others who can not "comprehend" the mystery to reject it outright. As an important leader in the London academic community, he weakens the relative importance of the doctrine. This was a crucial move on the part of the adversary towards the destruction of the Christian faith in the West in the 18th and 19th centuries.

Christians, on the other hand, are called to humility, especially when faced with the ultimate metaphysical mysteries. When they look at the problem of the unity and particularity in philosophy, they explain the impossibility with the "incomprehensible" doctrine of the Trinity. God is One and God is Three. Meanwhile, humanist philosophers only pretend to resolve these impossibilities. When Christians set out to resolve the problem of metaphysical causality in determinism and indeterminism, they explain that the solution to this impossibility is incomprehensible as well. For example, if everything in the universe happens by ultimate determinist or indeterminist forces, human responsibility and free will disappear. But Christians resolve this intellectual conundrum handily by acknowledging God's personal and sovereign rule over His creation. We say that God foreordains the free actions of men, and we have no idea how He does it! These mysteries serve as major foundation stones for the Christian worldview. We openly acknowledge tension in these apparent paradoxes, and demand humility from arrogant men who attempt to explain infinitude by human finitude. That the rational humanist mind refused to these mysterious truths was an important impetus to the apostasy in the West.

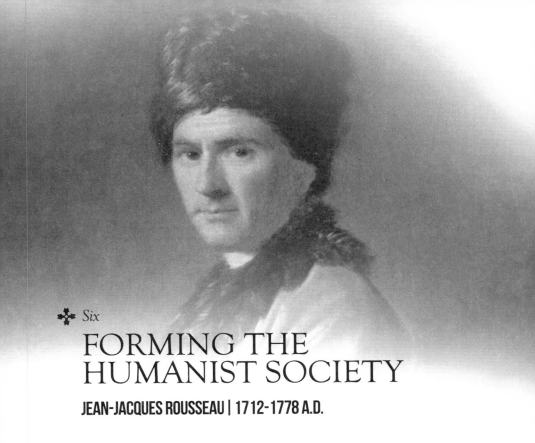

Six

FORMING THE HUMANIST SOCIETY

JEAN-JACQUES ROUSSEAU | 1712-1778 A.D.

T he great philosophers presented in this book are all intellectual giants who exerted enormous influence upon the Western world. Their ideas set the direction for entire nations, cultures, and civilizations. They formed the worldview that undergirds the thinking and life of the average person living in Europe, Asia, and America today. Few others in the history of the world have exerted this much influence upon the lives of so many people. Their ideas were utterly ruinous. Temporarily, they threatened the kingdom influence of Jesus Christ in the Western world. It is important that my reader gain a sense of the sheer magnitude of the powerful ideas that eroded a Christian civilization in the West and elsewhere around the world. After 1,500 years of Christian dominance, these men managed to empty the churches, secularize education, paganize the culture, eradicate the nuclear family economy, and build the modern humanist state. A few of them (like John Dewey and Friedrich Nietzsche) self-consciously realized and openly acknowledged their opposition to

Jesus Christ Himself. Herein lies a challenge to the faith of the Christian believer. Would these men set themselves against the influence and efforts of the risen Christ? If Jesus Christ is ruling on the right hand of the Father, this can only be seen as a temporary setback. If we believe that Christ is head over all principalities and powers in the present era, we can be sure that these humanist giants and the ideas they espoused will soon fall. They will tumble like Dagon before the Ark of the Covenant.

> *"What is the exceeding greatness of His power to us-ward who believe, according to the working of His mighty power, which He wrought in Christ, when He raised Him from the dead, and set Him at His own right hand in the heavenly places, far above all principality, and power, and might, and dominion, and every name that is named, not only in this world, but also in that which is to come: And hath put all things under His feet, and gave Him to be the head over all things to the church"* (Eph. 1:20-22).

INFLUENCE

Of all the modern Nephilim, the most imposing figure may very well have been the French philosopher Jean-Jacques Rousseau. He was the pivotal philosopher who gave birth to the modern age, which historians generally agree began in 1820. When Will Durant set out to write his extensive history of the world, he dedicated an entire volume to Jean-Jacques Rousseau. Says Durant, Rousseau "had more effect upon posterity than any other writer or thinker of that eighteenth century in which writers were more influential than they had ever been before."[1] Rousseau's fingerprints are all over the institutions of the modern world. Schools, churches, and governments have incorporated his ideologies in their organizational methodologies. For example, governments antedating the modern age barely consumed 5-10% of their national incomes.[2] After Rousseau, democratic statism came to dominate almost every nation in the world, and now most governments consume over 50% of their national income. The political, social, and educational institutions that provide the modern context for life on planet earth were very much defined by this man. In turn, the churches were forced

---

1. Will and Ariel Durant, *Rousseau and Revolution* (New York: Simon and Schuster, 1967), 3.
2. www.usgovernmentspending.com

to accommodate the social systems imposed upon them. Tragically, the political revolutions in France, Germany, China, and Russia that ended in the deaths of hundreds of millions of people were rooted in Rousseau's revolutionary doctrine. Karl Marx's communist ideologies, including the elimination of private property ownership, initially appeared in Rousseau's *Social Contract*.

Historian Paul Johnson recognizes Rousseau as the most influential of all of the philosophers who gave birth to the modern world. In Johnson's words, Rousseau was:

> *"the first of the modern intellectuals, their archetype and in many ways the most influential of them all. Older men like Voltaire had started the work of demolishing the altars and enthroning reason. But Rousseau was the first to combine all the salient characteristics... the assertion of his right to reject the existing order in its entirety; confidence in his capacity to refashion it from the bottom in accordance with principles of his own devising; belief that this could be achieved by the political process; and, not least, recognition of the huge part instinct, intuition, and impulse play in human conduct."[3]*

The first of the modern revolutions took place in the 1790s under the auspices of Maximilien Francois Marie Isidore de Robespierre, the chief architect of the French Revolution. Rousseau had the most significant influence on the revolutionary Robespierre, although Rousseau was dead by the time the revolution commenced. Robespierre was particularly proud of his acquaintance with the philosopher behind the revolution. In a letter to Rousseau, he wrote, "I saw you during your last days, and the memory remains a source of pride and joy. I contemplated your august features, and saw on them marks of dark disappointments to which you were condemned by the injustice of mankind."[4] If ideas have consequences, it was the ideas of Jean-Jacques Rousseau that brought about the spirit of revolution, the reign of terror, the guillotine, the forced redistribution of wealth, and 40,000 dead bodies. Regrettably, the horror did not end with Robespierre's execution. Biographer Otto Scott wrote, "Robespierre died, but folly has a virulence that outlasts its inventor. He inspired more Communes, more Voices of Virtue, more Lenins and Castros and Maos,

3. Paul Johnson, *Intellectuals* (New York: Harper and Row, 1988), 2.
4. Otto Scott, *Robespierre: The Fool as Revolutionary* (Windsor: The Reformer, 1995), 18.

more murder and hatred, more death and misery, than any other of the Sacred Fools that have emerged to plague honest men."[5] Rousseau was to Robespierre what Marx was to Lenin and Mao. First come the ideas, and then the consequences. What was it that Jesus Christ told us? *"Ye shall know them by their fruits."*

It is hard to pinpoint which of Rousseau's writings were most influential, for *Social Contract* shaped political states everywhere, but *Émile* may have been the most damaging of all. The book was radical for its day. When Rousseau told fathers they owed "their children to the state,"[6] he laid out a fundamental social view that would dominate for the next three centuries. Plato had alluded to this in *The Republic*, but no other empire or nation had ever used language which required such absolute subservience to a civil magistrate as this. You would have had to search long and hard to find any small city state over the 4,000 years of world history leading up to Rousseau's life that mandated a compulsory attendance law in order to indoctrinate hundreds of millions (if not billions) of citizens in statist ideologies. Rousseau's ideas provided the fertile ground that the statist educational theory needed to thrive in the 19th and 20th centuries. This philosopher's vision for statist education found acceptance in Prussia at around the same time of the publication of *Emile* (1763-1765). It would take another century before America incorporated these compulsory attendance laws - the modern statist system was finally in place when the state of Mississippi finally adopted the law in 1917.[7]

ROUSSEAU'S LIFE

As with the other great apostate minds, Rousseau backslid out of a rich Christian heritage. Born in Geneva, Jean-Jacques Rousseau was the grandson of a Calvinist preacher. His mother died within a week of his birth, and his father abandoned him to a boarding school in his tenth year. Five years later, he set out to wander around Switzerland on his own. Still homeless and rootless at sixteen, he attempted to commit adultery with

---

5. Ibid. 233, 234.

6. Jean-Jacques Rousseau, *Emile* (London: Everyman, 1911), 19.

7. Prior to the modern age, there were only a few attempts to establish government-mandated, compulsory attendance. Joshua Ben Gamla attempted it in Israel shortly before God brought judgment upon that nation for its gross disobedience and rejection of Christ. During the outset of the enlightenment, Scotland also dabbled a little with this ill-conceived idea.

another man's wife, commencing a long life of serial fornication. As an adult, Rousseau's philosophy turned sharply towards humanism, which some believe was related to his antipathy to the biblical view of human nature. Tragically, he noted in his writings that followers of Christ would not make good citizens[8] Such dangerous words would pave the way for the persecution of Christians at the hands of France and other humanist nations. He also revived the old myth that it was Christianity that had weakened the Roman state and brought about the fall of Rome. This is not to say that Rousseau did not believe in God or did not advocate some of the truths of Scripture here and there throughout his writings. In a nation where a thousand years of Christianity still permeated the culture, it would have been imprudent for this apostate to avoid God altogether. In 1765 France, the establishment would not have paid much attention to a self-proclaimed atheist.

Nevertheless, the apostasy from Christian orthodoxy was moving along smartly in Rousseau's day. Throughout his writings Rousseau clearly exalted human reason over divine revelation. He repudiated the doctrine of hell, rejected original sin outright, denied miracles, and considered all religions as equally credible.[9] These are still daring movements for an 18th century apostate - even John Locke's theological discrepancies fifty years earlier were tame in comparison.

Twenty years before *Émile*, a life-changing event occurred with the philosopher when his live-in girlfriend birthed his first child. Immediately, Rousseau bundled up the child and deposited it on the steps of an orphanage. This happened to be during the dead of winter, a time when babies disposed of in such a way had a scant chance of survival. In subsequent years, the wretch had a total of five children and each received the same derelict treatment. Sadly, there are no records concerning the gender of the children, for Rousseau never cared about such things. Concerning this "great" philosopher's gross moral failure, Paul Johnson writes, "What began as a process of personal self-justification—gradually evolved into the proposition that education was the concern of the State. By a curious chain of infamous moral logic, Rousseau's iniquity as a parent was linked to his ideological offspring, the future totalitarian state."[10]

8. Jean-Jacques Rousseau, *Social Contract*, 4.8
9. Jean-Jacques Rousseau, *Emile*, 274-330.
10. Paul Johnson, *Intellectuals*, 23.

"Ye shall not afflict any widow, or fatherless child. If thou afflict them in any wise, and they cry at all unto me, I will surely hear their cry; And my wrath shall wax hot, and I will kill you with the sword; and your wives shall be widows, and your children fatherless" (Exod. 22:22-24).

Jean-Jacques Rousseau was the prototypical liberal hypocrite who kills his babies in the morning and argues passionately for welfare redistributions to the indigent in the afternoon. Incredibly, Rousseau referred to himself as the greatest lover of mankind who ever lived. "I love myself too much to hate anybody," he once noted. His raw hubris and narcissism were altogether without limit. "If there were a single enlightened government in Europe," he told somebody, "it would have erected statues to me... It will then be no empty honor to have been a friend of Jean-Jacques Rousseau." These words came from a man who abandoned his own children on the steps of an orphanage and refused to honor the mother of his children with even a wedding ring. His acquaintances were particularly annoyed by his obnoxious habit of urinating in public. His self-conceit knew no bounds. He would gush, "The person who can love me as I can love is still to be born. . .No one has ever had more talent for loving. . .I was born to be the best friend that ever existed. . .I would leave this life with apprehension if I knew a better man than me. . .Show me a better man than me, a heart more loving, more tender, more sensitive. . .Posterity will honour me. . .because it is my due. . .I rejoice in myself. . .my consolation lies in my self-esteem."[11]

Rousseau's live-in girlfriend stayed with him for thirty-three years despite the fact that he "never felt the least glimmering of love for her." In retrospect, Rousseau may have been the prototypical narcissist. He wrote, "The sensual needs I satisfied with her were purely sexual and were nothing to do with her as an individual... I told her I would never leave her and never marry her." All the while, he maintained a relationship with another woman, Sophie d'Houdetot, whom he described, "The first and only love of all my life." Evidently, she didn't think much of him; after his death, she called him "a pathetic figure... an interesting

11. J.H. Huizinga, *The Making of a Saint: The Tragi-Comedy of Jean-Jacques Rousseau* (London: H. Hamilton, 1976)

APOSTATE

madman."[12]

It is fitting that this is the father of the secular state and the modern compulsory public education system. He is the father of the world where 40-50% of children are born outside of wedlock and the state promises womb-to-tomb social security for everyone. This is the madman who constructed our modern world. He had "immense influence" on John Dewey.[13] Now, billions of people follow his ideas over the wisdom of the old Christian order. As social systems continue to crumble around us, future generations will look back in disbelief at the foolishness of those who accepted Rousseau's thinking without question. They will wonder why so many people were taken by the ideas of a lunatic. Then, they will know that "all those who hate wisdom love death" (Prov. 8:36). God has a way of teaching His truth by historical object lessons. He makes it easy for us to see why we shouldn't follow a self-consumed narcissist who urinated in public and abandoned his five children on the steps of an orphanage. What makes the lesson so rich is that it is only learned after test-driving his prescribed social order for three hundred years!

Rousseau was highly influential, hopelessly utopian, wildly arrogant, and outrageously popular among academics. He was the archetypal humanist philosopher who lives in an ivory tower, loving mankind but hating any real person he ever met - especially his own family, children and common law wife. In his writings, Rousseau provided some insight into what he was thinking when he abandoned his children on the steps of an orphanage: "How could I achieve the tranquility of mind necessary for my work, my garret filled with domestic cares and the noise of children?" i.e. How could he ever create a utopia for the rest of the world without providing a hell for his own children? By the end of his sad life, Rousseau was hated by almost everybody who knew him. But the tragic part of the story is that most of the world loved him and followed him as they developed their democracies, their socialist states, their literature, schools, and fragmented families. This deranged "madman" created a new world in his own image. Now, Rousseau's orphanage is much expanded in the form of government-funded day schools, kindergartens, preschools, daycares, and foster care! In our country, over 50% of children born to women under 30 years of age are born without

12. Johnson, *Intellectuals*, 19, 27.
13. "Emile," in *Encyclopedia Americana*, Vol. 10 (New York: Americana Corporation, 1958), 294.

fathers,[14] and 64% of children under six are left alone for large portions of the day.[15] The state controls almost all of the education programs in most developed countries around the world, and parental freedoms are increasingly disappearing in the European Union and America.[16]

It would be difficult to construct a fictional character as twisted, pathetic, or evil as Jean-Jacques Rousseau. Yet, he is treated as a sort of god by many modern thinkers. Incredibly, Immanuel Kant, the great philosopher of the 19th century described Rousseau as one who possessed "a sensibility of soul of unequaled perfection." Leo Tolstoy, the towering literary genius from Russia said that Rousseau and the Gospel had been "The two great and healthy influences of my life." Percy Shelley referred to him as "a sublime genius," and John Dewey, the father of modern education, praised Rousseau as "The greatest educational reformer of modern times."[17] We are incredulous. What spell did this man cast upon the philosopher class and the whole world that came after him? How could men of such intellectual stature reduce themselves to such foolishness in their commendations of a fool? There was something profoundly perverse and unsound about Jean-Jacques Rousseau and his ideas. If this be the case, there must be something very misguided with those minds who cannot find any problem with him. *There must be something very wrong with our world.*

"Ye shall know them by their fruits. Do men gather grapes of thorns, or figs of thistles? Even so every good tree bringeth forth good fruit; but a corrupt tree bringeth forth evil fruit. A good tree cannot bring forth evil fruit, neither can a corrupt tree bring forth good fruit. Every tree that bringeth not forth good fruit is hewn down, and cast into the fire. Wherefore by their fruits ye shall know them." Matthew 7:16-20.

14. http://www.nytimes.com/2012/02/18/us/for-women-under-30-most-births-occur-outside-marriage.html?pagewanted=all&_r=0
15. Mary Eberstadt, *Home Alone America: The Hidden Toll of Day Care, Behavioral Drugs, and Other Parent Substitutes* (New York: Sentinel HC, 2004)
16. "Constricting Childhood: The Expansion of Compulsory Attendance Laws" http://www.hslda.org/courtreport/v16n5/v16n501.asp
http://www.thenewamerican.com/world-news/europe/item/13503-homeschoolers-flee-persecution-in-germany-and-sweden
"Parental Rights in the Schools: Do they exist after Palmdale?" http://www.educationlawconsortium.org/forum/2007/papers/Marino2007.pdf
17. Arthur Huebsch, "Jean-Jacques Rousseau and John Dewey: A Comparative Study and a Critical Estimateof Their Philosophies and Their Educational and Related Theories and Practices." (unpublished doctoral thesis, School of Education, New York University, 1930)

PHILOSOPHY

From the very first words of *Social Contract*, Rousseau veers off the biblical track and abandons his Christian roots. He writes, "Man is born free; and everywhere he is in chains."[18] The words sound good to the humanist mind, but not to the mind of the man trained to think according to a biblical anthropology. Man is born enslaved to sin (Rom. 6:16, Ps. 51:5, Eph. 2:1), and this constitutes his basic problem. However, the modus operandi of humanist leaders is always to point out man's tertiary problems, promising a redemption that fails to address the root issue. In the end, the humanist misses the root problem by a mile and his solutions are no solutions at all. He riles up the masses against their social systems and their local fiefdoms, only to shift them over to another form of tyranny under large, powerful nation states. Thus, the humanist moves his people from the frying pan into the fire, because he is unwilling to deal with man's primary issue. Jesus Christ, addresses a nation enslaved to the Roman power when He says, "Whosoever commits sin is a servant of sin. . .If the Son will make you free, you will be free indeed" (John 8:34-36).

In *Discourse on the Origin of Inequality*, Rousseau explicitly rejects the biblical view of man, which describes man's nature as sinful and depraved (Rom. 3:9-18). According to Rousseau, primitive, natural man has no depraved nature, but he is "perfect in *potentio*."[19] It is rather a wrongly-ordered society that is responsible for the bad things in the world. Of course, Rousseau points at the old Christian order as the aberrant society and the source of modern man's problems. He wants to replace Christian society with something better. At root, he believes that the right social system, the right ideas, and the right civil rulers in power will form man into a better creature. Whatever the "old order" has yielded is unacceptable to Rousseau, so he advocates a revolutionary agenda that must involve the state.

Rousseau continues in the *Social Contract*:

> *"The problem is to find a form of association which will defend and protect with the whole common force the person and goods of each associate, and in which each, while uniting himself with all, may still*

18. Jean-Jacques Rousseau, *Social Contract*, Introduction
19. Jean-Jacques Rousseau, *Discourse on the Origin of Inequality*, 1.2

obey himself alone, and remain as free as before."[20]

Here, Rousseau's utopian pipe dreams are supposed to draw in the gullible masses. He proposes a world of maximum freedom through "autonomy" where man is a law to himself. Somehow, the state is supposed to protect everyone, yet the individual is left to "obey himself alone," which is the goal of humanism. Natural man or humanist man wants to be left alone to "obey himself alone." Of course, this is not freedom - in the biblical perspective, this is sin. When Eve succumbed to the temptation in the garden, the devil promised that she could determine good and evil for herself (Gen. 3:5). As modern man rejects God as Lawgiver, and seeks to "obey himself alone," he is self-consciously embracing the original sin committed by Adam and Eve in the garden. Thus, the source of law for Rousseau is man, while the source of law for the Christian is God. Of course, fallen man is more than happy to take the place of God and become his own lawgiver. Contrary to Rousseau's hopes and aspirations, this sinful inclination does not produce maximum freedom nor does it release man from his chains. In the end, this rebellion always heightens governmental tyranny, which is exactly what happened in nations that followed Rousseau's ideas.

The founding fathers of this country would have rejected Rousseau's words out of hand. For example, Benjamin Franklin is known for his quip, "Either you will be governed by God, or by God, you will be governed!" That is, either man must submit himself to the laws of God, or he will find himself tyrannized — by God's sovereign ordination. These men understood the importance of obedience to the laws of God, while Rousseau did not.

But it gets worse. Rousseau's overweening confidence in human nature and his rejection of God's law produces a dreadful social theory. He admires the "natural" man who is born free and "lives for himself," but he hopes that this man will grow into the ideal "citizen," a slave of the socialist state. This man is "but the numerator of a fraction, whose value depends on its denominator; his value depends upon the whole, that is, on the community. Good social institutions are those best fitted to make a man unnatural, to exchange his natural independence for dependence: to merge the unit in the group, so that he no longer regards himself as

20. Jean-Jacques Rousseau, *Social Contract*

APOSTATE

one, but as a part of the whole, and is only conscious of the common life."[21]

Thus, Rousseau cannot find the happy medium between the ultimacy of the individual and the ultimacy of the corporate body. He cannot draw a fine line between the "one and the many" or between the anarchy of the individual who does whatever he wants to do and the tyranny of the corporate state that dictates all human action. Christians believe that the one and the many are equally ultimate in God Himself, the Trinity. In the self-consistent Christian mind, God is both one and three. This is what balances out a Christian social order, because Christians understand that both individual liberty and the structure of the corporate body politic are important for a stable society. At this point, however, the Western World had *already rejected Trinitarian Christianity* as having nothing to do with philosophical knowledge or social orders. Therefore the Western world devises its own political and social systems, based on unaided human reason sans God's revelation. The state becomes ultimate for Rousseau. The individual unit entirely merges into the group, and the individual no longer regards his own individuality. This harmful philosophy has been and continues to be the source of all draconian tyrannies, social programming, bureaucratic machines, and Orwellian nightmares which have abridged the freedoms for billions of people over the last two centuries.

George Washington, America's first President was strongly influenced by the Christian worldview when he wrote, "*Government is like fire—a dangerous servant and a cruel master.*" Our founding fathers did not trust government with unlimited power because of a right understanding and a fundamental mistrust of the nature of man. Rousseau did not share this anthropology, so he created a world of tyranny, social disintegration, moral decay, and civil unrest.

It is hard to comprehend the deceptive and dangerous character of Rousseau's social theory until we trace his ideas through to their ultimate consequences in France, Russia, China, and elsewhere. Rousseau's ill-fated words from *Discourse on Inequality* influenced Karl Marx, and then served as a fundamental operating principle for almost every modern nation.

21. Jean-Jacques Rousseau, *Emile*, 8.

"The first man who, having fenced in a piece of land, said, 'This is mine,' and found people naïve enough to believe him, that man was the true founder of civil society. From how many crimes, wars, and murders, from how many horrors and misfortunes might not any one have saved mankind, by pulling up the stakes, or filling up the ditch, and crying to his fellows: Beware of listening to this impostor; you are undone if you once forget that the fruits of the earth belong to us all, and the earth itself to nobody."[22]

Before the revolutions, Rousseau happily attributes all the horrors and misfortunes on earth to private property. But now, after all of his bloody revolutions have run their course, we look back and discover that it was actually Rousseau and his messed-up anthropology, sociology, and ethical theories that brought about the horrors and misfortunes!

It is obvious from the quote above that Rousseau rejected the eighth commandment. When God wrote "Thou shalt not steal," He established private property ownership. Moreover, in passages like Exodus 20:15 and Deuteronomy 19:14, the Bible requires a respect for private property and the means of production. Jesus Christ also confirmed this in Matthew 20:15, when the landowner in His parable claimed the right to determine the wages for his workers without government intervention. According to Christ, an employer has the right to set unequal pay for his workers as long as they accept the terms.

Jean-Jacques Rousseau was an original big-government socialist at heart. He resolved the conflict between the will of the individual and the will of the people by insisting that the will of the people prevail. He refused to address this tension by submitting all individuals and social systems to the laws of God (the Trinitarian God).

For any social system based upon human reason, it is easier to err on one side or the other, than to hold to a metaphysical mystery that allows for both the "one" and the "many" to operate simultaneously. Some humanists want to turn individual man into god. Others will turn the corporate expression of man (the state) into god. Although Rousseau is tempted towards the first option, he settles for the second because he would rather deify corporate, democratic man, to the abandonment of individual liberties. Of course, he also had to reject family and church

---

22. Jean-Jacques Rousseau, *Discourse on Inequality*, 2.1

community as important elements of the human social system. As with many of the Enlightenment men, he held marriage in low esteem, and never married.

ROUSSEAU'S PHILOSOPHY OF EDUCATION

Will and Ariel Durrant summarize Rousseau's *Émile* in these words: "Rousseau wanted a system of public instruction by the state. He prescribed many years with an unmarried tutor, who would withdraw the child as much as possible from parents and relatives."[23] Rousseau's weakness as a parent is evident in the very first section of his book *Emile*, where he at first entertains the notion that fathers ought to educate their own children, and then dispensed with it altogether as impractical.

Per Rousseau, the father is expected to raise the child for the state, first and foremost. "A father owes men to humanity, citizens to the state."[24] Rousseau also refers to Plato's *Republic* as "the finest book ever written on education."[25] As it turns out, Plato's ideal social theory is radically antithetical to a Biblical social theory; I quote: "The wives of our guardians are to be common, and their children are to be common, and no parent is to know his own child, nor any child his parent... A woman, I said, at twenty years of age may begin to bear children to the State, and continue to bear them until forty." In order for the humanist vision of society to progress, it is essential that family relationships are eventually obliterated. Father-son relationships are unimportant to the humanist mind. The God-ordained covenant relationships of family and church are impediments to the humanist vision of the authoritarian, anonymous, all-powerful state. This was the pattern of Rousseau's life with his own father and his own children, and he passed it on to future generations through his influential writings. Further in *Émile*, we find that Rousseau is impressed by a Spartan woman who did not care that her five sons were slain in battle. It was their winning of the victory for Sparta as a nation that brought her to rejoicing.

Rousseau reveals more of his agenda for education in the 1755 publication *A Discourse on Political Economy*, when he took the word

---

23. Will and Ariel Durant, *Rousseau and Revolution* (New York: Simon and Schuster, 1967), 179.
24. Jean-Jacques Rousseau, *Emile*, 19.
25. Ibid. 8.

"economy" or "*oikonomia*" and applied it to the government of a nation.[26] Translated from the Greek, the word means "the vision of the family." But in the first paragraph of his essay, Rousseau takes the word "family" and applies it to "that great family the state." Rousseau the vagabond, the man without a family must turn the state into his family. He further clarifies, "Government ought the less indiscriminately to abandon to the intelligence and prejudices of fathers the education of their children, as that education is of still greater importance to the State than to the fathers."[27]

Over previous centuries, education had been a matter of family and church jurisdiction. In order to bring about the powerful modern nation state that is so important to his vision, Rousseau understands that government-funded education is indispensable. In order to move modern nations towards total government by democracy, education would have to come under the purview of the state. The state-controlled education system would then become a juggernaut, a force that would be irrepressible by any "conservative" or "distributist" coalition. This is the only way in which the state can replace the family, and bring the majority of the population into dependence upon state welfare and state employment. As the state replaces the family by its welfare programs, education programs, medical programs, and economic systems, eventually fathers become obsolete. This destroys family economies and creates a society where the majority of children are raised without fathers involved in their lives and the majority of marriages end in divorce. Rousseau goes on to describe education as "the most important business of the State."[28] What a genius! Given that no other empire in the history of mankind had pulled off this level of total government involvement in the lives of the citizens as envisioned by Rousseau, his visionary capabilities were nothing short of phenomenal. For these ideas to have borne such enormous influence upon so many nations, so many institutions, and so many humans in our world, *there must have been higher, spiritual forces at work.*

To the Christian mind trained in biblical truth, Rousseau's educational program is revolutionary and appalling. His religious instruction compromises almost every doctrine of the Christian faith. He completely

26. Jean-Jacques Rousseau, *A Discourse on Political Economy*, Introduction
27. Jean-Jacques Rousseau, *A Discourse on Political Economy*, Section II
28. Ibid.

rejects the wisdom of the book of Proverbs. If the book of Proverbs told us "A," Rousseau says "Not A." Here are a few choice nuggets:

"It is not part of a child's business to know right and wrong."[29]
"Give your scholar no verbal lessons."[30]
"Never make him say, 'Forgive me,' for he does not know how to do you wrong."[31]
"He deserves neither punishment nor reproof."[32]
"The only natural passion is self-love or selfishness taken in a wider sense. This selfishness is good in itself."[33]

Christians ought to recognize that this social theory counters a biblical social theory. However, because many Christians frame their ethical and social systems by Jean-Jacques Rousseau and Karl Marx more than by the Bible, they have unknowingly and enthusiastically participated in this vision. They have effectively followed the apostasy and adopted a humanist worldview.

But those who use Scripture to determine the jurisdictional boundaries of family, church, and state instantly recognize the revolutionary and destructive nature of Rousseau's program. They know that state ownership of children is tyrannical and antithetical to freedom as explained by the prophet Samuel in 1 Samuel 8:11-13. They find that the enslaving of children to state-controlled economies and corporations is a shame to a free people (Nehemiah 5:5, 6). They are horrified by the elimination of family economies. They are repelled by a state-controlled system of education since there is no example of it in Scripture, let alone any mandate for it. Throughout the Scriptures, God requires fathers to oversee and control the education of their children (Deut. 6:7-9, Eph. 6:4, 1 Thess. 2:11, Col. 3:21, the whole Book of Proverbs). Normatively, fathers and mothers raise their children. They teach their children and work towards family economic goals together. This is assumed in the fourth commandment (Exod. 20:10, also reference Matthew 4:21, Genesis 29:9, 1 Samuel 17:15, etc.). Revolutionary social systems such

29. Jean-Jacques Rousseau, *Emile*, 64.
30. Ibid. 66.
31. Ibid.
32. Ibid.
33. Ibid. 66, 67.

as those proposed by Jean-Jacques Rousseau destroy family economies, family inheritance, family care for the elderly, family charitable systems, family-based voting, and family-centered education.

CONTRIBUTION TO THE ROMANTIC PERIOD

The Enlightenment alone, with its focus on the supremacy of human reason, was insufficient to bring about the political and cultural revolutions of the 19th and 20th centuries. It is true that Rousseau starts out as a firm believer in human reason. Before long, he follows every other humanist philosopher as he crosses the line from rationality and reason to irrationality and unreasonableness. Inevitably, the self-sufficient, arrogant humanist will abandon tradition and history. He rebels against the past and casts off the old social norms and morals. He takes on the revolutionary spirit, and he will trust in his own heart and feelings regardless of the consequences. This is how Rousseau bridged the Enlightenment into the Romantic era. Rousseau is identified as the first of the Romantic thinkers. There would have been no Marx, no Nietzsche, and no Wagner without Jean-Jacques Rousseau's worldview of Romanticism. There would have been none of those bloody, senseless revolutions without Rousseau's revolutionary doctrine.

The historians are right - Jean-Jacques Rousseau was the most influential humanist thinker of the last 500 years. His ideas formed the contours of modern life more than any others. He prepared the way for the social political, and cultural revolutions that destroyed the family, eroded political freedoms, and unraveled entire civilizations. When the story is written of the decline and fall of Western civilization, Jean-Jacques Rousseau will head the first chapter. If the team of men who brought the Western world to its knees were arranged in a pyramid, the name "Jean-Jacques Rousseau" would take its place at the top.

Seven

FORMING THE HUMANIST ETHIC

JEREMY BENTHAM | 1748-1832 A.D.

JOHN STUART MILL | 1806-1873 A.D.

BERTRAND RUSSELL | 1872-1970 A.D.

Jeremy Bentham plays an indispensable part in the story of apostasy in that he was the first notable philosopher in the modern world who was a self professed atheist and an apologist for homosexuality. His better-known disciple, John Stuart Mill, carried on his legacy into mainstream English society. Both men rejected biblical law outright, advocating a new ethical theory based upon human reason known as "utilitarian ethics." They set the stage for the humanist ethical methodology and political liberalism that permeates the political states in most nations today.

Jeremy Bentham was the original liberal. He was a dead-to-rights opponent of the old Christian order and English Common Law, as represented by William Blackstone. Best known for his *Commentaries on the Laws of New England*, Blackstone conventionalized the laws that made up the old Christian order, replete with biblical references. All English-speaking nations received the great heritage of Christian law by way of Blackstone's commentaries and his advocacy for English Common Law.

But when Bentham first heard Blackstone's lectures at sixteen years of age, he said he heard "no small part of the lectures... with rebel ears."[1] He made no secret of his steadfast opposition to the Christian faith and his commitment to overturn the 1,000 year heritage of faith in the West. Among his "intellectual" friends, he would refer to Christianity as "the Jug," (short for "the juggernaut"). Although he was brought up under the tenets of the Church of England, he did not accept this or any other Christian creed.[2] His parents had named him after the Old Testament prophet Jeremiah, preferring the New Testament Greek nomenclature "Jeremy."[3]

According to G. W. Foote, a Bentham devotee and progressive in his own right, Jeremy Bentham served as the great apostle of radical humanism.

> "Bentham exercised a profound influence on the party of progress for nearly two generations. He was the father of Philosophical Radicalism, which did so much to free the minds and bodies of the English people, and which counted among its swordsmen historians like Grote, philosophers like Mill, wits like Sydney Smith, journalists like Fonblanque, and politicians like Roebuck. As a reformer in jurisprudence he has no equal. His brain swarmed with progressive ideas and projects for the improvement and elevation of mankind; and his fortune, as well as his intellect, was ever at the service of advanced causes. His skepticism was rather suggested than paraded in his multitudinous writings, but it was plainly expressed in a few special volumes. **Not Paul, but Jesus**, published under the pseudonym of Camaliel Smith is a slashing attack on the Great Apostle. "The Church of England Catechism Explained" is a merciless criticism of 'that great instrument for producing mental and political slaves.'"[4]

Thus, Bentham represented well the 18th century enlightened humanist, who set himself in opposition to the Apostles of Christ, the canonized Scriptures, and 1,700 years of Christian churches. His objective in this book *Not Paul, but Jesus* was to prove that "the Epistles of

1. Charles Milner Atkinson, *Jeremy Bentham: His Life and Work* (London: Methuen, 1905), 17.
2. Ibid. 210.
3. Ibid. 2.
4. Jeremy Bentham, *Not Paul, But Jesus*

APOSTATE

Paul... form no part of the religion of Jesus."[5]

By this time, the apostates were coming into their own. Even Jean-Jacques Rousseau would never have professed his apostasy in such stark terms as did Bentham. Still, atheism was hardly mainstream in the 1820s. In his most strident defense of atheism, Bentham had to write under the pseudonym, Philip Beauchamp. He brought together his most succinct collection of blasphemous thoughts in a work called, *Analysis of the Influence of Natural Religion on the Temporal Happiness of Mankind* (1822), in which he unashamedly attacked all religion, natural and supernatural. "Religion," he wrote, "has inflicted the deepest injury upon humanity."[6] He mocked at an "Invisible Being" who is pleased or displeased by human action, and punishes those who displease Him.[7] Christians may view God's thoughts and ways to be incomprehensible, but then Bentham takes them to be "capricious and insane." The arrogance of this man is breathtaking - with him human reason sits enthroned, and unless God explains Himself to the satisfaction of human reason, He loses His right to exist! If Bentham is god, and his mind is the standard of rationality, then of course God cannot be God. After all, there can only be one God if we are talking about the ultimate source of truth, ethics, and reality. As long as Bentham is god, there can be no competition with him. However, we would politely disagree with this dead god (Bentham died in 1832). According to the Christian worldview, *the God of the Bible is God*. He created the universe, and by definition His intelligence must far exceed the limitations of the human intellect. This is our worldview. We assume that God is incomprehensible, and yet knowable as far as He reveals Himself to us.

> "O the depth of the riches both of the wisdom and knowledge of God! how unsearchable are His judgments, and His ways past finding out! For who hath known the mind of the Lord? Or who hath been His counselor? Or who hath first given to Him, and it shall be recompensed unto Him again? For of Him, and through Him, and to Him, are all things: to whom be glory for ever. Amen." (Rom. 11:33-36).

5. Jeremy Bentham, *Not Paul But Jesus*, Introduction
6. Jeremy Bentham, *Analysis of the Influence of Natural Religion on the Temporal Happiness of Mankind* (1822), Preface
7. Ibid, Chapter 2

Not surprisingly, Bentham was also the driving force behind the re-introduction of homosexuality to Western culture. He would defend homosexual activity as long as it did not produce "bad consequences."

As he approached the end of his life, Bentham ordered his body to be dissected in a public anatomy lecture after which his skeleton and head were to be preserved in a wooden cabinet called an "Auto-icon." He wanted the Auto-icon to include his actual head, mummified for all to see. This macabre scene represents the worldview of a man who rejected the resurrection and gloried in his own death. The famous postmortem display of Jeremy Bentham includes a wax head on a wax body made to resemble the living Jeremy Bentham, with his mummified head lying at his feet. That is all that is left of the proud, dead man. While the man lived he mocked the resurrected King of kings and those that served Him. Now, who is laughing?

INFLUENCE

While it is true that Jeremy Bentham is less known than some of the great philosophers treated in this book, his influence is obscured only by the "glory" of his disciples. Actually, John Stuart Mill may have been the most influential English philosopher of the 19th century. He is generally considered the father of political liberalism, an ideology that argues for moral libertinism while downplaying the importance of economic and political freedom. In order to identify the true causes behind the fall of Western civilization, one must delve into the fraternity of apostates and the discipleship of atheists. Indeed, there would have been no John Stuart Mill had there been no Jeremy Bentham. I would take Bentham as more significant than Mill in the scheme of things, in light of the fact that Jeremy Bentham was John Stuart Mill's godfather. John Stuart Mill's father, James Mill, raised his young son on Bentham's utilitarianism from his earliest years. The families were so close that John Stuart lived with Samuel Bentham, Jeremy's brother, for a time as a young man.

This generational legacy of atheism flourished through the 19th century. While Jeremy Bentham's atheism was left half concealed in the closet as demonstrated by his habitual use of pseudonyms, John Stuart Mill just let it all out. He was a self-professed atheist. Towards the end of his life, John Stuart Mill bequeathed his foul heritage to another famous man of the 20th century. Shortly before he died, he agreed to serve as godfather to Bertrand Russell. Thus, in this unholy legacy of covenant rebellion, the most well-known atheist of the 19th century served as the chief inspiration for the life of the most influential atheist of the 20th century. Finally, Bertrand Russell died in 1970 leaving a highly-symbolic, unbroken heritage of apostasy and atheism, extending from Bentham's birth in 1748 to Russell's death 222 years later. These men presided over the apostasy of the Western Christian world, and Jeremy Bentham was responsible for initiating this line of apostasy. He was a true Nephilim who spawned a generational heritage of unmitigated evil.

John Stuart Mill was also the world's most significant early proponent of feminism and gender egalitarianism, although once again Jeremy Bentham is still recognized as the grandfather of the movement.[8] This was essential for the dissolution of the family in the Western world. Mill laid the groundwork for "free" sex, no-fault divorce, "liberated" women, abortion and abortifacient pills, and the destruction of the old socio-economic system that was based on the nuclear family. It may be fair to say that no single man has influenced more political leaders in the last 200 years than John Stuart Mill, with the possible exception of Karl Marx. According to the *Stanford Encyclopedia of Philosophy*, "Mill's greatest philosophical influence was in moral and political philosophy, especially his articulation and defense of utilitarian moral theory and liberal political philosophy."[9] Jeremy Bentham's shadow falls far and wide into every legislative chamber, every university, and every community in every nation around the world.

Bertrand Russell, the secular godson of John Stuart Mill is probably the most famous atheist of all time, still highly respected by modern academics. He was awarded the Nobel Prize for Literature in 1950, and he is considered the father of modern analytical philosophy. Russell is most famous for his pamphlet, "Why I Am Not a Christian." To complete this continuous, generational apostasy in the line of the great Nephilim, Bertrand Russell personally mentored another important philosopher of the 20th century, Ludwig Wittgenstein.

These are the English philosophers that formed the worldviews of the modern world. Was it some strange coincidence that the English empire disintegrated between 1800 and 1970, the era in which the liberal ideas

8. "History of Feminism," http://en.wikipedia.org/wiki/History_of_feminism#Jeremy_Bentham
9. David Brink, "Mill's Moral and Political Philosophy," in *Stanford Encyclopedia of Philosophy* <http://plato.stanford.edu/entries/mill-moral-political/>

of Bentham, Mill, and Russell prevailed? These liberal philosophers were the "gods" that Rudyard Kipling attacked in his poem, "The Gods of the Copybook Headings" in 1919. Kipling alludes to the biblical truths that still remained in the copybooks that children were using in schools through the 19th century. The "Gods of the Marketplace" were the progressive ideas taught by men like John Stuart Mill and Bertrand Russell.

THE GODS OF THE COPYBOOK HEADINGS
RUDYARD KIPLING

As I pass through my incarnations in every age and race,
I make my proper prostrations to the Gods of the Market Place.
Peering through reverent fingers I watch them flourish and fall,
And the Gods of the Copybook Headings, I notice, outlast them all.

We were living in trees when they met us. They showed us each in turn
That Water would certainly wet us, as Fire would certainly burn:
But we found them lacking in Uplift, Vision and Breadth of Mind,
So we left them to teach the Gorillas while we followed the March of Mankind.

We moved as the Spirit listed. They never altered their pace,
Being neither cloud nor wind-borne like the Gods of the Market Place,
But they always caught up with our progress, and presently word would come
That a tribe had been wiped off its icefield, or the lights had gone out in Rome.

With the Hopes that our World is built on they were utterly out of touch,
They denied that the Moon was Stilton; they denied she was even Dutch;
They denied that Wishes were Horses; they denied that a Pig had Wings;
So we worshipped the Gods of the Market Who promised these beautiful things.

When the Cambrian measures were forming, They promised perpetual peace.
They swore, if we gave them our weapons, that the wars of the tribes would cease.
But when we disarmed They sold us and delivered us bound to our foe,
And the Gods of the Copybook Headings said: "Stick to the Devil you know."

On the first Feminian Sandstones we were promised the Fuller Life
(Which started by loving our neighbour and ended by loving his wife)
Till our women had no more children and the men lost reason and faith,
And the Gods of the Copybook Headings said: "The Wages of Sin is Death."

In the Carboniferous Epoch we were promised abundance for all,

By robbing selected Peter to pay for collective Paul;
But, though we had plenty of money, there was nothing our money could buy,
And the Gods of the Copybook Headings said: "If you don't work you die."

Then the Gods of the Market tumbled, and their smooth-tongued wizards withdrew
And the hearts of the meanest were humbled and began to believe it was true
That All is not Gold that Glitters, and Two and Two make Four
And the Gods of the Copybook Headings limped up to explain it once more.

As it will be in the future, it was at the birth of Man
There are only four things certain since Social Progress began.
That the Dog returns to his Vomit and the Sow returns to her Mire,
And the burnt Fool's bandaged finger goes wobbling back to the Fire;

And that after this is accomplished, and the brave new world begins
When all men are paid for existing and no man must pay for his sins,
As surely as Water will wet us, as surely as Fire will burn,
The Gods of the Copybook Headings with terror and slaughter return!

"The fool hath said in his heart, there is no God." Psalm 14:1.

MAN-CENTERED ETHICS

When philosophers speak of a "worldview" they refer to a basic framework of propositions that concern the broad areas of reality, truth, and ethics. As the Western world abandoned the fundamental constituents of a biblical worldview, humanist philosophers set about to develop new ethical approaches. It was Jeremy Bentham who took Aquinas' challenge to build up philosophical knowledge on human reason in the area of ethics. Doubtless, Aquinas would have been shocked at the results of this radical separation of philosophical knowledge from sacred knowledge that came about with Bentham's theory of utilitarianism. Surely, Aquinas would never have embraced the sexual sins that Bentham endorsed according to his new moral criteria.

Chapter 1, Section 1 of Bentham's *Principles of Morals and Legislation* opens with this important radical statement: "Nature has placed mankind under the governance of two sovereign masters - pain and pleasure. It is for them alone to point out what we ought to do, as well as to determine what we shall do."[10] This remarkable opening is, first, a statement that defines the naturalistic metaphysic. According to this worldview perspective, there is no personal Creator, only nature that "has placed mankind under the governance of two sovereign masters." Bentham also rejects God as Lawgiver, transferring the ultimate ethical authority from God's standard of good and evil, to man's perception of pain and pleasure. "It is for [pain and pleasure] alone to point out what we ought to do." According to this new ethical criteria, that which causes pleasure is a right thing to do, and that which causes pain is a wrong thing to do. Bentham's use of the word "sovereign" is also significant. This constitutes a radical departure from the old Christian order. For almost two thousand years, Christianity had recognized God as the only sovereign, especially in the area of ethics. In the early 5th century, Augustine spelled out this fundamental Christian truth in the bluntest terms in his *Confessions*, "For as among the government of men, the great authority is obeyed in preference to the lesser, so God must be obeyed above all."[11] By the 17th century A.D, one of the earliest founding fathers of the American colonies, John Winthrop was still hanging on to the last remnants of the old Christian worldview when he wrote, "The determination of law belongs properly to God: He is the only lawgiver; but He hath given power and gifts to man to interpret His laws."[12]

What remains after 200 years of Jeremy Bentham and these humanist ethical theories is unrelenting ethical chaos. What would the "liberals" of the 18th century think of homosexual marriage, transgendered six year old children, and government-funded orgies at state universities?[13] Recently, a "Christian" legal organization made the news when it took up the fight for the rights of transvestites in public schools in Virginia.[14] Then, a "Christian" television actor expressed slight regret over his participation in a popular situation comedy that makes light of homosexuality, sexual

10. Jeremy Bentham, *Principles of Morals and Legislation*, 1.1

11. Augustine, *Confessions*, Book III

12. John Winthrop, *American Historical Documents*, (New York: P.F. Collier and Sons, 1910), 90, 105.

13. http://landmarkreport.com/andrew/2013/01/sexual-education-center-at-canadian-university-hosts-orgy-party-for-students

14. "Virginia School District Considers Cross-Dressing Ban for Students," *The Rutherford Institute* <https://www.rutherford.org/publications_resources/tri_in_the_news/virginia_school_district_considers_cross_dressing_ban_for_students>

orgies, and bestiality.[15] The road to Gomorrah is slippery, and it is coated with the Teflon of utilitarianism and pragmatism, and those who exempt themselves from the slide are few and far between. While the masses wander in a wasteland of ethical confusion, sadly very few professing Christians find an anchor in a biblical standard.

This breakdown of all moral standards is evident also in modern art forms, language, music, movies, news casts, dress, billboards, textbooks, novels, the practice of law, and documentaries. The murder of children is called "choice," and the murder of the elderly is "humane." Miserable, unnatural perversions are "gay and rejoicing" activities. The abomination of witchcraft is sold to children as harmless fun. Even the worst forms of evil such as cannibalism and murder are made voyeuristic fodder in today's motion pictures and music. A recent documentary excused cannibalism as "making a statement." There are now university professors commending incest as "a fulfilling experience" in some cases.[16]

> "Woe unto them that call evil good, and good evil; that put darkness for light, and light for darkness; that put bitter for sweet, and sweet for bitter!" (Isaiah 5:20)

If all that is evil is called good, what is there left to call evil, but one thing, those Christians that uphold the objective, eternal law of the Creator of heaven and earth. Christians are now referred to as "homophobes," accused of hating or fearing homosexuals. Now, these are the criminals who are subject to large fines for speaking against certain sexual sins (as defined by God's law).[17] Bentham's ethical theory is in the driver's seat. Christians who subscribe to God's holy law in all of their spheres of activity and influence, Christians who preach the law as a means of convicting sinners of their sins and driving them to Christ, Christians who use the law as a restraint to the potential wickedness of men, are treated as intolerant, narrow-minded, and criminal. It is only the Christians who hold to God's authoritative, unchanging standard in order to call incest

---

15 "'Two and a Half Men' Actor Apologizes for Trashing Show," *Latino.FoxNews.com*, http://latino.foxnews.com/latino/entertainment/2012/11/28/two-and-half-men-actor-apologizes-for-trashing-show/>

16. http://www.lifesitenews.com/news/archive//ldn/2007/jul/07073008, German Government Promotes Incestuous Pedophilia: http://townhall.com/columnists/michaelbrown/2012/09/11/here_comes_incest_just_as_predicted/page/full/

17. http://www.lifesitenews.com/news/supreme-court-muzzles-free-speech-in-canada-crushes-born-again-christian-ac

and cannibalism evil. Now it is only the Christians who are the evil ones in the mind of the new humanist. Effectively, the battle was won by the turn of the 20th century, as Christians surrendered the principle issue: *by what standard may we define right and wrong?* Somewhere between 1700 and 1900, most of the organized Christian church in Europe and America took a strong stand against the Law of God. They created an unhealthy dichotomy between law and gospel, and took on the new ethics of the apostasy. By the 20th century, there were plenty of Christian socialists, prohibitionists, suffragists, fundamentalists, progressives, and other do-gooders. But few were interested in using the law of God to define human ethics.

BENTHAM'S UTILITARIANISM

Jeremy Bentham summarizes his new ethical theory with these words,

"By the principle of utility is meant that principle which approves or disapproves of every action whatsoever, according to the tendency it appears to have to augment or diminish the happiness of the party whose interest is in question: or, what is the same thing in other words, to promote or to oppose that happiness. I say of every action whatsoever, and therefore not only of every action of a private individual, but of every measure of government." [18]

Thus, utilitarianism recommends that action which produces the most pleasure or happiness for the most people in the long run. As it turns out, the internal weaknesses of this theory are manifold, and Bentham's ideas have been thoroughly discredited by philosophers and Christian apologists alike. Despite all of the fatal flaws, incredibly, the theory remains the most popular ethical rule for political, legal, and social systems in our day. Consider that,

1. Bentham argues his position on the basis of the fact that most people act like utilitarians. However he engages circular reasoning; he assumes that what people already do is what they ought to do. This may explain why the theory is so popular, but he fails to consider that the majority of people may be ignorant or morally depraved, and therefore

18. Jeremy Bentham, *Principles of Morals and Legislation*, 1.2

APOSTATE

are not doing what they ought to do.

2. Should some people prefer pain over pleasure, then the actions appropriate for one might be inappropriate for another.

3. The theory is unworkable if the principle "No pain, no gain" applies at all. Moreover, finite human minds would have difficulty determining how much pain would produce the most gain, good, or pleasure. What might produce happiness in the short term may not produce happiness in the long run, and vice versa. Often, there is a trade off here. So, how could anyone possibly determine which is to be preferred, and how to go about achieving the right balance between short term pain and long term gain?

4. Happiness itself is hard to define. How much pleasure is too much pleasure? Is there anything more to life than sexual pleasure and material well-being and comfort?

5. Finite, mortal men are incapable of applying this theory. They can neither define the good ends for which men ought to strive. What is the ultimate good for the individual and society? Moreover, they cannot possibly know what would produce the most good in the long run, because it is impossible to know all of the effects of any given action. There are millions, if not billions of possible consequences of any single action.

6. Could the greatest good and the highest form of happiness come about by suicide, or by the elimination of the species? Some might argue that we humans are a miserable lot, and evolution should take another course.

When men reject God as the Source of creation and ethics, there is no absolute by which to judge an ultimate good. Why are we bound to salvage the human species? Perhaps it would be better to destroy the globe, and start over with some other solar system.

UNLEASHING THE PLAGUE OF HOMOSEXUALITY

The problem of homosexuality has shown up from time to time in different places and at different times in history. The Greeks experimented with it for awhile, and the Romans tolerated it. But, the God of the Bible does not tolerate it with his covenant people, nor with pagan states like Sodom and Gomorrah (as is clear from Judges 21 and Genesis 21). That is why the influence of Jesus Christ upon the civilized world resulted in the virtual disappearance of these pagan practices. Wherever a Christian society develops, homosexuality eschews the light and settles back into the closet. For example, the Roman Caesar Phillip the Arab, influenced by Christianity, is recognized as the first Caesar to introduce a law against homosexuality (penalizing male prostitution). By the end of the 4th century, legislation against passive homosexual acts was incorporated into the Roman Empire. The Theodosian Code, a compilation of laws published in 429 AD, included "death by sword" for homosexual coupling.[19] This virtually put an end to the public advancement of homosexuality in the Western world... until Jeremy Bentham.

Bentham's work *Offenses Against One's Self* was not published until 1931 for its strongly offensive nature, although it was written in 1785. This is the first attempt among several on his behalf to open the door for homosexuality and pedophilia in the modern world. Appalling though it may be to a sensitive Christian conscience, the Greeks and Romans did not discriminate between homosexuality and homosexual pedophilia in their acceptance of these sins. In his radical apostasy and perverted mind, Jeremy Bentham does not discriminate either. Thankfully, the conscience of the modern courts, legislatures, and citizens still reprehend pedophilia. Recently, the NCAA practically shut down Penn State University's football program and a coach was imprisoned for life because he was trying to practice the sorts of the things the Greeks used to do in their Gymnasiums.[20] Clearly, the influence of Jesus Christ and His followers upon Western civilization has not entirely disappeared. However, Jeremy Bentham would have been disappointed. In his foul little book, he laments the fact that "among the modern nations [homosexuality] is comparatively rare." "In Edinburgh or Amsterdam," he writes, "You scarce hear of it two or three times in a century. In Athens and in ancient Rome in the most flourishing periods of the history of those capitals, regular intercourse between the sexes was scarcely much more common.

19. "Homosexuaity in Ancient Rome," *Wikipedia* <en.wikipedia.org/wiki/Homosexuality_in_an-cient_Rome>

20. Prisbell, Eric, "NCAA Hands out Severe Punishment for Penn State" *USAToday*, <http://usato-day30.usatoday.com/sports/college/football/bigten/story/2012-07-23/ncaa-penn-state-punishment-sanctions/56427630/1>

It was upon the same footing throughout Greece: everybody practiced it; nobody was ashamed of it."[21] Bentham condemns sexual activity that might become habitual or excessive. But in keeping with his utilitarian ethical theory, he refuses to recognize any moral difference between heterosexual activity and homosexual activity.[22]

It is hard to believe Bentham's statistics on the prevalence of homosexuality or pedophilia in cities like Amsterdam and Edinburgh - with only a case or two in a hundred years! Things have changed a bit in Amsterdam and Edinburgh. In San Francisco, for example, at least 15% of the population (94,000 people) claim to be habituated homosexuals. The homosexual population is also high in Seattle (12%), New York (6%), Chicago (6%), and Los Angeles (6%).[23] Six percent of British men have committed sodomy, and four percent of the marriages conducted in the Netherlands are now between homosexuals. Most of the Dutch (who come from a strong Christian traditional heritage) now support homosexuality. It is only the Muslims who maintain any degree of opposition to it in this old apostate Christian nation. According to a survey released in October of 2011, fully 90% of the ethnic Dutch view homosexuality as moral, but only 30% of Turks and 25% of Moroccans approve of it.[24]

Surely, it is no exaggeration that the problem is now at least a billion times worse than it was 230 years ago. The spirit of Jeremy Bentham has swept across the planet like a cloud of locusts. Over the last twenty years, thousands of homosexual clubs have spread into public high schools, and it is not unusual to hear stories about 12-year-old boys from Christian homes or homeschools accessing homosexual pornography on the internet. It is hard to say how many young boys end up snared in this bear trap. Suffice it to say that the problem is in order of magnitude worse than it was a generation ago. This is Nephilim work.

---

21. Jeremy Bentham, *Offenses Against One's Self*
22. In Bentham's 1785 issue of the essay on "Offenses Against One's Self," he uses words like "disgusting, "abominable," and "preposterous" to describe homosexual activity. However, in the Ogden transcription of his notes in 1814 and 1816, Bentham takes issue with all negative references to the practice, to include words like "unnatural" and "abomination." As the great "deformer" of the West, this man led the way to social acceptance of the worst possible moral offenses.
23. "Demographics of Sexual Orintation," *Wickipedia*, <en.wikipedia.org/wiki/Demographics_of_ sexual_orientation>
24. Johan van Slooten, "Homophobia Among Hindus in Holland" *Radio Netherlands Worldwide*, <http://www.rnw.nl/english/article/homophobia-among-hindus-holland>

"But whoso shall offend one of these little ones which believe in me, it were better for him that a millstone were hanged about his neck, and that he were drowned in the depth of the sea. Woe unto the world because of offences! For it must needs be that offences come; but woe to that man by whom the offence cometh!" Matt. 18:6, 7

It seems that (by the providence of God), something very dark and evil has slipped over Western society since the 18th century. Historians have studied public records from Plymouth colony in the 17th century and found that the divorce rate was 0.1% and the illegitimacy rate was about 1%.[25] Of course, there will be no state of perfection in a sinful, fallen world. However, where there are stable societies, dysfunctional conditions are kept to a minimum. So what can be said of our world today where the divorce rate is 500 times what it was in 1680 and homosexuality is a million times more prevalent in public high schools than it was 1950? Something happened in Amsterdam between 1810 and 2010. Bentham's ideas did not come into full fruition until the 1990's, and the harvest will come about in the next fifty years (in our children's generation). What will be the final results of this man's awful legacy? When the world finally emerges from this tragic era of human history, then all shall know surely that *something wicked this way came.*

In reference to the varying forms of evil in the world, the old catechism asserts, "Some sins by reason of several aggravations are more heinous in the sight of God than others."[26] That is, some sins are more noxious to God than others. Jeremy Bentham aside, the Bible insists on employing the word "abomination" for the more reprehensible sins, such as homosexuality. Moreover, there is no substantial difference between the Old and New Testaments' treatment of the sin. According to Leviticus 18:22, 20:13, Deuteronomy 23:17, 1 Corinthians 6:9, and Romans 1:26-27, it is a destructive sin which calls for both temporal and eternal judgment.

Although this potent moral position towards sexual sin may seem a little odd to the post-modern Christian, there is strong historical backing for civil restraints on gross sexual misconduct, (something Jeremy Bentham well understood). The Didache took a hard line against the

25. James Deetz and Patricia Scott Deetz, *The Times of Their Lives, Life and Love, and Death in Plymouth Colony* (New York: Anchor Books, 2000), 144-146.
26. *Westminster Shorter Catechism*, Question 83.

sin, and the Synod of Elvira (306 A.D.) instituted the most severe form of excommunication for church members who fell into it.[27] Later in the fourth century, St. Augustine wrote, "Offenses against nature are everywhere and at all times to be held in detestation and should be punished. Such offenses, for example were those of the Sodomites; and, even if all nations should commit them, they would all be judged guilty of the same crime by divine law, which has not made men so that they should ever abuse one another in that way. For the fellowship that should be between God and us is violated whenever that nature of which he is the author is polluted by perverted lust."[28]

In another era, these sorts of sins were typically considered unmentionable for fear that the mere reference would defile the hearer. Back in the 16th century, Martin Luther referred to the sin only a few times. In his commentary on the story of Sodom, Luther wrote, "I for my part do not enjoy dealing with this passage, because so far the ears of the Germans are innocent of and uncontaminated by this monstrous depravity; for even though disgrace, like other sins, has crept in through an ungodly soldier and a lewd merchant, still the rest of the people are unaware of what is being done in secret. The Carthusian monks deserve to be hated because they were the first to bring this terrible pollution into Germany from the monasteries of Italy... The heinous conduct of the people of Sodom is extraordinary, inasmuch as they departed from the natural passion and longing of the male for the female, which is implanted into nature by God, and desired what is altogether contrary to nature. Whence comes this perversity? Undoubtedly from Satan, who after people have once turned away from the fear of God, so powerfully suppresses nature that he blots out the natural desire and stirs up a desire that is contrary to nature."[29] This man could have been writing of 21st century America. When this sin was unleashed upon the Western world in full force, it was as if Satan himself was released from the pit.

Christian ethical commitments do not rely on the whims of cultural relativism. Pedophilia and homosexuality are wrong because God says they are wrong in His Word (Gen. 19:1-11, Lev. 18:22, Lev. 20:13, Judges 19:16-24, Rom. 1:18-32, 1 Cor. 6:9-11, 1 Tim. 1:8-10). There is no other basis by which to establish morality. Pedophilia is wrong because rape,

27. Synod of Elvira, Canon 71
28. Augustine, *Confessions*, Book 3
29. Martin Luther, *Commentary on Genesis 19*

homosexuality, and sexual behavior outside of the bounds of marriage are wrong. This is clearly defined by God's law. Granted, some homosexuals have reacted against this by suing Bible publishers for publicizing these "negative" references to homosexuality.[30] Meanwhile, quite a number of apostatizing churches and individuals are busy trying to reconcile biblical moral statements with homosexual behavior.[31] They engage in the highest order of blasphemy.

As we have seen in earlier chapters, the separation of human reason from the influence of sacred doctrine created the realm of "natural law." However, if one reverts to "natural law," he will eventually use it to excuse all kinds of atrocities! Animals kill their mates, eat their young, and engage in homosexual activity all the time. If men are animals, then what in the world is rape? What might have been "natural" in natural law in 1600 A.D. is quite different than what it is in 2000 A.D. Having ignored God's law in the pulpits and the civil magistracy for several hundred years, men will excuse any kind of behavior by way of their "natural law" theology. After four hundred years of "suppressing the truth in unrighteousness," it's time to get re-acquainted with the special revelation of the Scriptures in the area of ethics!

> *"These are wells without water, clouds that are carried with a tempest; to whom the mist of darkness is reserved for ever. For when they speak great swelling words of vanity, they allure through the lusts of the flesh, through much wantonness, those that were clean escaped from them who live in error. While they promise them liberty, they themselves are the servants of corruption: for of whom a man is overcome, of the same is he brought in bondage" (2 Peter 2:17-19).*

CIVIL GOVERNMENT

Without question, Bentham's primary influence is evident in modern civil governments, specifically in how legislators make their ethical decisions. In his book *The Principles of Morals and Legislation*, Bentham insists that legislators should only interfere "in broad lines of conduct." He comes off as a civil libertarian of sorts when he writes, "With what

---

30. "Gay Man Sues Publishers over Bible Verses," <http://usatoday30.usatoday.com/news/religion/2008-07-09-gay-bible_N.htm>

31. http://www.infowars.com/queen-james-bible-clumsily-cleanses-scriptures-of-homophobia/

APOSTATE

chance of success, for example, would a legislator go about to extirpate drunkenness and fornication by dint of legal punishment? Not all the tortures which ingenuity could invent would compass it: and, before he had made any progress worth regarding, such a mass of evil would be produced by the punishment, as would exceed, a thousand-fold, the utmost possible mischief of the offence."[32]

In some respect, Bentham is right to reprimand legislators who go beyond their bounds to fix things they should not fix. How many millions of pages of legislation attempt to regulate every area of our lives today? However, it is impossible for the human mind to determine where these "broad lines of conduct" lie. Using Bentham's utilitarian principle, legislators argue for hours over how a certain gun regulation will decrease crime or increase crime. Each side brings their limited, biased studies to bear on the debate. They throw their statistics at each other to prove their point. What they fail to understand is that cause-and-effect relationships are very hard to establish, especially when analyzing human behavior, with all of the complicating interactions and factors that play. Besides, how could we possibly determine how a certain policy legislated in 2013 A.D. would affect life in 2050 A.D., 2105 A.D., and 2450 A.D? It would be impossible to determine the repercussions of any single decision made in a court of law or legislature!

Bentham argues forcefully against laws that regulate sexual behavior (whether public or private in nature). Does he anticipate the damage that homosexuality, fornication, and pornography would bring about to a society where 53% of children are born without fathers (a rate seven times higher than the illegitimacy rate in the 1960s); where half of marriages end in divorce; and where children are twenty times more likely to be physically or sexually abused in a non-nuclear family? He doesn't know the answer to this. He could take a wild guess and the rest of us could trust this "smart" fellow, or. . .we could rely more on divine revelation.

As it turns out, the biblical approach to civil law generally agrees with Bentham's broad principle. The Bible does not allow the government to get involved in regulating every area of our lives. If one were to put all of the biblical laws addressing civil crimes in one document, it would hardly cover a page or two. Most of these laws address what the Bible would call "severe" abominations. Instead of regulating people for

32. Jeremy Bentham, *The Principles of Morals and Legislation*, Chapter 17

sins like drunkenness and drug abuse and for building homes without permits, etc., the Bible would only impose a civil punishment in cases of gross negligence. For example, if a drunk driver (with a previous record of driving drunk) kills somebody while driving under the influence of alcohol, he is subject to the death penalty. Thus, the Bible does not recommend a government with a billion regulations and a million bureaucrats. Biblical law imposes responsibility on the populace, and maximizes liberty while punishing severe crimes of negligence (Exod. 21:29). Nevertheless, the Bible does part ways with Bentham on the matter of "sexual freedom." Divine revelation recognizes the family as the basic social unit. Biblical law is careful to preserve the family as the foundation of human society, and prevent the sort of destruction we are experiencing now in the Western world. That is why there are laws against the sexual sins of adultery (Deut. 22:22-25), fornication (Deut. 22:28), homosexuality (Lev. 18:22), bestiality (Lev. 20:15), and certain forms of incest (Lev.18:6-17, 20:10-12). Some believe these Old Testament principles only apply to God's covenant people, but Leviticus 18:27, 28 gives the basis for these laws and applies the principle to pagan nations as well.

> "For all these abominations have the men of the land done, which were before you, and the land is defiled; that the land spue not you out also, when ye defile it, as it spued out the nations that were before you."

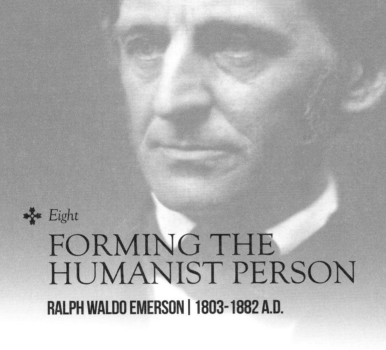

❖ *Eight*

FORMING THE HUMANIST PERSON

RALPH WALDO EMERSON | 1803-1882 A.D.

R alph Waldo Emerson was born in 1803 in Boston, Massachusetts, the son of a Unitarian minister. At this time in America's history, the Latitudinarians and Unitarians had made concerted progress in destroying the Christian faith in America. The first incursion of Unitarianism in this country came in 1747 when Jonathan Mayhew took the pulpit of the old West Church in Boston, Massachusetts. This was a religion rooted in human rationalism that stood in strong resistance to the incomprehensibilities of the Trinitarian God. Mayhew, a graduate of Harvard College, revived the old subordinationist heresy which taught that Christ was lesser in nature to the Father. Harvard produced another important Unitarian minister in Charles Chauncy, who pastored the First Church in Boston from 1727 through 1787. The pastors coming out of Harvard College were typically ahead of the game in the theological decline, while the churches were slower to adopt these new ideas. It wasn't until 1782 that the first church in Boston (King's Chapel) officially accepted the Unitarian faith.

Some apostasies are generational, and the Emerson family certainly did their part to fully support the American rejection of the Christian faith. Some of the earliest roots in New England Unitarianism and Christian apostasy are found in the famed Ralph Waldo Emerson's family. In fact, Ralph's father, William Emerson Jr., named one of his other sons "Charles Chauncy Emerson" after the previously mentioned Boston Unitarian. Ralph Waldo Emerson's grandfather died in 1776, before Unitarianism was adopted by the Boston churches, but he is reputed to have been a minister of Unitarian persuasion himself.

During Ralph's early formative years, his Aunt Moody Emerson introduced him to Hinduism and Neoplatonism. It was her unorthodox leanings that prepared the young boy's fertile mind for the polytheistic and pantheistic ideas that would eventually form a radical new religion called "transcendentalism."

At 14 years of age, Ralph matriculated to Harvard College, where he began to question the most fundamental tenets of Christian orthodoxy. Young Emerson wrote in his journal, "Who is he that shall control me? Why may not I act and speak and write and think with entire freedom? What am I to the Universe, or, the Universe, what is it to me? Who hath forged the chains of wrong and right, of opinion and custom? And must I wear them?"[1]

If God is the sovereign ruler of the universe, the Source of man's reality, ethics, and truth, then Emerson wanted nothing of it. He self-consciously professed his desire to be god. If anything, this constituted the basic article of his new-found "faith."

INFLUENCE

To this point, we have considered the great philosophers from England, France, and Germany. But Emerson is widely recognized as "the leading voice of intellectual culture in the United States,"[2] His transcendentalism deeply influenced America's most notable writers

---

1. Joel Porte, ed., *Emerson in His Journals* (Cambridge: Harvard University Press, 1982), 38.
2. "Ralph Waldo Emerson," *Wickipedia*, http://en.wikipedia.org/wiki/Ralph_Waldo_Emerson

APOSTATE

including men like Herman Melville, Walt Whitman, Henry David Thoreau, and Robert Frost. Melville referred to Emerson as "a great man."[3] The American literary critic, Harold Bloom, calls Emerson, "The prophet of the American Religion."[4] He points out that liberal, mainline Protestant Churches as well as Mormonism and the Christian Science religion all owe a great deal to the seminal ideas of Ralph Waldo Emerson.

Incredibly, Harvard College Divinity School would occasionally invite Emerson to speak about his pantheistic ideas to the student body. Since Emerson had rejected any semblance of Christianity or Unitarianism in his thinking and writing, he preached to the future religious leaders of America about the "god" in all of us. For a short time the university pushed back against his progressive, anti-Christian ideas. However in 1866, Harvard awarded him a doctorate degree, and the alumni elected him to their Board of Overseers. So then, at the highest echelons of American society, the nation had embraced the religion of secular humanism; it would take another 150 years to mass-produce the apostasy into the K-12 schools, the churches, and the wider culture.

The Christian worldview progressively disintegrated in 19th century America under the leadership and tutelage of Ralph Waldo Emerson. What everybody took for granted in the 17th century as basic Christian orthodoxy was called into question in the 18th century and forthrightly rejected in the 19th century. At one time, kings, merchants, clergy, farmers, and tradesmen in Europe and America almost universally accepted a biblical view of ethics and reality. The Christian heritage persisted a bit longer in America than it did in Europe. As late as 1776, American states like Delaware, Maryland, and Pennsylvania required all those who served in public office to take an oath affirming belief in the Triune God. Delaware's constitution included this oath for public office, "I, A____ B____, do profess faith in God the Father, and in Jesus Christ His only Son, and in the Holy Ghost, one God, blessed for evermore; and I do acknowledge the holy scriptures of the Old and New Testament to be given by divine inspiration."[5]

These fundamental allegiances were discontinued in the 19th

3. Ibid.
4. Ibid.
5. http://avalon.law.yale.edu/18th_century/de02.asp

century. What had reigned in the hearts and minds of men in Europe for 1500 years (since the Council of Nicea in 325 A.D.), collapsed between 1750 and 1850. Western countries which had held to the cultural common denominator of a Trinitarian God for centuries, quickly surrendered it in the face of powerful philosophers and literary figures like Emerson and Locke. America's religious commitments capitulated to liberal modernists, Unitarians, and cults in the 19th century, with Ralph Waldo Emerson at the forefront of the apostasy. *He was a true giant, a Nephilim of the modern world.*

THE MORALITY REVOLUTION

Jeremy Bentham is credited as the brave progressive to have set the door ajar for the introduction of homosexuality and the subsequent moral collapse of the Western world. It was an uphill battle to stand against 1500 years of Christian influence in the West. Bentham's nemesis, William Blackstone, a British judge, argued strongly for the death penalty for homosexuals in his Commentaries published in 1769. At the birth of this country, all thirteen American colonies provided death penalty laws for sodomy or "buggery."[6] As late as the 1780s, the civil magistrate in England executed men for public acts of sodomy, and Theodosius Reade and William Smith were prosecuted for the crime on April 10, 1780.[7]

Obviously, definitions and perceptions of morality have changed dramatically in 200 years. In the old Christian world, there were some sins considered socially egregious, that which was considered more harmful to the social fiber of a civilization. If the Bible considered the sin "abominable" and corrupting of the land itself (Lev. 18:22-29; 20:13), Christian society would take these warnings at face value. At the turn of the 19th century, however, all of that changed. The agenda of the new humanist faith extended beyond a rejection of Christian theology and epistemology. Now the apostates wanted the removal of Christian morals and social morals. They were reaching for something more - what they really wanted was the destruction of a civilization. Naturally, such an ambitious program could never be accomplished in a few short years. After the philosophers and universities replaced a God-centered epistemology

6. "Homosexuality Laws," *Conservapedia* Jul 25, 2011 <http://www.conservapedia.com/Homosex-uality_laws>

7. "Burke Proposes Abolition of the Pillory" Nov. 7, 2011 <http://pilloryhistory.com/burke.html>

with a humanist epistemology, the cultural and literary leaders set out to foment a moral revolution in ethical philosophy and behavior.

At a time in America's history when homosexual acts were unmentionable in civilized society, the greatest literary figures of the day, Ralph Waldo Emerson and Walt Whitman were writing poetry that incited these unnatural passions. In his journals, Emerson dreamed of a "tremendous affair" with a college classmate named "Martin Gay" and wrote poems with homosexual intonations.[8] Whitman wrote the "Calamus" poems, intended to evoke homosexual passions. Over the years, many sordid facts have been collected concerning the homosexual exploits of Walt Whitman, none of which are worth recounting here. Suffice it to say, this was new territory for the 19th century, but it was an important step towards the unraveling of Christian morality in the Western world.

Two hundred years after Emerson, the homosexual culture is practically ubiquitous. A judge in Missouri recently held that high school students had the right to access homosexual websites in public schools in that state.[9] Thousands of homosexual clubs are now meeting in high schools throughout the country, a new phenomenon which was practically unheard of prior to the 1990s.[10] Today, almost every major television network now features programs that place homosexual behavior in a positive light, and some states require homosexual indoctrination for students in K-12 schools.[11] At the turn of the 19th century, you would not have found any such immorality legitimized in even the worst dens of evil in Boston and New York City.

> *"Or do you not know that the unrighteous will not inherit the kingdom of God? Do not be deceived: neither the sexually immoral, nor idolaters, nor adulterers, nor men who practice homosexuality, nor thieves, nor the greedy, nor drunkards, nor revilers, nor swindlers will inherit the kingdom*

---

8. Caleb Crain, *American Sympathy: Men, Friendship, and Literature in the New Nation* (New Haven: Yale University Press, 2001), 159, 163.

9. Hollingsworth, Heather, "Federal Judge Orders Camdenton Schools to Stop Blocking Gay Websites," *News Tribune.com*, Feb. 16, 2012 <http://www.newstribune.com/news/2012/feb/16/federal-judge-orders-camdenton-schools-stop-blocki/>

10. http://www.citizenlink.com/2010/09/30/the-truth-about-glsens-school-climate-report/

11. "Study: Number of Gay Characters on TV at All Time High," *Fox News.com*, Oct. 5, 2012 <http://www.foxnews.com/entertainment/2012/10/05/study-number-gay-characters-on-tv-at-all-time-high/>, and "California Governor Signs Bill Requiring Schools to Teach Gay History," *CNN.us*, Jul 14, 2011, <http://articles.cnn.com/2011-07-14/us/california.lgbt.education_1_california-governor-signs-bill-gay-history-state-textbooks?_s=PM:US>

of God. And such were some of you. But you were washed, you were sanctified, you were justified in the name of the Lord Jesus Christ and by the Spirit of our God" (1 Cor. 6:9-11).

PHILOSOPHY

Thanks to the training he had received from his aunt, Emerson commenced his literary work with an intellectual commitment to Eastern philosophy. Today, a significant segment of American culture is steeped in Eastern mysticism in the form of "New Age" thinking. The Pew Forum Research Center estimates that a quarter of Americans believe in reincarnation and that there is spiritual energy located in physical things such as mountains, trees or crystals,[12] In the cosmic war of the worldviews, it was Ralph Waldo Emerson and Henry David Thoreau that invited these insidious ideas into the North American continent. In his seminal work, *Walden*, Thoreau writes:

> *"In the morning I bathe my intellect in the stupendous and cosmogonal philosophy of the Bhagavad Gita, since whose composition years of the gods have elapsed, and in comparison with which our modern world and its literature seem puny and trivial; and I doubt if that philosophy is not to be referred to a previous state of existence, so remote is its sublimity from our conceptions. I lay down the book and go to my well for water, and lo! there I meet the servant of the Brahmin, priest of Brahma, and Vishnu and Indra, who still sits in his temple on the Ganges reading the Vedas, or dwells at the root of a tree with his crust and water-jug. I meet his servant come to draw water for his master, and our buckets as it were grate together in the same well. The pure Walden water is mingled with the sacred water of the Ganges."*[13]

Except for Latitudinarians perhaps, most people who call themselves Christians believe that Hinduism is a false, pagan religion. In a world of thousands of demonic deceptions, it is just one more bypath to hell for billions of men, women, and children. Evidently, Satan and his minions used Emerson and Thoreau to bring this thinking into the Western

12. http://www.pewforum.org/other-beliefs-and-practices/many-americans-mix-multiple-faiths.aspx
13. Henry David Thoreau, *Walden*

world. It is still hard to believe that Americans could ever embrace a pagan religion like Hinduism; however, America was ripe for apostasy when Emerson and Thoreau came along. When a nation is already turning from the true and living God, it easily embraces Hinduism, Islam, Demonism, and even human sacrifice, to show its spite for the true faith.

The Eastern worldview of Hinduism and New Age thinking is replete with internal contradictions. Eastern philosophy reduces all of human knowledge to nothingness, by obliterating all distinctions in a monist conception of reality. Fundamentally, there is no difference between that which is God and that which is not God in the Eastern mind; there is no difference between that which is me and that which is you, or that which is good and that which is evil, or that which is true and that which is not true. Emerson explains his metaphysical perspective in his essay, "Nature:"

> "Standing on the bare ground, – my head bathed by the blithe air, and uplifted into infinite space, –all mean egotism vanishes. I become a transparent eye-ball; I am nothing; I see all; the currents of the Universal Being circulate through me; I am part or particle of God."[14]

Here is Emerson's worldview in raw form, as he proceeds to obliterate all distinction between Creator and creature. Man becomes a part of "god," the oneness of being - this is the essence of Eastern Hindu thought.

The biblical faith holds steadfastly and unmistakably to a Creator-creature distinction. "Know ye that the Lord He is God: it is He that hath made us, and not we ourselves" (Ps. 100:3). If there is such a thing as truth and falsehood, there could be no wider disparity between the biblical theology and Emerson. Those who hold that "all is one" are not Christians. They have the wrong worldview and the wrong god. They have deceived themselves with a worldview incapable of maintaining the preconditions for all of human thinking, coherent logic, and social interaction.

From a Christian point of view, this is gross idolatry in its blatant denial of the true and living God and its incorporation of man into the godhead. The god you choose to serve is important. Should you choose to believe in a false god, you will be guilty of violating the first

14. Ralph Waldo Emerson, *Nature - An Essay*, Section 1.

commandment, "Thou shalt have no other gods before me" (Exod. 20:3). Transcendentalists, humanists, Hindus, and Muslims who will not repent of this idolatry, will have "their portion in the lake that burns with fire and sulfur" (Rev. 21:8).

From the beginning of human philosophical inquiry, the Eastern monists have never been able to resolve some foundational questions. For example, if all is one, how can there be change and movement in the universe? Emerson recognizes this conflict within his worldview in his book, *The Oversoul*, but he could never quite resolve it. Instead of enthusiastically embracing this false worldview that couldn't even begin to explain these basic questions, Emerson should have embraced the truth of the Trinity—where God (the ultimate reality) is One and Three at the same time. He should have admitted that only the incomprehensibilities of a Triune God could explain the impossibilities of human philosophy. The permanent oneness of reality and the fluid manyness of change are only possible in a universe governed by the Triune God, who is both the One and the Many.

TRUST YOUR HEART

The creed of any church or group of individuals is usually known by the clichés used most frequently in the liturgy and "spiritual talk." It is often more effective to discern their "creed" from their political speeches, church pep-talks, favorite songs and movies, inspirational motivational seminars, and conversations, than from their actual "statement of faith." What are the clichés that are dropped with greater frequency? What elicits the most emotional support from the audience? This is the means by which we determine what people *really* believe. If we surveyed the familiar liturgy of the religion of "Americanism," we would find tidbits of Emersonianism strewn throughout. "Trust your heart" and "Follow your heart" is the Apostle's Creed of American religion. In philosophical terms, this creed advocates romanticism, irrationalism, and relativism. Emerson wrote,

> *"To believe your own thought, to believe that what is true for you in your private heart is true for all men, – that is genius. Speak your latent conviction, and it shall be the universal sense; for the inmost in due time becomes the outmost,— and our first thought is rendered back to us by*

the trumpets of the Last Judgment. Familiar as the voice of the mind is to each, the highest merit we ascribe to Moses, Plato, and Milton is, that they set at naught books and traditions, and spoke not what men but what they thought."[15]

Emerson's caricature of Moses is utterly ridiculous when he insists that, "The highest merit we ascribe to Moses.. is that [he] . . .spoke...what [he] thought." Had Moses prophesied in this manner, he would have been subjected to the death penalty, according to what he himself wrote in Deuteronomy 18:20. "But the prophet, which shall presume to speak a word in my name, which I have not commanded him to speak, or that shall speak in the name of other gods, even that prophet shall die."

We may well wonder how Emerson dared to drag Moses into his religion of self-worship. Naturally, he wants to make every man his own god, his own epistemological authority, and his own source of truth. While Plato and Emerson may have made up their own truth as they went along, this certainly was not the case with Moses! As the prophet of the living God, Moses communicated solely that which God wanted him to communicate. He revealed God's Word. He thought God's thoughts after Him. To equate the prophetic words of Moses to the philosophical meanderings of Plato (who worked his own autonomous human mind to produce a philosophical arrangement of propositions that were not inspired by God), is deception of the highest order.

Emerson looked within himself for truth, and rejected anything revealed by the old bards and prophets. To Emerson, it was not possible that a Creator (separate from the creation) might communicate transcendent truth through human prophets. That possibility is simply disallowed in Emerson's worldview, leaving man as the only possible source of truth for Emerson.

All of this is diametrically opposed to the wisdom of the ages communicated to us through God's transcendent Word. The Proverbs specifically warns against the very thing Emerson advocates: *"He who trusts his own heart is a fool." (Prov. 28:26).*

Moreover, God has what it takes to make known His words of truth (Proverbs 22:20, 21). God's words give light and understanding to the simple (Ps. 119:130). From Scripture, we understand that the god of this

15. Ralph Waldo Emerson, *Self-Reliance*

world has blinded the minds of those who do not believe (2 Cor. 4:4). As a Christian worldview expands across the world and replaces the old pagan disorder, there is only one explanation for what brings about this new order. "God, who commanded the light to shine out of darkness, hath shined in our hearts, to give the light of the knowledge of the glory of God in the face of Jesus Christ " (2 Cor. 4:6).

ETHICAL RELATIVISM

Ralph Waldo Emerson was one of the first self-conscious relativist thinkers of the day. Assuming that the universe is in constant flux, Emerson concludes that truth and ethics must be in constant flux as well. He believes that each new social more is always incorporated into "some more general law presently to disclose itself."[16] The goal of human existence is to advance to "higher forms." But all virtues are what he describes as "initial" virtues, not constant, absolute virtues. "The terror of reform," Emerson writes, "is the discovery that we must cast away our virtues, or what we have always esteemed such, into the same pit that has consumed our grosser vices."[17] As Emerson's ideas were incorporated into American academia and public life, the progressive agenda would always replace the old virtues with "new" virtues, which, usually turn out to be recycled "grosser vices" tossed into the pit a few generations earlier. Thus, "homophobia" has replaced homosexuality as the new vice; we will have to wait and see which new vices and virtues will emerge in the ethical chaos the world has inherited from Ralph Waldo Emerson.

> *"Woe unto them that call evil good, and good evil; that put darkness for light, and light for darkness; that put bitter for sweet, and sweet for bitter! Woe unto them that are wise in their own eyes, and prudent in their own sight! " (Is. 5:20,21).*

16. Robert Spiller, ed., et al, *The Collected Works of Ralph Waldo Emerson, Vol. 2* (Cambridge: Harvard University Press), 181.
17. Ibid. 187.

Nine

FORMING THE HUMANIST POLITICAL STATE

KARL MARX | 1818-1883 A.D.

arl Marx has had more impact on actual events, as well as on the minds of men and women, than any other intellectual in modern times."[1] These are the words of Paul Johnson, arguably the most prominent historian of the modern age. Was he exaggerating the case when he wrote this of Marx? Doubtful.

Given that Marx's ideological progeny includes the likes of Josef Stalin, Mao Tse Tung, Pol Pot, and Fidel Castro, there is no other man in recorded human history responsible for as many deaths as this "humanist of humanists." The other apostates we've discussed thus far retained varying degrees of consistency to atheism or anti-Christian sentiments, while Marx openly gloried in his total rejection of theism. Whereas the mass murderers of the 20th century might have had some slight association with the ideas of Jean-Jacques Rousseau and Jeremy Bentham, most of them would have freely acknowledged Karl Marx as

---

1. Paul Johnson, *Intellectuals* (New York: Harper and Row, 1988), 52.

their ideological father. He was a Lutheran turned-atheist, a Nephilim in the true biblical sense:

> *"There were giants in the earth in those days... the same became mighty men which were of old, men of renown... The earth also was corrupt before God, and the earth was filled with violence." (Gen. 6:4,11).*

The total number of citizens killed by the Roman Emperors is estimated to have been between 2 million and 8 million over a period of 400 years. Yet this is a just fraction of the number of lives lost under Marxist ideologues in the last century. We emerge from the bloodiest century in all of recorded history, and what shall come in the next century in Western Europe and America is an unknown. Thus far, the body count lies between 85 million and 200 million.[2]

WARNING

The life of Karl Marx is a deeply disturbing tale from the beginning to the end - a living nightmare, a true taste of hell. In his personal testimonies, we find striking similarities with the Bible's record of the thoughts, intentions, words, and actions of Satan himself (Isaiah 14:12-15, Matt. 4:1-10), Cain (Gen. 4:1-8), and Judas (Matt. 26:49). They are not pleasant meditations, so the reader should be careful to place them in the context of Jesus' sovereignty, His redemption, and His final judgment of all that is evil.

Karl Marx was born in 1818, and he was baptized into the Lutheran church in 1824. If the pen is mightier than the sword, then nobody captured this truism better than Marx. He was a furious, prolific writer of poems, plays, philosophy, and political diatribe. His first written work, *The Union of the Faithful with Christ*, indicates that he had some understanding concerning the nature of the Christian church and the believer's relationship with Jesus Christ. As a 17-year-old high school student at the Trier Gymnasium, Marx wrote, "Through love of Christ we turn our hearts at the same time toward our brethren who are inwardly bound to us and for whom He gave Himself in sacrifice." Thus far, so

---

2. "Mass Killings under Communist Regimes," *Wikipedia* <http://en.wikipedia.org/wiki/Mass_killings_under_Communist_regimes> accessed on Feb. 27, 2013, and "20th Century Democide," *Hawaii.edu*, Nov. 23, 2002 <http://www.hawaii.edu/powerkills/20TH.HTM> accessed on Feb. 27, 2013.

good.

It wasn't long after this however, that a very strange and horrible change came about in the young man's life. A dark spirit shrouded his poetry and plays. Gross blasphemy poured from his tormented heart and pen. "I wish to avenge myself against the One who rules above," he wrote. At first pass, it appears to be the words of the devil himself. More rational minds might conclude that these are words of a madman in an insane asylum screaming incoherencies, but reliable sources have it that these words came from Marx. This is well beyond anything Rousseau or Locke dared to write, but the 19th century apostasy had well matured by the 1830s and 1840s. Could this most influential social thinker of the 19th century have been possessed by the god of this world, the prince of demons himself?

The young Marx wrote the following lines in his poem *Invocation of One in Despair*: "So a god has snatched from me my all, in the curse and rack of destiny. All his worlds are gone beyond recall. Nothing but revenge is left to me. I shall build my throne high overhead." Marx dreamt of destroying the world that God had created. In another poem, fittingly named *Human Pride*, he wrote: "Then I will walk triumphantly, like a god, through the ruins of their kingdom. Every word of mine is fire and action. My breast is equal to that of the Creator." It is blasphemy of the highest order, reminiscent of the thoughts of Lucifer contained in Isaiah 14:12-15.

> *"How art thou fallen from heaven, O Lucifer, son of the morning! how art thou cut down to the ground, which didst weaken the nations! For thou hast said in thine heart, I will ascend into heaven, I will exalt my throne above the stars of God: I will sit also upon the mount of the congregation, in the sides of the north: I will ascend above the heights of the clouds; I will be like the most High. Yet thou shalt be brought down to hell, to the sides of the pit." (Isaiah 14:12-15).*

In another piece of work called *The Last Judgment*, Marx openly mocked God and referred to the judgment as nothing but a dream. In still another peculiar poem, called *The Player*, Marx speaks in the first person as one demon-possessed: "The hellish vapours rise and fill the brain, Til I go mad and my heart is utterly changed. See this sword? The prince of darkness sold it to me. For me he beats the time and gives the signs. Ever more boldly I play the dance of death."

From the beginning, Karl Marx's agenda was destruction, which is characteristic of all demonic agendas (1 Pet. 5:8). The king of the demons in Revelation 9:11 is *Apollyon* or *Abaddon* in the Hebrew, which is translated "The Destroyer." The words he uses in his play, *Oulanem* just exude with an overweening commitment to annihilation. "Yet I have power within my youthful arms to clench and crush you [i.e., personified humanity] with tempestuous force, while for us both the abyss yawns in darkness. You will sink down and I shall follow laughing, Whispering in your ears, 'Descend, come with me, friend.'" When the time comes for Oulanem's death at the end of the play, the protagonist screams out, "Ruined, ruined. My time has clean run out. The clock has stopped, the pygmy house has crumbled. Soon I shall embrace eternity to my breast, and soon I shall howl gigantic curses on mankind." And the play ends with more foul imprecations from the pit and supremely evil intentions, "If there is a Something which devours, I'll leap within it, though I bring the world to ruins—the world which bulks between me and the abyss I will smash to pieces with my enduring curses."[3]

Christians would recognize these words as originating from the mind of the prince of the bottomless pit. It is as if Apollyon, the Destroyer himself, was released to work his destruction on the earth. Any student of Marx's life and work must grapple with the spiritual and moral implications of these dark sayings. Is the author sincere as he expresses these wildly angry sentiments? Why does he announce his evil intentions to the world? Why do political leaders, the university elite, and billions of people around the globe still accede to his basic agenda? Some have passed these poems and plays off as vindictive hatred for the "idea" of God on the part of an atheist. Most scholars would dismiss these concerns as merely conspiratorial and superstitious drivel. However, the poems are apparently important enough to be included on Marxists.org, a website dedicated to the "rebirth" of Marxism. There is no reason to doubt that Marx took himself seriously as he wrote these words. As far as history records, he never recanted these works or corrected himself. If hundreds of millions of dead bodies may be counted the fruits of this man's work,

3. Marx, Karl, *Oulanem*, <http://www.marxists.org/archive/marx/works/cw/volume01/index. htm> accessed on Feb. 27, 2013

does this not prove the legitimacy of these early writings, and the compact that the young Marx made with the devil?

Surely the weakening the Christian faith in Western culture and the destruction of an entire civilization must require more than a single man. Without the work of John Locke, Jean-Jacques Rousseau, Immanuel Kant, and Hegel eroding the epistemological roots of the Christian West, it would have never happened. A host of philosophers have planted the seeds of destruction in social, economic, cultural, and education systems, but not many will admit to purposefully working a destructive agenda. Only Karl Marx was self-conscious and honest and purposeful enough to profess his intentions to the world! *He fully intended to destroy mankind and to consign the whole world to hell.* As already mentioned, the Bible presents the devil as intensively evil and destructive. The sentiments we read from the pen of Karl Marx could very well have been the devil's own. In a letter written on March 2, 1837, his father expressed concern that a demon may have alienated young Marx's heart. Marx's father may have been commenting on the poems Karl sent him on his 55th birthday. "My soul was true to God, is chosen for hell," He wrote, "I am great like God. I clothe myself in darkness like him."

Richard Wurmbrand wrote on Karl Marx's religious commitments in his book *Satan and Marx*: "Lunatcharski, a leading philosopher who was once minister of education of the U.S.S.R., wrote in *Socialism and Religion* that Marx set aside all contact with God and instead put Satan in front of marching proletarian columns. It is essential at this point to state emphatically that Marx and his comrades, while anti-God, were not atheists, as present-day Marxists claim to be. That is, while they openly denounced and reviled God, they hated a God in whom they believed. They did not question His existence, but rather challenged His supremacy. When the revolution broke out in Paris in 1871, the Communard Flourens declared, 'Our enemy is God. Hatred of God is the beginning of wisdom.'"[4]

As would be expected, Karl Marx's life was a disaster. He had seven children by his wife, Jenny. Continuing in the shameful tradition of Descartes and Rousseau, he produced a child out of wedlock with his house maid, Helene Demuth. Eleanor, his favorite daughter, married Edward Eveling, a Satanist known for his blasphemous lectures on "The

---

4. Richard Wurmbrand, *Satan and Marx* (Westchester: Crossway, 1990), 29.

Wickedness of God" and for his poems to Satan. If that wasn't horrible enough, Marx starved three of his children to death, five of his children died prematurely, and the two daughters who outlived him committed suicide. Thus ends the miserable, tragic life of Karl Marx.

THE CHARACTER OF THE MAN

The character trait most carefully honed in the life of Karl Marx was surely *hatred*. Unlike Rousseau, he did not profess to love anyone, for he was entirely comfortable with his hatred. In 1856, Marx wrote a foul little piece on *The Jewish Question*, in which he blamed the Jews for corrupting the world. He also wrote an article for the *New York Tribune* in which he suggested the complete elimination of the Jews; in Marx's words, "The fact that the Jews have become so strong as to endanger the life of the world causes us to disclose their organization, their purpose, that its stench might awaken the workers of the world to fight and eliminate such a canker." He also referred to the Slavic people as "ethnic trash" and prophesied eerily, "Their very name will vanish."

Karl Marx's life was filled with violent, explosive arguments with his family, which led to a complete breach of relationship with his mother and occasional separations from his wife. According to Jenny, his life was one continual row.[5] One of his acquaintances described Marx in a poem, "Dark fellow from Trier in fury raging, His evil fist is clenched, he roars interminably, As though ten thousand devils had him by the hair." Not surprisingly, he advocated terrorism and mob violence. Karl Heinzen, a fellow revolutionary, reported that Marx would routinely inform others: "I will annihilate you." Paul Johnson links this rage to his legacy.

> "He was never in a position to carry out large-scale revolution, violent, or otherwise, and his pent-up rage therefore passed into his books, which always have a tone of intransigence and extremism. Many passages give the impression that they have actually been written in a state of fury. In due course, Lenin, Stalin, and Mao Tse Tung practiced, on an enormous scale, the violence which Marx felt in his heart and which his works exude."[6]

5. Johnson, *Intellectuals*, 70.
6. Ibid. 72.

INFLUENCES

The great influences in Karl Marx's life included German philosophers Immanuel Kant and G.W. F. Hegel, as well as Jean-Jacques Rousseau and Charles Darwin. In fact, he dedicated his book *Das Kapital* to Charles Darwin with the words, "In deep appreciation—for Charles Darwin." Marx recognized the value of Darwin's theory of "survival of the fittest" as a framework for his own meta-historical theory of class struggle.

Immanuel Kant was one of the most significant philosophers of the modern age. We will not study his work in this book, because he merely echoed the seminal work of René Descartes and John Locke (humanist rationalism and empiricism). According to the *Stanford Encyclopedia of Philosophy*, "The fundamental idea of Kant's 'critical philosophy'— especially in his three Critiques: *The Critique of Pure Reason* (1781, 1787), *The Critique of Practical Reason* (1788), and *The Critique of the Power of Judgment* (1790) — is human autonomy. He argues that the human understanding is the source of the general laws of nature that structure all our experience; and that human reason gives itself the moral law, which is our basis for belief in God, freedom, and immortality."[7] In other words, truth is derived from man as the ultimate source - not God. Without Descartes and Locke, there would have been no Kant and Hegel; and without Kant and Hegel, there would have been no Marx.

PHILOSOPHY

The Communist Manifesto is the quintessential document of the 21st century, a good summary of Marx's ideology and work. In the *Manifesto*, Karl Marx concludes that Christianity is a non-issue by the 19th century. He rightly recognizes that the ancient religions were overcome by Christianity, but then he maintains that "Christian ideas succumbed in the 18th century to rationalist ideas." In fact, he can see his political theory aiding in the complete eradication of religion in the world: "Communism abolishes eternal truths, it abolishes all religion, and all morality."[8] Marx speaks prophetically; with the death of the Christian faith in mainstream western thought and life, the now autonomous man

---

7. "Immanuel Kant," *Stanford Encyclopedia of Philosophy*, May 20, 2010 <http://plato.stanford.edu/entries/kant/> accessed on Feb. 27, 2013
8. Marx, *The Communist Manifesto*, Section II

invents a godless world, free of the ancient ethical and social systems imposed upon him by the Christian religion.

Karl Marx is an idealist, with his own explanation of history, his own explanation of man's problems, his own ethical standard, and his own salvation plan for man. He rejects everything God has to say about all of that. So he presents his own ideas. Like all humanist idealists, he wants to be god. However, a god predestines the future and determines his destiny and that of his own kind. If Marx can explain the meaning of history on his own terms, then he reasons that he should be able to predestine the future. Of course, all of this is futile. He cannot possibly explain the complexities and the meaning of history, nor can any man determine the future. He cannot develop any absolute ethical standard on his own, and thereby define mankind's problems; and he certainly can never save man by the work of the state.

Marx interprets all of history by way of a "class warfare" model, a struggle for "freedom" and "equality." Obviously, he believes that economic inequality is an injustice that must be rectified by revolution and forced redistribution of the wealth. He is fiercely committed to his own standard of righteousness, which for a piece of cosmic dust (that cannot assume any absolute in a chance, meaningless universe), is utterly ridiculous. Regrettably, Marx's class-warfare motif played into the hands of the underprivileged in Russia, China, Cuba, and other nations, where men and women were already suffering under a greater degree of enslavement than elsewhere in the Western world.

For Karl Marx to react so negatively to economic inequality is to contradict his basic worldview. Why should a man who rejects the idea of "eternal truths, religion, and morality" commit so strongly to his own "moral" agenda? If there is an evolutionary, survival-of-the-fittest mechanism at work in a materialist universe as suggested by Charles Darwin, why not conclude a capitalist theory of economics? A materialist, evolutionary metaphysic could equally justify either a communist or a capitalist approach to economics. The humanist's attempts to explain history and to construct moral systems and social orders will always be arbitrary and groundless. Even if there was conflict between the classes, why should it be a problem according to Karl Marx's view of the world? I understand why Scripture considers class conflict and class envy as sinful, since it is a violation of God's tenth commandment. But why should Marx consider class conflict or class inequalities evil, when he rejects God's definitions and God's absolutes? Eliminating class conflict by egalitarian measures neither solves the root problem of sin, nor the inclination towards covetousness that resides in the evil hearts of men.

We know that the Bible condemns slavery, just as it condemns disease, death, debt, and divorce (Prov. 22:7, Mal. 2:16, 1 Cor. 7:21-23, 1 Cor. 15:26). Yet the Bible recognizes slavery as an inevitable by-product of sin in a fallen world, along with other evil consequences such as disease, divorce, debt, and death. Man's fundamental problem is that he has sinned against God, by transgressing God's laws. Thus, the problem of slavery is solved only when we address the problem of sin, which can only be solved by the sacrificial, atoning work of Jesus Christ. Liberty—a release from slavery—comes mainly by discipling the nations through the teaching of the Bible and working it into the warp and woof of families and individuals, masters and servants, political tyrants and their minions.

Marx opposes all forms of economic inequality, even if both the worker and employer would agree to the terms of employment. Instead of dealing with the sin of covetousness, Karl Marx makes the problem worse by institutionalizing envy and redistributing wealth in an effort to address this new "sin" of economic inequality. However, the Bible does not condemn inequality in pay scales, even for people doing the same work (Matt.20:1-15). In his parable, Jesus insists that a landholder should be able to pay his workers whatever he would like to pay them, as long as the employees agree to it at the outset of the work. *An inequality in pay scale does not amount to inequity or injustice*, according to the law of God. Moreover, the same passage in Matthew 20 actually condemns the envying of those who received more money than the others (vs. 15). Elsewhere in Scripture we find the law of God specifically forbidding the redistribution of the wealth. Also, biblical passages like Exodus 23:3, 6, 7 and Exodus 30:15 caution government officials not to countenance the poor man in his cause, or to set a higher tax rate for the rich than for the poor.

Humanist solutions to the problem of sin and slavery in this sin-cursed world will always turn out to be counter productive. Karl Marx's solution has failed, and it will always fail. He brought about more slavery and death to the billions of men and women who found themselves ensnared in the Marxist revolutions of the 20th and 21st centuries. All they did was trade one form of slavery for another. As sinful men tend to do when they reject the salvation provided by the Lord Jesus Christ, Karl Marx tried to rectify one injustice with more injustices. Petty tyrannies of the old world were replaced by a far more aggressive and extensive, highly centralized, bureaucratic tyranny.

THE ABOLITION OF THE FAMILY ECONOMY

Although the subject is rarely addressed by opponents of Marxism, Karl Marx's most radical agenda includes the abolition of the family based economy. At the onset of the industrial revolution, Marx could see that many capitalist corporations were already disintegrating the family by employing men, women, and children apart from the home economy. So he resolves to throw the argument back into the face of the capitalists: if capitalism could exploit children and destroy family-integrated economies, then Marx would make more effective work of it by his statist system. Moreover, Marx argues, "the family exists only among the bourgeoisie," and "the proletarians are torn asunder, and their children transformed into simple articles of commerce and instruments of labor."[9] If those employed by the capitalists are unable to sustain their own well integrated family economies, then how can the capitalists argue against the communist abolition of the family? This, of course, is nothing new; in fact it is the same Utopia proposed by Plato and Rousseau.

The Communist Manifesto, Karl Marx's most well-known work may be the single most influential document of the last two centuries. At the core of the document is this highly significant statement:

> "We destroy the most hallowed of relations, when we replace home education with social."[10]

Importantly, Marx realizes that the core battle in the war of the worldviews must be fought in the area of education, and specifically in government control of education. Before 1848, very little education was a product of large bureaucratic, democratic governments. For thousands of years, education was considered the responsibility of families, churches, and small communities, and was carried out under

9. Ibid.
10. Ibid.

their direction. Karl Marx understands that the nuclear family and its commitment to direct the education and upbringing of children was the one impediment to the all-consuming state. Home education was the core issue then and continues to remain the core battle to this day. Marx knew that without home education, the bonds between generations would gradually erode and the state would assume a more dominant role, generation by generation. One of the last American Congressmen to argue for a reduced role for the state retired in 2012. In his farewell address, Congressman Ron Paul stated, "Expect the rapidly expanding homeschooling movement to play a significant role in the revolutionary reforms needed to build a free society with Constitutional protections. We cannot expect a Federal government controlled school system to provide the intellectual ammunition to combat the dangerous growth of government that threatens our liberties."[11]

The covenant relationships of family and church were deadly to the statist agenda. Without the destruction of "the most hallowed of relations," the totalitarian state would never be successful at achieving its objective. Thus, Marx held that family economies and marriage must be replaced with an "openly legalized community of women."[12] After 150 years of steady progress, this Marxist vision is finally being realized the world over. The majority of households in America are now led by single women. Over 50% of children born to women under 30 years of age are illegitimate (this percentage is an increase from scarcely 5% in 1960, and 1% in the 1800s).[13] Half of marriages now end in divorce. Since 1960, women have killed billions of their own children through abortion, the abortifacient birth control pill, and emergency contraception. They do so to maintain their independence in the "community of women." For the past five years, Hillary Clinton, the United States Secretary of State has been busy exporting birth control pills and abortion to third-world nations. It is an effort to emancipate women from the "slavery" of marriage and family-economies, and enslave them to the large statist economic systems. In the 2012 American elections, 70% of single women

11. Ron Paul, "Last Speech: Ron Paul's Farewell to Freedom," *Fox Nation*, Nov. 17, 2012 <http://nation.foxnews.com/ron-paul/2012/11/15/last-speech-ron-pauls-farewell-freedom> accessed on Feb. 27, 2013

12. Karl Marx, *The Communist Manifesto*, Section II

13. Jason DeParle, and Tavernise, Sabrina, "For Women Under 30, Most Births Occur Outside Marriage," *NY Times*, Feb 17, 2012, <http://www.nytimes.com/2012/02/18/us/for-women-under-30-most-births-occur-outside-marriage.html?pagewanted=all&_r=0> accessed on Feb. 27, 2013

and 98% of single black women voted for the more socialist presidential candidate.[14] Karl Marx's agenda proceeds as designed. This man of the Nephilim class has virtually accomplished his agenda in every developed and undeveloped country around the world. *Something wicked this way came.*

THE TEN PLANKS

Marx leaves no doubt as to the agenda of the *Manifesto*. In the second section, he writes, "The theory of the Communists may be summed up in the single sentence: Abolition of private property."[15] But he is a practical man, and he knows that this agenda will not be accomplished overnight. Therefore, towards the end of the document, Marx lays out a blueprint for implementing the agenda, virtually all of which violates biblical law. Here are the ten planks with the corresponding biblical worldview perspective.

Plank #1. Abolition of property in land and application of all rents of land to public purposes.

The Bible forbids the confiscation of private property by the government. It is a great sin to remove the ancient landmarks (property markers), or to confiscate the property of the fatherless (Prov. 23:10). King Ahab, as the first acting communist was soundly condemned when he confiscated Naboth's vineyard (1 Kings 21:4-27). Jesus also taught that a landowner had the right to set the wages for his employees (Matt. 20:15). Moreover, the eighth commandment assumes the lawfulness of private property ownership when it forbids stealing.

Plank #2. A heavy progressive or graduated income tax.

The Bible disallows unequal taxation for public-works projects. Since God would not permit graduated taxation for the construction of the tabernacle or the temple, the same principle ought to be applied to all forms of coercive taxation for projects like building the city hall (Exod.

---

14. http://todayhealth.today.com/_news/2012/11/07/15001360-new-voter-bloc-emerges-single-women?lite
15. Karl Marx, *The Communist Manifesto*, Section II

30:15, Lev. 19:15). When it comes to the civil magistrate, God does not want the government to "countenance the poor man in his cause" (Exod. 23:3).

Plank #3. Abolition of all rights of inheritance.

The Bible condemns inheritance taxation according to the same principle condemning property taxation. Israel's inheritance is divided up in Deuteronomy 21:15-17, and the state is not mentioned as a "beneficiary."

Plank #4. Confiscation of the property of all emigrants and rebels.

The Bible forbids the oppression of immigrants (Exod. 12:49).

Plank #5. Centralization of credit in the banks of the state, by means of a national bank with state capital and an exclusive monopoly.

The Bible opposes the pride-oriented, humanist penchant to centralize power. This is the clear message contained in Genesis 9, when men wanted to "make a name" for themselves and build a huge tower and city at Babel. Christians simply cannot commit to an agenda that centralizes power.

Also, the Bible certainly does not prohibit trade in gold and silver. In fact, it seems that this is the preferred means of monetary exchange. Inevitably, the centralization of power in banking leads to artificial manipulation of the means of exchange. Assuming God knows what He's talking about in the Book of Proverbs, a debt-based economy manipulated by power-brokers in Washington is not a very good idea. For example, Proverbs 20:10 warns of the manipulation of the value of trade commodities: "Diverse weights, and diverse measures, both of them are alike an abomination to the LORD." When the government artificially adjusts the value of money, it is imposing false weights and measures on an entire society. Forbidding the free exchange of coinage and certificates that are properly backed by something of known value is also a violation of Christian liberty (Matt. 20:15).

Plank #6. Centralization of the means of communication and transport in the hands of the state.

When the Roman state tried to control the communication of the Gospel in the streets of Judea, the Apostles told the officials,"We ought to obey God rather than men" (Acts 5:29). If controlling the means of communication includes forbidding the public communication of the Gospel (which is how communist countries handled it), there is a violation of Christian liberty and God's law.

Plank #7. Extension of factories and instruments of production owned by the state; the bringing into cultivation of waste lands, and the improvement of the soil generally in accordance with a common plan.

Jesus insisted that the landowner had the right to do as he saw fit with his own resources (Matt. 20:15). The Bible also provides for restitution in cases where an individual harms the property or person of others (Exod. 22:1-4), but there is nothing in God's law that legitimizes the regulative state that the socialists brought to the world since the turn of the 20th century. The Bible plainly disapproves of governments owning more than 10% of the people's property, persons, and income (1 Sam. 8:15ff).

Plank #8. Equal obligation of all to work. Establishment of industrial armies, especially for agriculture.

The Bible describes the enslavement of daughters to other landowners (let alone governments) as a cursed thing (1 Sam. 8:15ff, Neh. 5:1-10). Enslaving one's wife to a centralized, governmental-economic machine is even worse.

Plank #9. Combination of agriculture with manufacturing industries; gradual abolition of all the distinction between town and country by a more equable distribution of the populace over the country.

The Bible generally discourages the centralization of power within cities (i.e. Babel). Nevertheless, the Bible allows freedom for those who wish to live in cities or in rural areas.

Plank #10. Free education for all children in public schools. Abolition of children's factory labor in its present form. Combination of education with industrial production, etc.

The Bible does not give the jurisdiction of education over to the realm of the state. The very definition of a tyranny in 1 Samuel 8:11-13 is the removal of sons and daughters out of home for service in the state. Moreover, it is the comprehensive and universal testimony of Scripture that the education of children is the responsibility of the family (Exod. 10:2, Deut. 5:14, Deut. 6:7-9, the entire Book of Proverbs, 1 Thess. 2:11, Eph. 6:4, etc.).

PROGRESS TOWARDS MARX'S AGENDA

Truly, it is hard to explain the wild enthusiasm with which the Western nations embraced Karl Marx's agenda. It wasn't until the 1950's that American conservatives and Christians in the West began to form any kind of an organized resistance against communist and socialist ideas. Previously, most Christians never thought of using biblical ethics to oppose evil agendas and evil people as we have laid it out in this book. Somehow, over the centuries, the Christian religion has been stripped of a distinctively biblical view of epistemology, metaphysics, and ethics. The Christian church was "absent without leave" in the "War of the Worldviews." With the publication of books like this, many Christians are back in the battle and we fully expect the righteous cause to prosper in years to come.

Nevertheless, it is astonishing to consider how many countries around the world have gladly adopted Marxist thinking, and incorporated the communist planks into their respective governments since 1848. America is no exception to the rule. The following summarizes the progress made thus far with the Marxist agenda in the United States:

1. We have seen property taxation incorporated into all fifty states. At the turn of the 19th century, only four states taxed property by valuation. Generally, states were using a biblically based, uniform capitation tax (Exod. 30:15). Illinois was the first state to formally adopt a constitutional provision for property taxation, and in 1834, Tennessee

passed a constitutional amendment enabling property taxation based on value. By 1848, eight states had incorporated a property tax that was in line with the Communist Manifesto. By 1896 most of the other states had followed suit.

2. A heavy, graduated income tax was incorporated in America, beginning in 1913 and has only increased since then. Roughly 75% of the total income tax collected in recent years is paid by the top 10% wage earners in the country.[16] According to a study produced by the Organization of Economic Cooperation and Development, the United States imposes the most progressive income tax in the world.[17]

3. Inheritance taxation has also been incorporated at the federal level and in 23 states (as of 2012).[18]

4. Immigrants are also subject to property taxation in most states in America.

5. After the long battle over the formation of a national bank in the days of Alexander Hamilton, Aaron Burr, and Andrew Jackson, the United States finally centralized control of all credit in 1913 by means of a federally-controlled Federal Reserve Bank, with the power to offer credit on a fractional reserve basis.

6. In America, there is still some freedom of transportation, and private ownership of the means of transportation. However, the FCC now regulates a large percentage of public communication systems, and the highways and the sky-ways are constantly monitored and controlled by the Federal Government and its agents. Over the last five years, Americans have increasingly submitted to body searches, seizures, and other tyrannical impositions at the hands of the Transportation Security Administration.

7. Since the early 20th century, over one-half of the property in the

16. http://www.heritage.org/federalbudget/top10-percent-income-earners?nomobile
17. http://taxfoundation.org/blog/no-country-leans-upper-income-households-much-us
18. http://www.smartmoney.com/taxes/income/estate-taxes-the-worst-places-to-die-1297801297458/

western states are owned and controlled by the Federal Government and its agents (the states).[19] Governmental planning departments for all land use have been established in almost every city, county, and state in America. These planning commissions were nonexistent prior to 1900. Most factories in America are not yet entirely owned by the government, however the government controls almost every department of labor (manufacturing, human resources, management, service, agriculture, etc.) with hundreds of thousands of pages of regulations and federal laws. Private industry may pretend to own the means of production, but they are at the mercy of the agencies that control their activities. Today, there are two government employees for every manufacturing worker in America.[20] Just fifty years earlier, it was the other way around - there were two manufacturing workers producing valuable products, for each one government employee in this country.

8. This plank speaks largely to the abolition of family economies. Marx intended for each individual to work as a part of the national economic machine. For 5,900 years, families worked as family economies. Wives were helpers for their husband's dominion-taking efforts in the household economy. "The heart of her husband safely trusted in her, so that he would have no need of spoil" (Proverbs 31:11). But Marx was committed to put an end to these healthy family economies. In America, the family farm and the family business have now virtually disappeared. The vast majority of women work outside of the family economy at their government (or government regulated) corporate jobs.

9. When Marx wrote the *Manifesto*, the vast majority of the populace of developing nations lived in the rural areas. Obviously, this demographic made it difficult for the social planners and centralizing strategists to control the citizenry. Since then, huge numbers of the populace have relocated into large cities where they are subject to far more government control. In America, almost every urban area is extremely liberal

19. http://www.nytimes.com/interactive/2012/03/23/us/western-land-owned-by-the-federal-government.html?_r=0
20. http://online.wsj.com/article/SB10001424052748704050204576219073867182108.html

(controlled by the big government party).[21] This guarantees a steady shift towards more socialism in almost every state across America. In 2006, the world's urban population finally hit 50%, a major increase from 13% in 1900.[22]

10. In 1852, Massachusetts became the first state in America to pass a compulsory school attendance law, just four years after the publication of the *Communist Manifesto*. By 1918, all fifty states had incorporated compulsory attendance laws; the tenth plank of the Communist Manifesto was now well established in the United States of America. There are currently 50 million students enrolled in public schools in this country at a per-student cost of $11,467 per year.[23] It has become almost impossible to oppose the $600 billion public school monopoly in the face of the growing, totalitarian state in this country.

INFLUENCE

It is hard to comprehend how a committed atheist, communist, mass-murderer, and demon-inspired author had so much influence on so many people. While few Americans would openly admit their admiration for Marx, their commitment to Marxist ideals is undeniably obvious in almost every political election since 1848. If government expenditures as a percentage of the Gross National Income is any measure of socialism and the growing tyrannical state, this country has seven times the socialism it had in 1900.[24] The federal, state, and local government take of the GDP in 1900 was 7.8%. That compares to something in excess of 50% today. After 150 years of steady progress towards a Marxist agenda, most Americans still take pride in their "free" country. So why did America embrace Marxism with such unrelenting devotion? On the one hand, the Soviet form of Marxism was implemented by a few revolutions and a hundred million dead bodies. However, Marxism American style, came about by fifty consecutive elections, socialist education programs,

21. In the 2012 elections, the liberal cities won the election for the more liberal presidential candidate, Barack Obama. As one pundit wrote, " President Barack Obama won re-election with 322 electoral votes to Romney's 206. But had just four cities. . . been removed from the equation, Romney would have received 293 electoral votes to Obama's 245."
22. "Urbanization," *Wickipedia* <http://en.wikipedia.org/wiki/Urbanization> accessed on Feb. 27, 2013
23. http://nces.ed.gov/fastfacts/display.asp?id=372
24. http://www.usgovernmentspending.com/breakdown_2012USpt_13ps5n
http://www.usgovernmentspending.com/breakdown_1900USpt_13ps5n

a breakdown of the nuclear family, and a slow but steady increase of dependence upon government among the populace. The Marxists took Russia to hell in a casket of thorns, while they took this country down in a casket of velvet. Either way, the objective seems about the same.

A poll conducted by the BBC News in 1999 found that Karl Marx was the most influential thinker of the Millennium.[25] Not surprisingly, Darwin, Nietzsche, Aquinas, Kant, and Descartes also made the short list. Almost every mainstream academic article interfacing with Karl Marx describes the philosopher as a wonderful thinker, although his ideas were poorly applied (not to exclude Christian professors as quoted in the preface of this book). The praise from academic sources comes with nauseatingly monotonous frequency: "His work as a philosopher, social scientist, historian and a revolutionary is respected by academics today."[26] Indeed, it is considered the highest social faux pas among the academic elite to attack the sainted intellectuals that formed the modern mind and the modern world.

The facts are inescapable. Karl Marx was the most influential thinker of the Millennium in the minds of westerners. The academics, the masses, and their institutions have followed Karl Marx like the Pied Piper of Hamlin. They reason that if the man is the greatest influence upon our world, then it would be incongruous for the people influenced by him to critique him! To critique him, they would have to begin by acknowledging that they have taken a part in the greatest mistake, the greatest fraud, and the greatest miscalculation of all of history. As it turns out, this remarkable intellectual leader, the great architect who designed their world for them, also destroyed it. When will the masses admit their mistake? When will they come to grips with the fact that they have embraced a monster, and he has taken them to hell? At present, there are but a few free market advocates and conservative Christians who have come to realize the momentous errors committed in the last millennium. However, it will be evident to the rest of the world within another generation or two. Western civilization is almost finished.

"O LORD God, to whom vengeance belongeth; O God, to whom

25. "Marx the Millennium's Greatest Thinker," *BBC*, Oct 1, 1999 <http://news.bbc.co.uk/2/hi/461545.stm> accessed on Feb. 27, 2013
26. "The Economist "Marx's Intellectual Legacy," Dec. 19th, 2002, <http://www.economist.com/node/1489165>

vengeance belongeth, shew thyself. Lift up thyself, thou judge of the earth: render a reward to the proud. LORD, how long shall the wicked, how long shall the wicked triumph? How long shall they utter and speak hard things? and all the workers of iniquity boast themselves? They break in pieces thy people, O LORD, And afflict thine heritage. They slay the widow and the stranger, and murder the fatherless. Yet they say, The LORD shall not see, neither shall the God of Jacob regard it. Understand, ye brutish among the people: and ye fools, when will ye be wise? He that planted the ear, shall he not hear? He that formed the eye, shall he not see? He that chastiseth the heathen, shall not he correct? He that teacheth man knowledge, shall not he know? The LORD knoweth the thoughts of man, that they are vanity" (Psalm 94:1-8).

APOSTATE

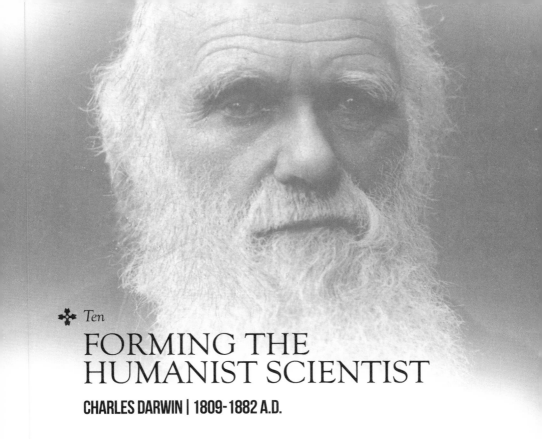

✤ *Ten*

FORMING THE
HUMANIST SCIENTIST

CHARLES DARWIN | 1809-1882 A.D.

Charles Darwin came from a long line of Christian apostasy that began with John Locke's ideological "children" of the 18th century. The Oxford Latitudinarians of the 17th century gave birth to the Unitarians of the 18th century, who gave birth to the Agnostics and Atheists of the 19th century. And, no family better personified this trend than the Darwin lineage. Charles's father, Robert, at first associated with the Unitarians and later referred to himself as a "free-thinker." Erasmus Darwin (1731-1802) was a pioneering humanist and an enlightenment thinker in his own right. Influenced strongly by John Locke and Jean-Jacques Rousseau, he advocated radical educational programs. Well before Charles Darwin entered the picture, Erasmus was one of the first evolutionists. He published a number of controversial books theorizing the evolution of man, a "Big Bang" sort of cosmology, and the transmutation of species.[1] In his poetic compositions, Erasmus

1. "Erasmus Darwin," *Wikipedia*, <http://en.wikipedia.org/wiki/Erasmus_Darwin>, accessed on Mar. 6, 2013.

Darwin presented nature as self-determining and independent of any Creator. In his words, "Nature is powerful and autonomous enough to break the supposedly exclusive society between God and spiritual beings."[2] Clearly, Erasmus Darwin rejected a God Who is involved in nature as Creator and Sustainer of all.

Well into the 19th century, it was still fashionable for England's bright young prodigies to enroll in the old Cambridge Seminary. The external religious forms continued strong, despite the worldview revolution that was radicalizing seminaries and universities. If we have learned anything about the breakdown of the Christian church, it is that the preeminent Christian seminaries must lead the apostasy. Charles Darwin entered Cambridge University in 1828 fully intending to prepare for the ministry. Early in his university experience, Darwin wrote that he "did not then in the least doubt the strict and literal truth of every word of the Bible."[3]

However, it wasn't long before Darwin's commitment to biblical truth faded. While his wife Emma continued in the Unitarian faith until the end of her life, Charles diligently labored to eliminate every vestige of the Christian faith from his thinking. This was no easy feat, but he applied interminable, determined effort to the task, achieving remarkable success in this thorough-going apostasy. In his autobiography, written towards the end of his life, he referred to the Christian faith as "manifestly false" and the Christian God as a "revengeful tyrant." The Bible, he said, is "no more to be trusted than... the beliefs of a barbarian."[4] Darwin's religious journey is a little hard to follow at points however, by the end of his life he claims the identification of "agnostic" as a "more correct description of my state of mind."

Although Darwin would make reference to a "Creator" in his public writings, he admitted in private letters that this was merely a marketing ploy intended to curry public favor. Darwin wrote, "I have long regretted that I truckled to public opinion, and used the Pentateuchal term of creation, by which I really meant 'appeared' by some wholly unknown process."[5]

November 24, 1859 may be the most important date in modern

2. Christopher Upham Murray Smith, *The Genius of Erasmus Darwin* (Burlington:Ashgate Publishing, 2005), 352.

3. Charles Darwin and Nora Barlow, *The Autobiography of Charles Darwin: 1809-1882* (New York: Norton, 1958), 57.

4. Ibid. 58.

5. Charles Darwin, *More Letters of Charles Darwin* (New York: Appleton, 1903), 272.

APOSTATE

history. The world would never be the same after the publication of Charles Darwin's magnum opus, *On the Origin of Species*. After 28 years of research and intense mental struggle, Darwin introduced his ideas to world that was waiting for an intellectual explanation for a materialistic ontology. The first print run sold out in a day.

In one sense, Darwin met a market need. The modern world was looking for an escape hatch from the Christian faith and the biblical God, and this was their opportunity. In our search for the forces that brought about this epochal apostasy, it is easy to oversimplify the equation. On the one hand, the great philosophical minds did provide the intellectual ammunition to lead the masses, but there were other spiritual forces at work. Apostasy was the "zeitgeist" or the spirit of the age. By the mid-19th century, millions of people were just looking for a reason to abandon the old faith, with its moral restrictions, realistic assessment of human nature, bloody atonement, and its suffer now, rewards later narrative.

Darwin worked powerfully on the psyche of the Western world. He could not disprove the existence of God. But if he could identify a natural mechanism for the development of the complexity of life forms, then there would be less of need for God as a causal force. Charles Darwin hypothesized that mankind and the various species of animals evolved by a form of natural selection in which the most physically-fit mutations (those that were better adapted to the environment) survived while the weaker died out. Darwin's hypothesis perfectly accommodated the growing deism and agnosticism of the day, because it took God out of the picture. If this was a viable explanation for the development of the complexity of biological life, then it rendered a Creator God obsolete in the process. These were heady times for modern man who thought he could rid himself of God!

But alas, over the years things did not go well for Darwin's hypothesis. Although much of the scientific world still embraces the macro-theory, many evolutionary scientists have now given up on gradualist mechanisms. Some evolutionists now postulate a strange, unproven mechanism called "punctuated equilibrium," which can hardly be considered a natural process and rather resembles supernatural creationism. Furthermore, no substantial evidence for transitional forms have been found in the fossil record, forms which might have helped identify a mechanism. Considering that scientists have never replicated cross-species evolution in a laboratory setting and the fossil record has added little substantiation to the theory over 150 years, the theory is more tenuous now than ever. Darwinism will not survive the test of time.

THE CHARACTER OF THE MAN

A careful reading of Darwin's autobiography and personal letters reveal a very strange man indeed. In the modern vernacular, he was a "twisted" individual. By his own admission, he was a sadist and he took great enjoyment from torturing and killing animals. He especially loved to kill birds by pounding on their heads with a hammer. From the time he was 17 years old, he dedicated his summers and autumns to killing animals (not for the meat, but for the sheer delight of killing).[6] While in our day this might bother a member of PETA, it should be particularly troublesome to the Christian who believes Proverbs 12:10. "The righteous man regards the life of his beast, but the tender mercies of the wicked are cruel." As he made plans for the voyage on the Beagle, Darwin included several guns in hopes that he might be able kill some "d— cannibals,"[7] Even as a child, he would beat puppies "simply from enjoying the sense of power."[8]

Entire books have been written on the subject of Darwin's psychological problems. He suffered from depression, agoraphobia, insomnia, vision alterations, hallucinations, malaise, vertigo, shaking, tachycardia, fainting spells, shortness of breath, trembling, nausea, vomiting, dizziness, muscle twitches, spasms, tremors, cramps and colics, bloating and nocturnal flatulence, headaches, nervous exhaustion, dyspnea, skin blisters, tinnitus, and sensations of loss of consciousness, and impending death."[9] According to Darwin's own testimony, his problems began at 16 years of age, and by the time he was 28, he was virtually incapacitated by his mental illnesses. These maladies were so chronic that Darwin Scholar Michael Ruse concluded that he must have been an "invalid" for the last 43 years of his life.[10]

6. Jerry Bergman, *The Dark Side of Charles Darwin* (Green Forest: Master Books, 2011), 127.

7. Charles Darwin, *The Correspondence of Charles Darwin*, vol. 1, *1821-1836* (New York: Cambridge University Press, 1985), 150.

8. Charles Darwin, *The Autobiography of Charles Darwin 1809-1882*, ed. Nora Barlow (New York: W.W. Norton, 1958), 27.

9. Bergman, 87.

10. Michael Ruse, "Is Evolution a Secular Religion?" *Science* 2003, http://www.sciencemag.org/content/299/5612/1523.full

In personal letters to friends, he wondered if his book *Origin of Species* might be the cause of "the main part of the ills which my flesh is heir to."[11] Dr. Jerry Bergman believes there was a strong connection between Darwin's religious apostasy and his psychoses. Drawing from Darwin's own admissions in his personal letters, Bergman writes, "His nagging, gnawing fear about murdering God caused a 'cold shudder to run through' him because of his fear that he had devoted his 'life to a fantasy... an illusion,' and a 'dangerous one' at that."[12]

Given that this is the character of the "brilliant" genius who popularized an evolutionary hypothesis for human origins, it should come as no surprise that he turned it to evil ends. In a book he wrote in 1871, *The Descent of Man*, he opened the door to the dreadful practice of eugenics, selective breeding of human beings to eliminate certain perceived genetic weaknesses. It is no great surprise that his cousin, Frances Galton pioneered early research in eugenics and prepared the world for Adolph Hitler and the eugenics programs in America. It is also no real surprise that Darwin enthusiastically endorsed Galton's book, *Hereditary Genius*, calling it a "great work." Nor is it any surprise that Darwin's own son George was an active supporter of eugenics and published an article on the "better breeding" of humans. Darwin enthusiastically defended his son's work in eugenics. Opposition to these ideas at the turn of the 20th century was all too rare, with little resistance coming from a severely weakened Christian church. However, G.K. Chesterton helpfully categorized these humanist ideas with the little quip, "If Darwinism is the doctrine of survival of the fittest, eugenics is the doctrine of survival of the nastiest."

DARWIN'S EPISTEMOLOGY

A man's worldview informs his science, his hypothesizing, and his interpretation of the data in his scientific inquiries. We are less interested in Darwin's science than we are in his worldview, through which he filters his scientific data and forms his hypotheses. If ideas have consequences, what are the fundamental ideas that yielded such dangerous consequences? As with many philosophers, Darwin's fundamental worldview comes into full fruition in his

11. Darwin, *Correspondence of Charles Darwin*, vol.7, 247.
12. Bergman, 117.

later writings. In a key passage in *The Descent of Man*, Darwin writes,

> *The same high mental faculties which first led man to believe in unseen spiritual agencies, then in fetishism, polytheism, and ultimately in monotheism, would infallibly lead him, as long as his reasoning powers remained poorly developed, to various strange superstitions and customs. Many of these are terrible to think of—such as the sacrifice of human beings to a blood-loving god; the trial of innocent persons by the ordeal of poison or fire; witchcraft, etc.—yet it is well occasionally to reflect on these superstitions, for they shew us what an infinite debt of gratitude we owe to the improvement of our reason, to science, and to our accumulated knowledge.[13]*

From the outset, Darwin assumes that men really are thinking independently of divine revelation when they devise their theistic conceptions. His grand assumption is that man reasons for himself in a world without God. According to Darwin, man ponders his own existence and surroundings while gradually working his way towards higher intelligence in the evolutionary process. He lumps monotheism in with the "primitive" religions of polytheism and fetishism. Also important to this survey, Darwin shudders at the notion that God would require a blood sacrifice or blood atonement for sin. This must include the Christian doctrine of atonement by the sacrifice of Christ, God's own Son on the cross. In the enlightened age of rank humanism, atheists are especially offended by this doctrine and typically regard it as primitive and repulsive. Further on in the passage, he expresses relief that highly evolved modern man has finally abandoned these old "superstitions and customs." According to Darwin's theory of knowledge, a right understanding of reality is entirely dependent upon man's improvement of his own reason and science. There is no place for special revelation or any revelation from God whatsoever for Darwin.

How primitive man comes upon a conception of God in a world where God does not exist is a conundrum to the mind of the evolutionary naturalist. This argument forms Anselm's ontological argument for the existence of God. These religious conceptions demand an explanation,

---

13. In a recent book, *A Natural History of Rape*, evolutionists Craig Palmer, PhD, and Randy Thornhill, PhD. argue for an evolutionary basis for rape.

APOSTATE

and Darwin pulls an answer out of a hat. He opts for a psychological explanation, attempting to attribute man's spiritual nature to another animal trait. According to Darwin, all notions about the cruder religions and the "more advanced" monotheistic religions (such as Christianity) come from "the same high mental faculties," and God does not reveal Himself to man. Instead, the evolutionist must view man as alone in the universe, and therefore he will have to figure things out for himself. Darwin concludes that man is becoming more self-aware, more intelligent, more advanced, not because he submits to God's revelation but because he is evolving into a higher creature. For Darwin, religion is just a phase as the human species evolves into a higher form.

However, his explanation of the evolution of man is arbitrary and baseless, without historical evidence. Ancient civilizations did not have access to the applied science available today, but only because this technology requires significant manpower, division of labor, and multiple generations to develop. But archaeological research of ancient civilizations has uncovered amazing architectural feats, well developed art forms, complex mechanical devices, and advanced social systems, proof that ancient man was just as intelligent as modern man.[14] Where primitive, uncivilized tribes are discovered in recent centuries, it is clear that these peoples had little or no access to the covenant people of God, where divine revelation has enabled human culture, civilization, and society.

Significantly, in *Descent of Man*, Darwin rejects any discrete distinction between the animal kingdom and the human kingdom. "The mental faculties of man and the lower animals do not differ in kind, although immensely in degree."[15] This is a radical departure from Psalm 8. "Thou hast made him a little lower than the angels... thou hast put all things under his feet, all sheep and oxen..." The implications of Darwin's ideas are frightening, especially when it comes to human morality. If the human is no different from the animal, what then is rape or infanticide? What happens to moral authority, and how does human morality differ from random animal instinct and behavior? [16]

14. Don Landis, *The Genius of Ancient Man* (Green Forest: Master Books, 2012)
15. Charles Darwin, *The Descent of Man*, Chapter 6
16. Ibid, Chapter 5

DARWIN AND EUGENICS

By far the most controversial element of Charles Darwin's legacy is the Adolph Hitler connection. If modern humanists still recognize one villain in history, Hitler usually makes the list. Therefore, evolutionists must repudiate any connection between Darwin and the German Nazi, and carefully avoid references to Darwin's support of eugenics. For our purposes, this consideration is of essence. In accordance with the immortal words spoken by Jesus Christ, we cannot separate ideas and consequences, teachers and their fruits. What follows is the most egregious section of Darwin's *Descent of Man* (Matt 7:20):

> *"With savages, the weak in body or mind are soon eliminated; and those that survive commonly exhibit a vigorous state of health. We civilised men, on the other hand, do our utmost to check the process of elimination; we build asylums for the imbecile, the maimed, and the sick; we institute poor-laws; and our medical men exert their utmost skill to save the life of every one to the last moment. There is reason to believe that vaccination has preserved thousands, who from a weak constitution would formerly have succumbed to small-pox. Thus the weak members of civilised societies propagate their kind. No one who has attended to the breeding of domestic animals will doubt that this must be highly injurious to the race of man. It is surprising how soon a want of care, or care wrongly directed, leads to the degeneration of a domestic race; but excepting in the case of man himself, hardly any one is so ignorant as to allow his worst animals to breed.*

> *The aid which we feel impelled to give to the helpless is mainly an incidental result of the instinct of sympathy, which was originally acquired as part of the social instincts, but subsequently rendered, in the manner previously indicated, more tender and more widely diffused. Nor could we check our sympathy, even at the urging of hard reason, without deterioration in the noblest part of our nature. The surgeon may harden himself whilst performing an operation, for he knows that he is acting for the good of his patient; but if we were intentionally to neglect the weak and helpless, it could only be for a contingent benefit, with an overwhelming present evil. We must therefore bear the undoubtedly bad effects of the weak surviving and propagating their kind; but there*

appears to be at least one check in steady action, namely that the weaker and inferior members of society do not marry so freely as the sound; and this check might be indefinitely increased by the weak in body or mind refraining from marriage, though this is more to be hoped for than expected."[17]

In true Nephilim style, the author weaves and bobs. He is slippery, purposefully inconsistent, and ominously vague. Deceptive obfuscation only accentuates the evil character of men who toy with the idea of racial extermination. In the first sentence in the quotation, Darwin *almost* approves of the "survival of the fittest" mechanism operating among the savages who do not "check the process of elimination." He half-heartedly recommends a limitation on marriage for the weaker and inferior members of society. But he reveals his true agenda, while admitting to his own inconsistencies, as he holds on to something called the "noblest part of our nature." At some point however, the "overwhelming present evil" will trump the contingent benefit, and the surgeon will just have to "harden himself" whilst performing the operation. This is how Darwin opens the door to powerful social planners who will centralize power and act on these fateful propositions. Later, Friedrich Nietzsche picks up on this and corrects Darwin's purposeful inconsistencies, providing the link to Adolph Hitler.

Apologists for Darwin have done their best to present this great oracle of naturalism in the best light. After all, he was the guru and the messiah for the humanist apostasy in the West. However, anyway you cut it the above quotation is evil incarnate. What spirit must have descended upon Darwin as he wrote those fateful words? This is the kind of writing that sets the agenda for the ultimate evil that shows up in future generations. *"Something evil this way comes."*

GENOCIDE

Regrettably, Darwin isn't done yet. In chapter VI, Darwin includes another frightening remark concerning extermination of races. *Warning: These may be the most evil words ever recorded in human history, as measured by the subsequent effects on human society.*

17. Ibid, Chapter 6

"At some future period, not very distant as measured by centuries, the civilised races of man will almost certainly exterminate, and replace, the savage races throughout the world. At the same time the anthropomorphous apes, as Professor Schaaffhausen has remarked (18. 'Anthropological Review,' April 1867, p. 236.), will no doubt be exterminated. The break between man and his nearest allies will then be wider, for it will intervene between man in a more civilised state, as we may hope, even than the Caucasian, and some ape as low as a baboon, instead of as now between the negro or Australian and the gorilla."[18]

Granted, the extermination Darwin speaks of is descriptive and not prescriptive. The silent presupposition underlying this writing is this: the descriptive forms the prescriptive. If the fittest survives in a tooth-and-claw world, then that is what is supposed to happen. (This argumentation is similar to that used by Jeremy Bentham.)

Charles Darwin isn't prescribing the extermination necessarily, but neither does he discourage it. His worldview already disallows all ethical absolutes governing human action, so now he lays out the ethically acceptable, natural process of human evolution. In view of the hundreds of millions of innocent men and women slaughtered in the succeeding century, the reader cannot help but feel the chill of his words. He writes as a cold, heartless, and detached scientist picking at a live human pinned to his mounting board. This genius Nephilim has less concern for the people groups to be eliminated than he does for the animals he destroyed with his little hammer. If the reader does not shudder a little as he reads these things, then Darwin has proven the point. We have entered a brave new world that fails to respect the human life created in the image of God.

It is a prophetic statement, an attempt to predestine the extermination of the "savage races." It is for Darwin to establish the metaphysical necessities of naturalist evolutionism. On the one hand, he does not argue for social imperative for eugenics and genocide, but neither does he argue against it. This is how Charles Darwin paved the way for the megalomaniacs of the 20th century who thought nothing of exterminating the Jews in Gemany, or the Slavics in the Soviet Union, or

18. Benjamin Wiker, *Ten Books that Screwed Up the World and Five that Didn't Help* (New York: Regnery, 2008), 10.

the Armenians at the hands of the Turks.

Against this sad legacy of racism, eugenics, and genocide stands the eternal truths of God's revelatory truth. The Bible acknowledges variance in culture, nationality, language, and skin pigment (Jer. 13:23), but there is no "racial" differentiation with a people who trace their lineage to Noah and Adam. God soundly condemned Miriam and Aaron for discriminating against Moses for his Ethiopian wife (Num. 12:1-12). As far as intermarriage is concerned, the Bible sees no issue with intermarriage across families and cultures except for the unequal yoking between believer and unbeliever, light and darkness (2 Cor. 6:14).

Certain atheist apologists have caviled against God's judgments recorded in the Old Testament (against Sodom and Gomorrah and other tribes in the land of Canaan). Such arguments however, fail to interact with the whole case. According to the Christian worldview, God is the ultimate Judge of the earth and the standard of all morality. If God should choose to judge an entire nation for its widespread use of infanticide, child sacrifice, and homosexuality, He performs His judgment based on morals (not on some cold, necessity in a naturalist-materialist world). Of course, those who are given to sins of infanticide, abortion, and homosexuality would be terribly offended by a God who should wish to judge them on the basis of His laws! The problem with atheists is that they have forfeited any absolute ethical standard, so they undermine their own right to argue any ethical case whatsoever.

Clearly God's law for all people today forbids the extermination of whole tribes and peoples, women and children even in warfare between nations (Deut. 20:13,14). It is only on this basis that we can claim genocide to be ultimately evil. In Christ's parable of the "Wheat and the Tares," He prohibits any kind of "religious jihad" (Matt. 13:30). We would argue that there is still a limited use for the civil magistrate for certain gross crimes, but none of this allows for the "extermination of the savage races." Rather, the Gospel is intended to reach every tribe and nation.

"And they sung a new song, saying, Thou art worthy to take the book, and to open the seals thereof: for thou wast slain, and hast redeemed us to God by thy blood out of every kindred, and tongue, and people, and nation" (Rev 5:9).

Every man, woman, and child, regardless of ethnic and cultural background, is made in the image of God. Some have lived in darkness and degradation for a longer period of time than others, such as the South Sea islanders and the Australian aborigines who had little access to the Christian West and the Christian gospel until the mid-19th century. In the 1870s and 1880s, missionaries like John Paton fought hard against Darwinian whites who were committed to eliminating the "savages" in Australia by mass murder.[19] Even Christian pastors like Charles Kingsley were convinced that "The black people in Australia cannot take in the gospel. . .poor brutes in human shape. . .they must perish off the face of the earth like brute beasts."[20] Theistic evolutionists were a sad lot from the beginning. In spite of Darwin and his ilk, the gospel has succeeded in reaching these far off lands, and thousands who at one time cannibalized one another now commune together at the Table of Christ.

Ironically, Charles Darwin was blessed with 1500 years of Christian heritage, but he abandoned it in favor of a godless, man-centered metaphysical and ethical outlook. If Darwin had been blessed with any moral, scientific, and economic improvement in Europe (as compared to the poor savages down in the South Sea Islands), it was only because Europe had a Christian, biblical heritage already formed between 33 A.D. and 1871 A.D. — the publication year for Darwin's ill-conceived book.

> "And then shall that Wicked be revealed, whom the Lord shall consume with the spirit of His mouth, and shall destroy with the brightness of His coming. Even Him, whose coming is after the working of Satan with all power and signs and lying wonders, And with all deceivableness of unrighteousness in them that perish; because they received not the love of the truth, that they might be saved. And for this cause God shall send them strong delusion, that they should believe a lie: that they all might be damned who believed not the truth, but had pleasure in unrighteousness" (2 Thess. 2:8-12).

THE INCREDIBLE INFLUENCE

19. John Paton, *Misionary Patriarch: The True Story of John G. Paton*, 1891 (San Antonio: Vision Forum, 2001), 262.
20. Ibid. 264.

OF CHARLES DARWIN

What possible influence could this agnostic, racist, mentally-ill sadist have had on any person or persons of intellectual or moral stature in the world? *Of course, his influence was titanic. According to multiple recent polls, Charles Darwin is still considered the most influential person in the world.* I know this doesn't say much about the character of the masses in the modern world.

Christians have their men of influence as well; Augustine, Chrysostom, Athanasius, John Bunyan, Brother Lawrence, Francis of Assisi, C.S. Lewis, and Thomas A'Kempis come to mind. These leaders have influenced millions, if not billions of people throughout history. To my knowledge, no historian has described these men as racists, sadists, or insane; nor do their autobiographies reveal anything of this nature. While they lived their own lives of humble repentance before God, they generally seemed to be at peace with God and men. Why then is Charles Darwin the patron saint of the modern men and women of our day? I merely inquire into the nature of human psychology at this point. Why did the masses run after men like Charles Darwin with such ardent affection and dedication over the last century? Evidently, the emotional bias towards apostasy pulls strongly on the Western psyche.

The lives and institutions of billions of people around the world from Japan and China to Russia, England, and America, were radically changed by Charles Darwin. This man's work has touched every person in every nation on earth through the educational, cultural, religious, and political institutions that affect their lives. Regrettably, Darwin's dreary influence still looms heavily over the whole world. His ideas have impacted the way *everybody* thinks. Godlessness prevails everywhere - in school classrooms, media, entertainment, and politics. Even for the average born again Christian, God is often a distant reality; He seems so very far away. We may look at His creation, but we scarcely see His fingerprints anymore. We seldom use terminology that speaks of "the Creation." Instead we speak of ecology, biology, reproductive systems, and rising atmospheric pressure. Charles Darwin's naturalistic materialism has so changed the Western metaphysic that the average person hardly senses God's providential interaction with the world, let alone His existence.

Goodreads.com conducted a poll amongst hundreds of thousands of readers who rated Darwin's *Origin of Species* as the most influential book in history, out-ranking *the Bible, the Koran,* and Marx's *Communist Manifesto.* In the worldwide war of worldviews, Darwin's naturalism and Marx's materialism are serious competitors against the theist worldviews of Islam and Christianity. Without question, humanism has given the theist religions a run for their money in the last two centuries. What remains to be seen is whether these relatively new, humanist ideas will have the staying power of the Christian worldview. Thus far, the Christian faith has outlasted every world empire since Rome fell in the 400s.

Nevertheless, it is the last century that captures our interest for the moment. Consider the following statistics contrasting the two worlds—before Darwin (we'll call it "B.D.") and after Darwin ("A.D").

B.D. - In 1900, 0.2% of the world were atheists (In 1850, there would have been fewer.).[21]

A.D. - In 2012, 21.3% of the world were atheists, 36% of 18-34 year old Brits claimed to be atheists/agnostics, and 63% of Brits claimed to be "not religious."[22]

B.D. - In 1850, 0% of the scientists of the day were self-described atheists.

A.D. - In 2005, 52% of the scientists in a survey conducted by National Opinion Research Center of Chicago, Illiniois said they had no religious affiliation (compare this to 14% of the general population who claim no religious affiliation).[23]

A.D. - In 2006, it was reported that 93% of the National Science Academy members were self-described atheists.[24]

This 2007 Pew Research study on Americans (below) showed a huge increase in the percentage of atheists by birth year.

Date of Birth	Percent claiming to be Atheist or Agnostic[25]
Before 1946	5%

21. "Religion and Belief, Some Surveys and Statistics," *Humanism.org.uk*, <http://www.humanism.org.uk/campaigns/religion-and-belief-surveys-statistics> accessed on Mar. 6, 2013
"Scientists May Not Be Very Religious, But Science May Not Be to Blame," *Phys.org*, Jul 3, 2007 <http://phys.org/news102700045.html> accessed on Mar. 6, 2013
22. J. Johnson, Jr., "The Atheist-Dominated National Academy of Sciences," *HumanEvents.com*, <http://www.humanevents.com/article.php?id=37503> accessed on Mar. 6, 2013
23. Bergman, 52.
24. http://www.humanevents.com/article.php?id=37503
25. http://www.pewforum.org/Unaffiliated/nones-on-the-rise.aspx

1946-1964	11%
1965-1976	14%
1977+	19%

Greg Graffin from Cornell University studied the religious backgrounds of 151 of the leading evolutionary biologists in the United States. He found that 98.7% of them had rejected a theistic faith and had become "functional atheists" as a result of their training in evolutionary biology. The famous atheist of the 21st century, Christopher Hitchens, claimed that "[Darwin's] doctrine of evolution... has removed in every thinking mind the last vestige of orthodox Christianity."[26]

All of the above data points to a significant increase in professed atheism in our world. The prevalence of atheists is at least one hundredfold higher than it was when Charles Darwin published *Origin of Species*. This is also confirmed in the testimonies of many contemporary atheists, where the road to atheism almost always began in a biology class or with some form of Darwinian thinking.

The theory of evolution affects a man psychologically more than logically. Though it was only a half-baked, poorly supported scientific hypothesis, it still appealed to men who were running from God. If God is unnecessary for the gradual development of complexity in certain life forms, then perhaps science could somehow eliminate the necessity of God as the source of all life forms, matter, and energy. What apostate scientists are looking for are pseudo-intellectual reasons to apostatize from the Christian faith. With the Darwinian hypothesis, they hope to find convenient justification for their apostasy. If man could separate God from his reality and origins, he would have no trouble separating Him from his ethics (which is the real issue). If he could separate God from ethics, he wouldn't have to worry about bothersome issues like guilt, God's judgment, God's law, or even God's redemption plan in Jesus Christ. Instead, he could be a law to himself, free to determine his own ethics and his own future in a world without God.

A few theistic evolutionists have argued that God, by His sovereign providence, directs a macro evolutionary process to bring about the world

---

26. Mayr, Ernst, "Reading On: Reactions to the New Naturalism," *Science and Philosophy*, July, 2000 <http://sciphilos.info/docs_pages/docs_Mayr_Dawin_css.html>, accessed on Mar. 6, 2013

as we see it today. However, it is impossible to reconcile this position with passages like Exodus 20:11 without equivocating on the Hebrew word for "day."

> *"For in six days the Lord made heaven and earth, the sea, and all that in them is, and rested the seventh day: wherefore the Lord blessed the sabbath day, and hallowed it" (Exod. 20:11).*

There are plenty of half way houses on the path to apostasy, and there are many who do not understand the deep devotion and the incorrigible commitments of the apostates. The Bible-believing Christian cannot reconcile a slow evolutionary process with these words without equivocating on the word *yom*. Does God wish for men to work for six indeterminate periods of time and rest for a seventh? Obviously, the commandment speaks of 24-hour periods - this is the plain meaning of the text. Any other interpretation requires exegetical gymnastics that would compromise the hermeneutical method for the rest of divine Scripture. If we haven't learned this lesson after 200 years of "scientific" criticism and religious apostasy, we will no doubt play a part in it. The young earth view of the creation is highly orthodox and bears strong historical roots over 2,000 years of Christian history. We are told that the only exception to this is found in Augustine of Hippo, but Augustine himself would not agree. Speaking of the Greek pagans, he wrote, "They are deceived, too, by those highly mendacious documents which profess to give the history of [man as] many thousands of years, though reckoning by the sacred writings we find that not 6,000 years have yet passed."[27] The testimony to a young earth is universal among the church fathers, including important figures as Barnabas, Justin Martyr, Irenaeus, Theophilus, Clement of Alexandria, Origen, and Hippolytus. We stand in good company. Without question, Darwinism was apostasy from the historical Christian faith.

Charles Darwin also had a profound effect upon John Dewey, the man who mainstreamed godless humanism and pragmatism in Western education at the turn of the 20th century. We will explore this connection more when we cover the contributions of John Dewey.

The well-known scientist Ernst Mayr summarizes the remarkable

---

27. Augustine, *The Literal Meaning of Genesis*, 1.12.10.

influence of Darwin in a well-publicized article written in 1999:

> *"A 21st-century person looks at the world quite differently than a citizen of the Victorian era did. This shift had multiple sources, particularly the incredible advances in technology. But what is not at all appreciated is the great extent to which this shift in thinking indeed resulted from Darwin's ideas. Remember that in 1850 virtually all leading scientists and philosophers were Christian men. The world they inhabited had been created by God, and as the natural theologians claimed, He had instituted wise laws that brought about the perfect adaptation of all organisms to one another and to their environment... The basic principles proposed by Darwin would stand in total conflict with these prevailing ideas... Eliminating God from science made room for strictly scientific explanations of all natural phenomena; it gave rise to positivism; it produced a powerful intellectual and spiritual revolution, the effects of which have lasted to this day."[28]*

This is clear testimony concerning the sea change in worldviews in the Western world. If the conflict between the humanist scientific apostasy and the epistemological authority of Scripture is important to the future of the faith, then Christians should be concerned with recent losses. At the present, it appears that these losses are accelerating in every country of Protestant or Roman Catholic heritage. Of the 110 Christian universities in America where the faith is still strongest, only about half teach creationism and oppose evolutionary Darwinism. Taking into account all public and private university instruction in this country, a mere 1% maintain a God-centered epistemology and metaphysic in the matter of origins.[29] The Darwinian theories dominate at least 99% of higher education instruction in America, and it is safe to say that that number is closer to 99.999% in Europe. In the war of the worldviews, this appears to be a complete rout! Of the thousands of museums and science centers in America, there are fewer than five which maintain a young earth, creationist perspective. Darwin's materialism has made progress since the Scopes trial of 1925. At this stage, his influence maintains almost complete sway over the scientific and educational institutions in

28. Charles Darwin, *The Descent of Man*, Chapter 3
29. Ken Ham, *Already Compromised* (Green Forest: Master Books, 2011)

the Western world. If not for the missionary movement that is hard at work spreading Christian gospel to every land, the kingdom of Christ would have languished.

By sheer numerical quantity, the last 100 years have produced the most extensive apostasy from the Christian faith in the history of Christianity. This apostasy has been largely confined to Europe, America, Australia, and Canada, however, it is only a temporary setback. The two-thousand year expansion of the Christian faith advances by ebb and flow as the waves of Christian influence hit the shores of continents around the globe. As a result, we have seen Christianity grow significantly in Asia and Africa over the last century. Two hundred years ago, about 95% of Christianity was confined to Europe and America. Today, professing Christians in the West comprise about 15% of the total number of Christians in the world (and these continents represent about 16% of the world population).[30]

But the specific impact that Charles Darwin has had on the lives of hundreds of millions of Christian families is overwhelming. This man was a key leader in the apostasy. It is an undeniable fact that the Christian faith was far stronger 150 years ago in England and America. In the 1850s, Americans from previous generations were generally orthodox Christians. Now, their 21st century grandchildren are pagans, atheists, homosexuals, witches, and atheist-scientists. The sheer numbers that will be in hell because of Charles Darwin's commitment to "murder God" is too much—and too torturous—to fathom.

> "Why boastest thou thyself in mischief, O mighty man? the goodness of God endureth continually. The tongue deviseth mischiefs; like a sharp razor, working deceitfully. Thou lovest evil more than good; and lying rather than to speak righteousness. Selah. Thou lovest all devouring words, O thou deceitful tongue. God shall likewise destroy thee for ever, he shall take thee away, and pluck thee out of thy dwelling place, and root thee out of the land of the living. Selah. The righteous also shall see, and fear, and shall laugh at him: Lo, this is the man that made not God his strength; but trusted in the abundance of his riches, and strengthened himself in his wickedness. But I am like a green olive tree in the house of God: I trust in the mercy of God for ever and ever. I will praise thee for

30. http://en.wikipedia.org/wiki/List_of_religious_populations

APOSTATE

ever, because thou hast done it: and I will wait on thy name; for it is good before thy saints" (Psalm 52).

From reading the plethora of biographic material available on Charles Darwin, it is clear that this man picked a fight with the God of the Bible, and he lost.

❖ *Eleven*

FORMING THE HUMANIST PSYCHOLOGY

FRIEDRICH NIETZSCHE | 1844-1900 A.D.

B y the turn of the 19th century, the amalgam of atheism, agnosticism, and general unbelief was gathering momentum. God was soon to be very distant from the modern mind.

Between the 18th and 19th centuries, Germany took the lead in the religious apostasy. Of all the first generation godless Nephilim, German Friedrich Nietzsche was the most aggressive and pugnacious - he was the leviathan of the apostates. This philosopher extraordinaire was outspoken in his opposition to Jesus Christ, and his apostasy was spectacular in the most negative possible sense of the word. Benjamin Wiker compares him with the modern light-weight atheists with whom we are familiar: "The best seller atheists around now (like Richard Dawkins, Christopher Hitchens, and Sam Harris) are pussycat atheists, not lions like Nietzsche who, if he were still around, would chew them up and spit them out in disgust."[1]

1. Benjamin Wiker, *Ten Books that Screwed Up the World and Five that Didn't Help* (New York: Regnery, 2008), 100.

APOSTATE

Born on October 15th, 1844, the son of a Lutheran pastor, Friedrich was baptized nine days later. Karl Ludwig, the boy's father selected Luke 1:66 for his baptismal verse: "Everyone who heard this wondered about it, asking, 'What then is this child going to be?' For the Lord's hand was with him." Both grandfathers and an uncle were all Lutheran ministers. Ironically, his paternal grandfather, Friedrich August Ludwig Nietzsche (1756–1826), wrote a number of Christian books, one of which affirmed the "everlasting survival of Christianity."

His father died when young Friedrich was five years old, and initially the boy aspired to the pastorate in the tradition of his father and grandfather. But then he happened to read Ludwig Feuerbach's skeptical treatise, *Essence of Christianity* in his 17th year.[2] This book paved the way to unbelief for the young man at a time when German higher criticism and humanist rationalism had widely infected the Lutheran church. As he read further in Schopenhauer's *The World as Will and Representation*, he was fully convinced of atheism. On Easter Sunday in 1865, he refused communion at the Lutheran church. In a letter to a friend, Erwin Rhode (1870), he included himself in the growing number who, "have completely forgotten Christianity." In God's providence this son of a Lutheran pastor would become a major leader in the dismantling of the Christian worldview in the West.

Nietzsche's ideas were extremely toxic, and his influence vast. In fact, this son of a pastor may have been the most *dangerous* philosopher of the last millennium. Nobody defied God with as much animate force and vigor as Nietzsche. By his own testimony, he fully intended to strike "a destructive blow against Christianity."[3] With astonishing hubris, he pronounced to the world, "the old god abolished and... I myself will henceforth rule the world."[4] What we find with Nietzsche is a remarkable, one-of-a-kind composite of unmitigated arrogance, unparalleled intellectual capability, and a demonic hatred of Christ. He declared himself to be "the most terrible opponent of Christianity,"[5] and then identified himself as *The*

---

2. As with many of the other apostates, Ludwig Feuerbach was raised in a devout, Christian home but abandoned the faith entirely during his university years under the tutelage of Hegel and Karl Daub. His was a classic case of rising academic arrogance, theological skepticism, and rebellion against his father. This German atheist profoundly influenced Karl Marx, Friedrich Engel, and Friedrich Nietzsche in their formative years.

3. Wiker, *Ten Books that Screwed Up the World and Five that Didn't Help,* 112.

4. Friedrich Nietzsche, *Beyond Good and Evil,* Section 208.

5. Friedrich Nietzsche, *Selected Letters of Friedrich Nietzsche,* Anthony Ludovici, trans. (Garden City: Doubleday, 1921).

Antichrist in a book with the same title published in 1888. Only three months after he made this grand declaration, this monstrous intellectual lost his mind, and for the last 11 years of his life Nietzsche was by all reports, certifiably insane. His sister cared for him until he died. In his insanity, he could not help but admit the truth of his own condition: "I am dead because I am stupid... I am stupid because I am dead." Commenting on Nietzsche, G.K. Chesterton declared, "The man who thinks without the proper first principles goes mad... thinking in isolation and with pride ends in being an idiot. Every man who does not have a softening of the heart, must at last have softening of the brain."[6]

> "And upon a set day Herod, arrayed in royal apparel, sat upon his throne, and made an oration unto them. And the people gave a shout, saying, It is the voice of a god, and not of a man. And immediately the angel of the Lord smote him, because he gave not God the glory: and he was eaten of worms, and gave up the ghost. But the word of God grew and multiplied" (Acts 12:21-25).

INFLUENCE

If any of the philosophers needed a public relations campaign, it would have been Friedrich Nietzsche. Despite his insanity, his ideas were indispensably instrumental in the development of modern philosophy and psychology. However, the man's virulent hatred of God, his connection to Adolf Hitler, and his insanity would have tarnished his image with the masses, except that his biographers and other academics have worked over time to prop up his reputation.

As faith weakened and apostasy metastasized in the West, the world demanded a "new morality" however fragmentary, inconsistent, and incoherent it would prove to be. Nietzsche's complete break with any possibility of ethical absolutes provided this new philosophical direction, and he greatly influenced the 20th century existentialists Karl Jaspers (1883-1969), Martin Heidegger (1889-1976), and Albert Camus (1913-1960). Without question, Nietzsche's philosophy was also formative in the thinking of the most popular philosopher of the 20th century, Jean-Paul Sartre. This well-known existentialist wrote on Nietzsche's philosophies in his exit exam for his graduation from the University of Sorbonne.

6. G.K. Chesterton, *Orthodoxy*, Chapter 1.

Friedrich Nietzsche is also considered by many to be the grandfather of the modern psychology taught in most universities and colleges. What a supreme, unparalleled irony that a man who was certifiably insane for at least eleven years out of his life should bear the title of the founder of humanist psychology! In his autobiography, Nietzsche described himself as the first psychologist. He wrote, "Before my time there was no psychology. To be the first in this new realm may amount to a curse."[7] Both Sigmund Freud (1856-1939) and Carl Jung (1875-1961) expressed admiration for Nietzsche. According to one source,

> *"Alfred Adler (1870-1937) developed an 'individual psychology' which argues that each individual strives for what he called "superiority," but is more commonly referred to today as 'self-realization' or 'self-actualization,' and which was profoundly influenced by Nietzsche's notions of striving and self-creation. The entire 'human potential movement' and 'humanistic psychology movement' (Abraham Maslow, Carl Rogers, Rollo May, etc.) owes a great debt to this line of thought. Even pop psychologists of 'self-esteem' preach a gospel little different from that of Zarathustra. The ruthless, self-assertive 'objectivism' of Ayn Rand (1905-1982) is difficult to imagine without the influence of Nietzsche."[8]*

Modern playwrights, George Bernard Shaw and Eugene O'Neill, also followed his philosophies in their plays.

Later philosophers, psychologists, and academics will gladly admit to the pervasive influence of Friedrich Nietzsche on practically every modern institution. Yet, only one in a thousand Christians will recognize his philosophies in their own perspectives, music, and culture. Thus, Christians are easily synthesized and their children tend to apostatize from the faith. *If you live in the modern world and spend any time with the books, media, movies, and music produced by it, then you should know something about the intellectual sources that frame most of it.* Following the political and social revolutions of the 19th century, came the all-important cultural revolution. Nietzsche and his friend, Richard Wagner played a vital part in the deconstruction of the entire Western world.

---

7. *Ecce Homo* [Behold the Man!], Conclusion.
8. Brians, Paul, "The Influence of Nietzsche," April 1, 1998, <http://public.wsu.edu/~brians/hum_303/nietzsche.html> accessed on Mar. 13, 2012.

FRIEDRICH NIETZSCHE AND RICHARD WAGNER

Every religion has its prophets and preachers, and the religion of man-centered humanism is no exception to the rule. The composer, Richard Wagner (1813-1883) was one of the important preachers in the cultural apostasy of the 19th century. As the pioneer composer of modern music, it is possible that Richard Wagner had more of an influence upon Nietzsche than Nietzsche had on him. There was surely a symbiosis of sorts between the two. Nietzsche referred to Wagner as "Germany's greatest living creative genius," and Adolf Hitler shared the sentiment.[9] Wagner himself explained the mission of his work in these words: "My task is to bring revolution wherever I go. . . only revolution can give us back the highest artwork."[10] This obviously appealed to Nietzsche, and the subsequent cultural revolution was an inevitable result of their mutual philosophical revolution against God.

In multiple instances in his writings, Nietzsche explicitly advocated Dionysus, the Greek god that symbolized all that is unrestrained, chaotic, dangerous, and unexpected, particularly embodying the unrestrained force of will and intoxication. In the last words of his autobiographical work, *Ecce Homo*, Nietzsche sets this Greek god against Christ. It would take more than a few heady books from an erudite philosopher to reach the masses and work the ideas into the warp and woof of a civilization - enter Richard Wagner's revolution in music. This was crucial to the massive cultural revolution of the 19th and 20th centuries that came of age in the 1960s. Somebody had to incarnate Dionysus into the music, where the force of emotion would overpower the orderly organization of melody and content. This musical Dionysian revolution captured the hearts and minds of several billion people in subsequent years. Without a cultural revolution in music, Nietzsche would not have had nearly the same impact on the world. As the dust clears after the social and cultural atom bombs fell on Western civilization, we can assess the causes of the devastation. Perhaps it was more Wagner than Nietzsche that did the damage - music can carry ideas into the heart of a man, better than prose. Historians chronicling the decline of Western civilization would do well

---

9. Adolf Hitler was fanatical in his appreciation of Richard Wagner. He reports to have heard Wagner's opera, *Tristan und Isolde* some thirty to forty times while he lived in Vienna. He is quoted, "Wagner's line of thought is intimately familiar to me, at every stage of my life I come back to him." Source: Shirer, William L. *The Rise and Fall of Adolf Hitler* (New York: Scholastic Book Services, 1961), 15-20.

10. Richard Wagner, *Art and Revolution*.

APOSTATE

to study the connections between Friedrich Nietzsche, Richard Wagner, and the popular music revolution of the 1950s and 1960s.[11]

PHILOSOPHY

Friedrich Nietzsche believes in the will to power. Or, to use a more familiar idiom, he holds that "might makes right." Higher culture was developed," says Nietzsche, when "men of prey who were still in possession of unbroken strength of will and lust for power, hurled themselves upon weaker, more civilized, more peaceful races... In the beginning the moral noble caste was always the barbarian class."[12] Make no mistake about it - these are words of Nephilim strength, containing the potential for much destruction. These words produced real bloodshed in the earth. Effectively, Nietzsche justifies the most tyrannical and cruel action where the strong prey on the weak in order to produce a higher culture or race of men. A generation later, the German leader, Adolf Hitler incarnated these ideas word-for-word in the dreadful Nazi Reich. Regrettably, that was not the extent of it as the spirit of this madman swept others into its force, racking up the body count in the succeeding century. The "unbroken strength of will" and "lust for power" certainly possessed Lenin, Stalin, Mao Tse Tung, Pol Pot, and other dictators as they lived out these destructive ideas. Nietzsche's chilling prophesies envision the blood bath that would ensue in the 20th century in his book *Beyond Good and Evil*: "The time for petty politics is over: the very next century will bring the fight for the dominion of the earth—the compulsion to large-scale politics."[13]

The popular atheists today (such as Richard Dawkins and Christopher Hitchens) will take up a great deal of time defending the moral virtues of atheism, while chiding the "awful immorality" of the God of the Bible. For some reason, they are fixated upon their own arbitrary, baseless systems of morality. These arguments are handily dismissed, by simply pointing out the internal inconsistency and incoherence contained within the Nietzschean worldview. For example, Nietzsche openly admits that the idea of morality is impossible where there is no Absolute. In a materialist universe without a God, there can be no standard by which moral actions

11. E Michael Jones, *Dionysos Rising: The Birth of Cultural Revolution out of the Spirit of Music*, (San Francisco: Ignatius Press, 1994).
12. Friedrich Nietzsche, *Beyond Good and Evil*, Chapter 9
13. Ibid. Section 208.

are to be measured. Yet if you read a paragraph or two of Nietzsche's writings, you find him filled to the brim with a moral outrage. But why all the moral outrage if humans are just advanced forms of cosmic dust randomly assembled in this form or that? Debating moral issues then makes no more sense than two dogs arguing over the benefit of table manners, or two pieces of dirt arguing over property rights.

However, Friedrich Nietzsche attempts self-consistency, claiming that he takes the world "Beyond Good and Evil." Nonetheless, we insist that he is not self-consistent enough, for he continues to cling to some transcendent purpose for man in his writings. For example, he says there is something "better" about tribes with "fidelity and courage" versus those without these virtues. He prefers suffering, nobility, unhappiness, and power over the "slave-like" virtues of patience, industry, humility, and pity. The goal of existence, according to Nietzsche, is more than survival (as Darwin held). It is the opportunity—or the ability—to discharge one's strength; he calls this "the will to power." But we press the question harder: "Why? Why should the discharge of strength add any meaning to life whatsoever?" If the next asteroid that careens into our atmosphere destroys all of life on planet earth, what is the purpose of this discharge of strength?

Nietzsche is inconsistent in other areas as well. On one hand, he praises the philosopher of the future who accepts a relativistic way of looking at the world. "All philosophers hitherto have loved their truths. But assuredly they will not be dogmatists."[14] This statement is easy to counter when we see that his will-to-power ethic is quite dogmatic. His goal is to get beyond the age-old Christian ethical definitions; yet for him, everything is subservient to his new ethic - the will to power. He is willing to employ "severity, violence, slavery, danger in the street and in the heart, secrecy, stoicism, tempter's art and devilry of every kind... everything wicked, terrible, tyrannical, predatory, and serpentine in man," as long as it "serves as well for the elevation of the human species."[15] But why elevate the species? What is it about the descriptive evolutionary process (highly questionable though it may be) that would prescribe the survival of the species? What is to say that the species should not die out, assuming his basic metaphysical perspective?

14. Friedrich Nietzsche, *Beyond Good and Evil*, 9.42
15. Ibid. 9.44

APOSTATE

Nietzsche also goes after the utilitarianism of John Stuart Mill and Jeremy Bentham, who argued for the greatest good and greatest happiness for the greatest number. If that be the human agenda, he counters, the weak would eventually overwhelm the gene pool, which would stymie the advancement of human culture. His agenda is slightly more self-consistent or honest than Darwin's eugenics plan in *Descent of Man*. Consistent with his morose disposition, Nietzsche rejects the notion of seeking happiness for others—or for oneself, for that matter. Nietzsche's motto is "No pain, no gain." But at the end of the day, why should one accept Nietzsche's definitions of "Good" and "Virtue" as any better than Mill or Bentham's definitions, or any other human being's definition? Why would "nobility" and the exercise of "power" be any better than industry, humility, and pity? After all, why should the human species survive? Why is it important that life develops into higher forms, if the universe has no transcendent purpose?

In the analysis of his thought, let us be careful not to minimize the sheer evil of Nietzsche's ethical agenda, especially in his preference for "Master Morality" as against "Slave Morality." He advocates Master Morality as that which promotes self-glorification. Master Morality inspires dread in others, as it exploits, injures, and gains preeminence over the weak. Meanwhile, Slave Morality wastes time in pity, generosity, patience, industry, humility, and friendliness.[16] Apparently Nietzsche was quite familiar with the Bible, because he chose a life ethic that exactly contradicts the teachings of Christ!

> "But Jesus called them unto him, and said, Ye know that the princes of the Gentiles exercise dominion over them, and they that are great exercise authority upon them. But it shall not be so among you: but whosoever will be great among you, let him be your minister; And whosoever will be chief among you, let him be your servant: Even as the Son of man came not to be ministered unto, but to minister, and to give his life a ransom for many" (Matt. 20:25-28).

The Bible clearly condemns self-glorification. When Herod sought glory for himself, God killed him for it (Acts 12:21-25). In terms of Nietzsche's ethical outlook, actually the Scriptures do commend self-

16. Ibid. 9.259, 260.

discipline and severity in the battle with the flesh (Matt. 18:9, 10), but it also condemns the exploitation of the weak in society as one of the highest forms of evil (Exod. 22:22-24, Psalm 10:18, Psalm 94:6, Prov. 23:10, Is. 10:2, Jer. 22:3, etc.). Fundamentally, Nietzsche favors tyranny, while the Bible repudiates it.

During his more rational moments, Nietzsche refuses to reckon with the ultimate implications of his mortality, finitude, and godlessness. By rejecting any ultimate source of truth, ethics, and purpose, he undermines *all* basis for any truth proposition. As with every humanist philosopher, he attempts to climb the ladder of knowledge. But the ladder rests on nothing, in an endless ocean of arbitrary notions. He finds no certainty for a first proposition. So how can he argue that his system of knowledge is better than any other system? Obviously, he cannot test the argument by any absolute standard, so in the end he must forfeit the argument. When the self-consistent humanist finally comes to the realization that there is no essential meaning in what he says, he is forced to abandon rationality completely, and opt for insanity. If according to his worldview, the brain is just another natural process in a purely material world then what are these immaterial ideas? If the brain is a collage of chemical reactions similar to the chemical processes that happen when grass grows in the yard, why should we take the ideas coming from the mind of these men seriously? Without an immaterial God as the absolute Source of wisdom and knowledge, there is no possibility for meaning or human rationality. The most self-consistent brilliant philosopher will either turn to God or turn insane.

Later in his life, Nietzsche ponders the philosophy of Nihilism, all the while hoping that his "Will to Power" scheme will somehow trump Nihilism. He envisions a "Super Man," as a higher form of human existence, engineered by man himself. Perhaps this unrealistic vision and futile project will silence the loud screams of Nihilism in the back of his head, "There is no purpose! There is no reason for being! There is no truth! There is no right and wrong!" But alas for Nietzsche, his own mind forces him into towards higher degrees of self-consistency, and so he loses his mind.

"All those who hate me, love death" (Prov. 8:36).

As Christians true to our worldview commitments, we must be *even more intensely aggressive* in our demands for self-consistency from Nietzsche and his ilk. We must hold the feet of these atheists to the fire, forcing them either to suicidal nihilism or to Christ. There are no other alternatives.

> *"Answer not a fool according to his folly, lest thou also be like unto him. Answer a fool according to his folly, lest he be wise in his own conceit"* (Prov. 26:4,5).

SATANIC INFLUENCE

Four years before he went insane in the clinical sense, Nietzsche published an odd collection of rambling ideas, entitled *Thus Spake Zarathustra*. He continued recording the prophecies of Zarathustra in his autobiography *Ecce Homo* months before his insanity incapacitated him. Here Nietzsche freely admitted, "I have not uttered a single word which I had not already said five years ago through my mouthpiece Zarathustra."[17] Now this introduces some interesting questions. If he is truly the great humanist philosopher who was supposed to have built up his philosophy on human reason, who in the world is Zarathustra? And why does he still speak (long after the old Zoroastrian prophet of the same name died)? As Christians, we are well aware of a spiritual world of principalities and powers beyond flesh and blood. Therefore, it seems plausible that these powers were influencing the tortured mind of this philosopher. What might the secular scholar say about a self-conscious humanist like Nietzsche giving credit to the revelations of some other being? Why does this pseudo-intellectual turn to these supernatural revelations as if appealing to a demonic intelligence? If the entire world followed Nietzsche, who were they following - a man or a demon?

Nietzsche signs off his autobiographical *Ecce Homo*, with one last defiant screech directed towards his arch-enemy, Christ.

> *"Dionysus vs. the Crucified."*

Whether it is the devil himself or Nietzsche himself set against Christ, it doesn't really matter. Opposition to the Creator of the universe is nothing but a futile dream for a creature confined to a world created by

17. Friedrich Nietzsche, *Ecce Homo*, Why I am a Fatality

God.

In the end, this atheist could not help but acknowledge the existence of God. It is the ultimate honesty, when natural man admits that he knows God and then confesses his hatred of Him. Nietzsche cannot ignore the reality of Jesus Christ, but he also states in no uncertain terms his vehement opposition to Him. He writes with unrestrained animus, "Christian morality is the most malignant form of all falsehood. . . The concept 'God' was invented as the opposite of the concept 'life'— everything detrimental, poisonous, and slanderous, and all deadly hostility to life, was bound together in one horrible unit in him."[18]

Thirty years after the first publication of *Thus Spake Zarathustra*, the German government printed 150,000 copies of this demonic, toxic creed for distribution among the army during World War I. This also paved the way for the Nazi nightmare of the succeeding thirty years. The consequences of these ideas upon the entire German nation and Adolf Hitler in particular were horrific.

Nietzsche's "will to power" is exactly opposite the Christian story of redemption. Our Savior, Jesus Christ entered His state of exaltation only after He experiences a state of humiliation at the cross. He stooped to rule, and He is the Lamb on the Throne (Rev. 7:17). Of course this irritated Nietzsche. It was the rule of Christ that bothered him so much. It was the "A.D." business on the calendars that tortured his mind. After 1800 years, this "Galilean" was everywhere! He could not stand the ever-reigning presence of Jesus Christ hovering over the Western world and the Western mind. So, this Nephilim picked a fight with the Crucified, the King of kings on the right hand of the Father. And he lost the battle.[19]

> *"But there were false prophets also among the people, even as there shall be false teachers among you, who privily shall bring in damnable heresies, even denying the Lord that bought them, and bring upon themselves swift destruction... And many shall follow their pernicious ways; by reason of whom the way of truth shall be evil spoken of. And through*

18. Ibid
19. I understand that many humanists disagree with me on this point. They cannot see the end of the Nephilim reign any time in the foreseeable future. They see the dominance of these men's ideas, and they are still excited about man's future without God. But the handwriting is on the wall. Whether we look at the social indices, the economic indices, the political stresses, or the cultural and moral condition of the nations, we arrive at the same conclusion. The heyday of humanism is long gone. This experiment with godless materialism is almost over.

covetousness shall they with feigned words make merchandise of you: whose judgment now of a long time lingereth not, and their damnation slumbereth not. For if God spared not the angels that sinned, but cast them down to hell, and delivered them into chains of darkness, to be reserved unto judgment; and spared not the old world, but saved Noah the eighth person, a preacher of righteousness, bringing in the flood upon the world of the ungodly... The Lord knoweth how to deliver the godly out of temptations, and to reserve the unjust unto the day of judgment to be punished" (2 Pet. 1:1-8).

Twelve

FORMING THE HUMANIST EDUCATION

JOHN DEWEY | 1859-1952 A.D.

J ohn Dewey was another key apostate from the Christian faith and quite possibly the most significant American philosopher of the modern age. If Nietzsche was the philosopher that prepared Germany for the 20th century and John Stuart Mill was the philosopher who prepared Great Britain for the 20th century, it was John Dewey who prepared the United States for the 20th century.

Dewey's apostasy was academic and intellectual, but it was comprehensive in scope. On one hand, he did not veer from the faith by way of "teenage rebellion" or sexual revolution. His apostasy came about by the slow and steady influence of the university as he immersed himself in higher levels of academic training. Since the advent of the secular universities from the 12th century in Europe or from the 17th century in America (Harvard College), these academic institutions have formed the juggernaut for undermining the Christian worldview in the West. This is hardly debatable, and the majority of public and private universities would admit this to be the case. The "conservative" or Christian battles with the liberalizing trends in cultural and political systems are futile unless the loyal opposition is willing to take on the problem of higher education. Buried at the heart of the secular university ideal are the ideas and forms that erode the faith and glorify human reason. It is the universities that have promoted the humanist ideals of Thomas Aquinas, John Locke, Jean-Jacques Rousseau, John Stuart Mill, Karl Marx, and Charles Darwin. John Dewey's story has been repeated a million times over the generations. It begins with humble fathers and mothers who raise their children in good Christian homes. They work hard to get their sons and daughters into the "big universities" so as to secure for them a "good classical education" in humanist epistemologies and ideologies. Then they watch their children forsake the faith, to their horror and dismay.

John Dewey was born of humble parents, his father a Congregationalist and his mother a Calvinistic evangelical. Reportedly, she was an outspoken evangelist, asking virtually everyone she met, "Are you right with Jesus?"[1] In 1884, young Dewey obtained his PhD from John Hopkins University and took his first teaching post at Michigan State University in Ann Arbor. He joined the "Student Christian Association," which at that time was one of the largest organizations on campus.[2] Dewey's first Sunday speech given to the Student Christian Association at MSU was on "The Obligation to Knowledge of God," in which he called belief "not a privilege but a duty." While at Michigan State University, he conducted a Bible class on the "Life of Christ." In the years that followed however, John's faith proved to be too shallow to survive.

JOHN DEWEY'S APOSTASY

In his first publication, entitled *Psychology*, Dewey argued that logic proved God a necessity. These theistic remarks invited a fiery response from his former instructors at John Hopkins University, G. Stanley Hall and William James. According to Larry Hickman, eminent researcher on the life of John Dewey, "Their criticism of his book, forced Dewey

---

1. Larry Hickman, Center for Dewey Studies, Southern Illinois University.
2. Needless to say, this is no longer the case. As of 2012, many universities are kicking Christian organizations off their campuses. See "Campus Crackdown: Restricting Religious Freedom" by Chuck Colson, Christian Post Opinion, <http://www.christianpost.com/news/campus-crack-down-restricting-religious-freedom-71563/> accessed on Mar. 14, 2013.

to re-examine his thinking and nudged him along the path toward pragmatism."[3]

The generational lineage of apostates is not hard to follow. As Providence would have it, Dewey's mentor, William James, was Ralph Waldo Emerson's godson, and his other mentor, G. Stanley Hall was another outstanding apostate in his own right. Hall was raised by devout parents with a rich Christian heritage dating back to the Mayflower Pilgrims on both sides of his family. His father was heartbroken to learn that his son wanted to attend college, but they reached a compromise by deciding on a seminary training in order to prepare the young man for the pastorate. This was the next best thing to farming in the minds of these solid Christian folk. Not surprisingly, it was G. Stanley Hall's college experience and his exposure to John Stuart Mill that propelled his apostasy.[4] He matriculated to a liberal German university, where after six years this farm boy's ideas was set, and his apostasy sealed. Hall was especially attracted to Charles Darwin's ideas, and turned into a full-blown eugenicist. According to one biographical source, "Hall had no sympathy for the poor, the sick, or those with developmental differences or disabilities. A firm believer in selective breeding and forced sterilization, Hall believed that any respect or charity toward those he viewed as physically, emotionally, or intellectually weak or 'defective' simply interfered with the movement of natural selection toward the development of a super-race."[5] Hall was a pioneer in psychology, in fact the first to earn a doctorate in psychology in America. He more or less invented the modern idea of adolescence. In true form to the radical humanist worldview, he completely rejected divine revelation in favor of human reason as the source of knowledge. According to Hall, Jesus was a fraud who "ordered his life with fidelity to the old oracles (the Old Testament prophecies), and man just invents his religion as he goes along to help him make it through life.[6] This was G. Stanley Hall, the high skeptic that shamed men like John Dewey into atheism.

No philosopher works in a vacuum, and John Dewey would never

3.Walker, Linda Robinson, "John Dewey at Michigan" *Michigan Today,* 1997 <http://michiganto-day.umich.edu/97/Sum97/mta1j97.html> accessed on Mar. 14, 2013.
4. Louis N. Wilson, G. Stanley Hall, A Sketch, P. 34 http://books.google.com/books?id=-WU-WAAAAIAAJ&pg=PA11&source=gbs_toc_r&cad=4#v=onepage&q&f=false.
5. "G. Stanley Hall," Wikipedia < http://en.wikipedia.org/wiki/G._Stanley_Hall> accessed on Dec. 25, 2012.
6 G. Stanley Hall, *Jesus the Messiah in Light of Psychology,* Vol. II, Chapter 6.

have taken his place in this historical pantheon of apostates had it not been for the other players in this historical drama. Dewey himself admitted to having been influenced by men like Jean Jacques Rousseau (for his education theory), Immanuel Kant, and Descartes (for his epistemological framework). Yet of the great humanist minds in history, Charles Darwin was the greatest in John Dewey's estimation, and that according to Dewey's famous article, *The Influence of Darwin on Philosophy*. It is hard to miss the unified front constructed by these philosophers over a period of 500 years. Together, they successfully dismantled the Christian order in the West.

The precise events of John Dewey's "religious journey" aren't entirely clear. Somewhere between 1884 and 1900, John Dewey abandoned the Christian faith. In his 1934 publication of "A Common Faith," Dewey still showed some approval of the "religious," but he rejected a supernatural God or any religion connected to the supernatural. He counted himself a "religious humanist," and his signature stands out prominently on the *First Humanist Manifesto* issued in 1933. John Dewey was one of the first card-carrying secular humanists in the modern world.

INFLUENCE

During the latter part of the 20th century, a few conservative movements formed in an attempt to save Western civilization from the hands of the progressive humanists. Their effort was too little and too late. There was nothing these conservative leaders could do to reverse the cultural, educational, and social trends set in motion by the apostates over the previous three centuries. Only a spiritual transformation in the hearts of the masses and a reformation in the church could stop this freight train. In 2005, a group of fifteen conservative leaders selected the most harmful books of the 19th and 20th centuries. John Dewey's book *Democracy and Education* came in fifth on the list behind Karl Marx's *Communist Manifesto*, Adolf Hitler's *Mein Kampf*, Mao Zedong's *Quotations from Chairman Mao*, and Alfred Kinsey's *Kinsey Report*.[7] Presumably, this group of conservatives were acutely aware of the critical role that education played in bringing about a humanist and Marxist vision for

7. "Ten Most Harmful Books of the 19th and 20th Centuries" *Human Events*, <http://www.humanevents.com/2005/05/31/ten-most-harmful-books-of-the-19th-and-20th-centuries/> accessed on Mar. 14, 2013.

the modern world.

If the battle for the future was to take place in education where the combatants grapple over the hearts and the minds of the succeeding generation, then John Dewey knew where to place his influence. There has never been a time in history in which so many people have been educated by the same centralized system paid for by the state and ordered by humanist philosopher-kings and social planners. Moreover, no single man has influenced as many people through the institution of state-based education than John Dewey. According to PBS.com, "[Dewey's] educational theories broke new ground and continue to wield influence at the dawn of the twenty-first century."[8] His influence in education spanned the globe, extending into modern nation states like Turkey, Japan, China, and the Soviet Union, all of which enthusiastically embraced his "modern" doctrines and methods in their public schools.

Until 1900, the *McGuffey Readers* curriculum used in American one-room school houses still retained references to Scripture, articles referencing the Ten Commandments, and some sense of the fear of God. By 1950, almost every textbook in America had been purged of references to God, Jesus Christ, the Christian church, and the moral laws of God. This complete national apostasy came about by the influence of John Dewey.

> *"The fear of the LORD is the beginning of knowledge: but fools despise wisdom and instruction" (Proverbs 1:7).*

Prior to the 20th century, John Locke and even Jeremy Bentham still retained some semblance of Christian manners, ethics, and religious language in their writings. By the 1930's however, humanists had achieved increased epistemological self-consciousness and self-consistency. The facades were down, and the pretenses had disappeared. Between the 1830s and the 1930s, these Christian affectations became passé and obsolete, especially for the intellectual elite. By 1930, humanism was ready to define itself in its true colors. As far as these progressives were concerned, God is not god, and man is god. Effectively, this was the message of the *Humanist Manifesto* of 1933, which historians generally

---

8. "John Dewey," *PBS.org*, <http://www.pbs.org/kcet/publicschool/innovators/dewey.html> accessed on Mar. 14, 2013.

agree was co-authored by John Dewey. The manifesto declares:

> "The universe is self-existing and not created... Man is a part of nature and has emerged as a result of a continuous process... Holding an organic view of life, humanists find that the traditional dualism of mind and body must be rejected... The nature of the universe depicted by modern science makes unacceptable any supernatural or cosmic guarantees of human values... A socialized and cooperative economic order must be established to the end that the equitable distribution of the means of life be possible... Man is at last becoming aware that he alone is responsible for the realization of the world of his dreams, that he has within himself the power for its achievement. He must set intelligence and will to the task."[9]

Clearly, the humanist agenda is godless, egalitarian, Marxist, and stridently man-centered. At this point in his life, Dewey was through with the halfway house apostasies of deism, Unitarianism, and closet atheism. The statement quoted above may be the most self-consciously humanist statement ever produced, for it strips God of His authority as the Source of human values (ethics) and as the sovereign Director of human destiny. Christian churchmen who wish to compromise on the centrality and sovereignty of God in man's reality should take careful note of the humanist position as stated here in clear terms. The issue at stake is the very "God-ness" of God. While rejecting "supernatural" values, the religious humanist will allow for no moral absolute. There can be no guarantees of any moral value whatsoever in this system of thought. Another fundamental element of the humanist agenda is man's complete sovereign control over his own destiny. But it is only a pretense. How can finite man ever control his own destiny? Doesn't it take omnipotence to predestine the outcome and "realize the world of his dreams?" How would a man control every asteroid that randomly pulls into this solar system and eliminates life on planet earth? How can he control the billions of possible causes and forces in this universe? The best the humanist can do is foster a dream that he will someday predestine the future, the world of his imagination. He can only hope that his dreams

---

9. Humanist Manifesto I, < http://www.americanhumanist.org/Humanism/Humanist_Manifesto_I>.

won't take him to hell.

While somebody as smart as John Dewey would never have seen a need for the wisdom contained in the old book of Proverbs, I trust my readers aren't that "smart." One simple proverb destroys the grand proclamations of the *Humanist Manifesto*: "A man's heart deviseth his way, but God directeth his steps" (Proverbs 16:9). It is not brute chance in an indeterminate universe that controls man's destiny, nor is it man himself. God and only God is sovereign over reality. This is the very essence of a Christian worldview.

JOHN DEWEY'S EDUCATIONAL THEORY

Dewey's educational theory is really quite simple: education is all about training the individual to fit into the social entity of the state. Sixty years earlier, Karl Marx set out to to "replace home education with social," in *The Communist Manifesto*. Effectively, Dewey stands in agreement with Marx as he writes in his own *Pedagogic Creed*, "The school is primarily a social institution."[10] All educational content is subservient to the social element—training the young person to belong to the social unit and pursue the objectives of the social unit (however unwise, ungodly, and unintelligent they may be). Dewey goes on in the *Creed*: "[Education] is the regulation of the process of coming to share in the social consciousness."[11] When this agenda is in place, everything else takes a back seat—all academic rigor, character training, the fear of God, dominion work in a free enterprise system, etc. From this point on, education becomes the playground for faceless social planners whose objective is to mold future society in public schools and universities. This system also directs the centralization of power in the nation's education from the local school districts into state departments, and then to a massive national "Department of Education." Centralized, institutionalized systems are not built for the individual child's needs, talents, and abilities. Inevitably, centralization and standardization of educational systems ruin individual academic achievement. Parents should know that the schools are not ultimately committed to academic excellence. Their chief purpose is to plug the children into the "social consciousness."

10. John Dewey, *My Pedagogic Creed*.
11. Ibid.

APOSTATE

Character is important for John Dewey, but his ideal is the same form of character that the communists aim for in their schools. Dewey elucidates, "The deepest moral training is precisely that which one gets through having to enter into proper relations with others in a unity of work and thought."[12] Obviously, human individuality is lost in this socialist institutional utopia, where the well-socialized individual is taught to move in herds, to get along in the system, and to meld ("maintain unity of thought and work") with the herd. The humanist model sees no need for the fear of God or the honor of parents, and they displace the covenant bodies of family and church with the all-consuming state. It is for this reason that modern teenagers are generally expected to rebel against their parents while conforming to the standards of popular culture and the uniform social systems incorporated by the socialist state. They are trained to break the Fifth Commandment while submitting to the order in their social institutions. According to God's book of education, character is important as well, but it is a character as defined by God. Fundamentally, the child must learn the fear of God and the honor of parents. This is what makes the well-ordered society by God's definition. At the root, these are radically different systems of education and they will produce radically different human societies.

Later on in the *Creed*, Dewey gets to the heart of his agenda. If any would doubt the religious nature of humanism, this should settle it once and for all. There is no neutrality in educational approaches. Dewey writes, "I believe that in this way the teacher is the prophet of the true god and the usherer in of the true kingdom of god."[13] Of course, he speaks of the kingdom of man, if Dewey's *Humanist Manifesto* is any indication of his religious commitment to man as god. Given that the teachers usher in the true kingdom of god, it is no wonder that almost every school bond levy is approved by the public school educated voters in every election around the country. The school has replaced the church as the center of the community in most urban and rural areas today. For Dewey, the public school teacher manages the process by which a child plugs into the "matrix" or the social consciousness. He or she serves as the agent of social reform, the pastor, the preacher, the prophet, and the shepherd in the church of the humanist, socialist state. Over 120 years

12. John Dewey, *The Quest for Certainty*, Chapter IX, The Supremacy of Method.
13. John Dewey, *My Pedagogic Creed*

later, we now see the consequences of this vision. The average high school graduate is barely literate, but he knows how to use a condom. He is far more likely to support socialism and homosexuality than his parents and grandparents in their generations. But he can't name two men who signed the Declaration of Independence, and he probably can't tell the difference between Groucho Marx and Karl Marx.

This worldview is quite different from the Christian worldview in that it presents an antithetical moral system, a wrong-headed view of reality, and an adversarial kingdom to the true Kingdom of God. Eventually, the social order proposed by the humanists will break down. It will squelch human creativity and freedom as it undermines Christian morality. Instead of ushering in the great kingdom of man, Dewey will yield social and academic disintegration and a curtailment of political freedoms. His utopia becomes a dystopia.

A biblical social view maintains the delicate balance between the individual and his society. The state cannot provide human relationship and community. Without the covenant bodies of family and church, society will err to the side of either anarchy or tyranny. In a humanist social situation, anarchy and tyranny play off each other until the system unravels. Four hundred years ago, the church took about 10% of a family's income, the state took 5%, and the family itself retained about 85%. Today, the church gets 1-2%, the state takes 60-75%, and the family retains a paltry 30%. The relative importance of family and church in people's lives is fairly minimal, thanks to the influence of Rousseau, Marx, and Dewey.

Contrary to what Dewey believed, the true prophet of God speaks only what God tells him to speak. The salvation message preached must be the gospel of Christ, and the church elders are held responsible for "preaching the Word." The family and church are the fundamental social units, and the family is responsible for the education and upbringing of children (Eph. 6:4, Deut. 6:7, 1 Tim. 5:8, etc.). Then, the state is responsible for prosecuting crimes like murder and robbery (Gen. 9:6, Exod. 21:1-5). This is the biblical social theory rejected by John Dewey.

THE EPISTEMOLOGY OF UNCERTAINTY

John Dewey's basic philosophical approach bridges the gap between modernist rationalism and post-modernist relativism, in which modern man crosses the epistemological divide between optimism and pessimism. Two centuries earlier, Descartes began with doubt, hoping to find certainty. Now John Dewey comes full circle, endorsing a philosophy of doubt in his book called *The Quest for Certainty*. He struggled valiantly to strike a balance between skepticism and dogmatism, but his main point was that certainty is heretical. Even the pursuit of certainty, according to Dewey, is futile. He writes,

> *"The concrete pathologies of belief, its failures and perversions, whether of defect or excess, spring from failure to observe and adhere to the principle that knowledge is the completed resolution of the inherently indeterminate or doubtful. The commonest fallacy is to suppose that since the state of doubt is accompanied by a feeling of uncertainty, knowledge arises when this feeling gives way to one of assurance."* [14]

In some ways, John Dewey is more honest and self-consistent than the earlier humanists, especially Descartes. Dewey's objective is to make us comfortable with the fact that modern man is uncertain and perplexed about all of the knowledge he has accumulated. In fact, he admits that the sheer magnitude of human knowledge has expanded exponentially, while certainty concerning his system of knowledge has diminished greatly. Dewey readily concedes that there can be no certain knowledge within this humanist philosophy that is built on human reason. Yet, he still refuses to admit the obvious: If there is no certain knowledge, then why do we listen to anything Dewey is saying? What possible truth might come from a man who cannot be certain about anything? This is a man standing on quicksand. He admits he stands on quicksand, yet he is quite sure that it is a good place to stand! Inevitably, unbelieving thought will migrate back into skepticism and irresolvable inconsistencies. This is what happens when men try to develop their systems of thought independently from God.

Was the Apostle Paul referring to John Dewey as he described the man who is "ever learning, and never coming to the knowledge of the truth." (2 Tim. 3:7)? In his philosophical meanderings, John Dewey comes across as intellectually brilliant. He uses big words, long sentences, and convoluted arguments that go on for multiple pages. In fact, he is so

14. John Dewey, *The Quest for Certainty*, Chapter IX, The Supremacy of Method.

"brilliant" that it can be hard to follow his system of thought. In the end, he finally admits that we cannot know anything for certain. John Dewey cannot possibly come to the knowledge of the truth because he denied the most basic truth of all—the existence of God and His Truth.

To the contrary, Jesus Christ comes across as one very certain of the truth. He also expects His hearers to be certain of the truth that He reveals, using words like this: "Truly, truly, I say unto you, unless one is born again he cannot see the kingdom of God" (John 3:3). Luke wrote his gospel in order that "you might know the certainty of those things, in which you have been instructed" (Luke 1:4). There is neither a hint of uncertainty nor doubt with the Apostle Paul as he writes, "For the which cause I also suffer these things: nevertheless I am not ashamed: for I know whom I have believed, and am persuaded that he is able to keep that which I have committed to him against that day" (2 Tim. 1:12). Of course, such strong language would have irritated John Dewey. These are what Dewey refers to as the "concrete pathologies of belief" that "spring from failure to observe and adhere to the principle that knowledge is the completed resolution of the inherently indeterminate or doubtful."

PRAGMATISM AND UTILITARIANISM

John Dewey is probably best known for his philosophy of pragmatism, which is a derivative of Bentham's utilitarianism. As previously noted, utilitarianism became the primary ethical philosophy for the social and political institutions of the Western world in the 19th century. Modern humanists loudly claimed to be securing the most good for the most people over the long run. It took about 100 years for the humanists to come to grips with the weaknesses of utilitarianism, fully admitting the charade. In a world without absolutes, how could anybody possibly know what *is* the highest good or what might produce it? After Friedrich Nietzsche, Jeremy Bentham, and John Stuart Mill's systems began to show their inherent inconsistencies and weaknesses, humanist man was desperate. He could no longer measure any ethical decision by an absolute standard, because he had openly rejected all possibility for an absolute in his atheistic, materialistic view of the world.

That's where philosophical pragmatism comes into play. Dewey was not the first pragmatist, but he was the humanist giant used to mainstream this philosophy throughout the Western world. Pragmatism effectively abandons any and all certainty for the ultimate ethical good or the desirable social goals. The pragmatist admits that we can never know what is that "good thing" for which man ought to seek. Therefore, the social and political leaders must choose an end (at random), and there is no reason to believe that this goal is any better than any other goal. The important thing is that the social programmers have chosen a goal for which we all ought to strive, and it is for the rest of us to get behind the project. It might be a totally worthless project in the end, but then how would you measure "total worthlessness" in a meaningless universe? Once the social leaders choose the goal, they invite the scientists into the conference room to explain how they will achieve this goal. Pragmatism will then identify the best means to achieve the ends. Put in the common vernacular, "The ends justify the means" even though the ends have no justification themselves. If a country needs a highway, it will confiscate as much property as necessary from the citizens to build that highway. If 80 million retiring baby boomers bankrupt the social security system, there is always euthanasia to eliminate those who will not contribute to the economy in the year 2050. If a country wishes to be the most powerful country in the world, then it will draft every man and woman into military service to make that happen. There is no higher law to which the democratic society shall submit as it pursues its programs. The powers of government choose the ends, and they will do whatever they need to do to accomplish those ends.

DEWEY THE PROPHET

Every religion has its prophets, and John Dewey may have been the greatest prophet of humanism. He was a true visionary—misguided and misguiding, of course—but a visionary nonetheless. In what might be his most transparent, prophetic moment, Dewey wrote an article called *The Influence of Darwin on Philosophy*. Incredibly, he freely and openly admitted to the humanist agenda that we have carefully outlined in this book. What follows is the salient part of the article:

> *"That the publication of the "Origin of Species" marked an epoch in the development of the natural sciences is well known to the layman. That the combination of the very words origin and species embodied an intellectual revolt and introduced a new intellectual temper is easily overlooked by the*

expert. The conceptions that had reigned in the philosophy of nature and knowledge for two thousand years, the conceptions that had become the familiar furniture of the mind, rested on the assumption of the superiority of the fixed and final [God and His Word]... In laying hands upon the sacred ark of absolute permanency, in treating the forms that had been regarded as types of fixity and perfection as originating and passing away, the "Origin of Species" introduced a mode of thinking that in the end was bound to transform the logic of knowledge, and hence the treatment of morals, politics, and religion.

"For 2,000 years [since the time of Christ], purposefulness accounted for the intelligibility of nature and the possibility of science, while the absolute or cosmic character of this purposefulness gave sanction and worth to the moral and religious endeavors of man.

"The Darwinian principle of natural selection cut straight under this philosophy. If all organic adaptations are due simply to constant variation and the elimination of those variations which are harmful in the struggle for existence that is brought about by excessive reproduction, there is no call for a prior intelligent causal force to plan and preordain them. God is a faded piece of metaphysical goods."[15]

The prophet of the New Humanism speaks, and he dances on the grave of the "old faith" and the "old God." He rightly points to evolution as the juggernaut of the new humanist revolution that captured modern societies and laid siege on education, science, culture, social systems, morality, and faith. Once Darwin has delivered man from the ultimate Creator and the ultimate Sustainer, man is freed from the Source of ethics and the Judge of the earth. He is relieved from all meaning, purpose, and absolutes! According to Dewey, this new philosophy "foreswears inquiry after absolute origins and absolute finalities."[16] In a recent documentary called *Expelled*, an evolutionary science professor from Cornell University, Dr. Will Provine, argues that if evolution is true then there can be no life after death, no transcendent purpose, no morality, and no free will. He

15 John Dewey, *The Influence of Darwin on Philosophy.*
16. Ibid.

APOSTATE

speaks of his own suicide. These academic leaders are finally embracing the logical conclusions of their worldview.[17] For these men, suicide feels like freedom, but what is freedom where there is no free will or purpose or meaning to life?

If God fades away in the conception of reality, absolutes fade, everything fades. Humanists prefer this, but they end up with more than they bargain for. When God fades, truth fades, so why seek truth? When God fades, ethics fade, so why argue for any kind of moral imperative? Man's reality fades, so why engage the struggle for life at all? When humanist man arrives at full self-consistency, he loses any and all transcendent purpose for life. That is when post modern man and his societies will commit suicide.

So what of the prophet? Does Dewey resort to hyperbole in his euphoria over Darwin, or is his historical assessment accurate? Has Charles Darwin singlehandedly dispensed with 2,000 years of "the fixed and the final," or God and His eternal Word? Has Darwin trumped Jesus Christ in the Western world as Dewey suggests? The hubris is breathtaking. It is true that the humanists could smell victory at the turn of the 20th century. After all, they were sitting in the driver's seat after 300 years of steady advancement into the fields of education, politics, culture, and literature. Certainly, it was an impressive apostasy at this stage—perhaps the most impressive in 2,000 years. In the minds of billions of people in the Western world, the reality of God had very much faded. There was the faithful Christian minority who fought hard to keep the fear of God and the worship of God in the science classroom and in the rest of life. But the loyal opposition was a bare remnant. In the storm of the humanist enlightenment, naturalism almost entirely consumed supernaturalism, even in the mainline church. Back in the 16th century, the masses in Europe bought indulgences because they were concerned about judgment and hell. They might have been cheap religious solutions, but at least people were still concerned that there was such a thing as God and hell fire judgment. The average person walking out of a grocery store today, whether of Catholic or Protestant heritage, could hardly be sensitive to these realities. The fear of God has largely disappeared from the Western mind.

Towards the end of the above quotation, John Dewey declares that

---

17. *Expelled - No Intelligence Allowed*, 2008, Directed by Nathan Frankowski

the old ideas will slowly give way to the new. Mankind will cease to ask the ultimate questions and rather begin to "improve our education, to ameliorate our manners, to advance our politics." Mankind will give up on transcendent principles and goals, and take on the burden of responsibility to map out our own destiny. He doesn't see the ideas of the old Christian order surviving. It is time to move on, per Dewey.

Well, a great deal has changed since John Dewey wrote those words. The "new" era of humanism is almost over. The optimism is fading. The empires are crumbling. The experiment is proving a failure. Now the 21st century man is thinking that Dewey and the rest of them may have miscalculated. This most spectacular experiment with apostasy and religious skepticism is now showing some cracks in the foundations - fissures eight feet wide. As the smoke clears, some still wonder. . .*What if God does exist?* What if John Dewey, the father of public education in America, had the wrong worldview? What if billions of people who were more informed by Darwin and Dewey than Moses and Paul have been led astray? What if the tiny remnant still holding on to 2,000 years of "the fixed and the final" are right? Are Dewey's theories turning out to be cataclysmic miscalculations? This kind of historical drama is not unusual in God's order.

Yes. We are still assuming that God exists.

> *"For the wrath of God is revealed from heaven against all ungodliness and unrighteousness of men, who hold the truth in unrighteousness; because that which may be known of God is manifest in them; for God hath showed it unto them. For the invisible things of Him from the creation of the world are clearly seen, being understood by the things that are made, even his eternal power and Godhead; so that they are without excuse: Because that, when they knew God, they glorified him not as God, neither were thankful; but became vain in their imaginations, and their foolish heart was darkened. Professing themselves to be wise, they became fools" (Romans 1:18-22).*

Thirteen

FORMING THE HUMANIST CULTURE

JEAN-PAUL SARTRE | 1905-1980 A.D.

Jean-Paul Sartre's life practically defined the 20th century man. His life almost spanned the century; in many ways he was the prototype of the modern age. Albeit espousing a new humanist religion, he was truly the pastor, the guru, the philosopher, and the guide for billions of youth from the 1940s into the 1970s.

Jean-Paul Sartre was an apostate in the truest sense of the term, having descended from seven generations of protestant ministers dating back to the 1660s. His mother's cousin was the well-known liberal protestant, Albert Schweitzer who sported a slightly tamer brand of skepticism from that which Sartre would espouse.[1] His grandfather on his father's side was an atheist doctor married to a devout Catholic. By the time Jean-Paul was born, his grandparents on both sides had already charted a course towards skepticism. Apostasy played an important part of this family's generational vision.

---

1. Annie Cohen-Solal, *Jean-Paul Sartre: A Life* (New York: The New Press, 2005), 19.

Jean-Paul lost his father before his second birthday, and during his early formative years, he and his mother lived with her father, Karl Schweitzer. Although his grandfather presented himself as a religious man, he conducted a number of adulterous affairs which no doubt badly influenced the young boy's future path. His mother remarried when he was twelve, but his relationship with his stepfather was generally nonexistent. For the remainder of his adolescent years, Jean-Paul carried out what we now call teenage rebellion. When he persisted in a pattern of stealing and lying, his stepfather finally took action and removed him from the house.

The spirit of rebellion was strong in the early 1900s, not only in Jean-Paul Sartre, but also in Ernest Hemingway, a popular author whom we shall treat later in the book. It was a cultural rebellion defended by G. Stanley Hall in his magnum opus entitled *Adolescence* (1904). Later in the 20th century, James Dean popularized teenage rebellion on the movie screen in *Rebel Without a Cause* (1955), and the sixties took it into the mainstream culture. Now, a century later, this teen rebellion is normative, and the institutions of media, culture, school, church life, and family life are all structured around the expectation of adolescent angst, discontent, and rebellion. In the early years of the 20th century, Jean-Paul Sartre served as the prototype of the man who cursed his father and did not bless his mother.

> *"There is a generation that curseth their father, and does not bless their mother... there is a generation whose teeth are like swords, and their jaw teeth as knives"* (Prov. 31:11-14).

What Sartre exemplified in his home life, he replicated in society as the archetypal rebel of the 1940s, 1950s, and 1960s. His primary interest was not political revolution, although he did join the communist party towards the end of his life. He drove a cultural revolution by way of a new, popular ethical philosophy called "existentialism."

As in the case of many of the other "great" philosophers covered thus far, Sartre's ideas were formed in college as he read the earlier humanists, especially Friedrich Nietzsche. For his exit exam at the University of Sorbonne he chose the topic, "Nietzsche's Writings and Contingency." This was one of the tight connections within the race of

APOSTATE

the Nephilim; without Nietzsche there would have been no Sartre.

Descartes had his temporary fling with fornication, and Rousseau had a few children out of wedlock, but Sartre's life was one continuous fifty-year celebration of debauchery. He was an alcoholic, a drug addict, and a serial fornicator over his 30 to 40 year writing career. Biographers report that he wrote his "best works" in a drunken stupor. While working on *The Critique of Dialectical Reason*, Sartre submerged himself in enough drugs and alcohol to kill a horse. In a 24-hour period, he would consume a quart of vodka, 200 mg of Corydrane, several grams of barbiturates, and two packs of cigarettes.[2]

Sartre's writings include an autobiographical collection of rambling comments that lend some insight into the mind of this apostate. He writes,

> *"I have been writing for exactly half a century, and for forty years I have lived in a glass prison... I realize that literature is a substitute for religion... Little by little, atheism has devoured everything. I have disinvested and secularized writing... [For 40 years, I have been thinking against myself].[3] I have systematically undermined the bases, yanked religion away from literature: no more salvation, nothing can save, besides, that is no longer the question... immortality is not the point."[4]*

His commitment to atheism and opposition to the Christian faith ("religion") is palpable. But there is angst, perhaps even guilt, and a sense of his own misery here. Does he countenance second thoughts? Why does he mention that salvation is irrelevant? Plainly, he is aware of his life's mission and the destructive force of "yanking religion." Reading Sartre's literary work, one gets the sense he is kicking against the pricks until his foot is a bloody mess. Perhaps the drugs deadened the pain a little in the process.

Further in his autobiography, he confesses to be the "Chronicler of Hell."[5] Almost the entire book is taken up with explaining the painful ordeal of expelling every vestige of God out of his life. Evidently, the Holy

2. Sartre crossed out this bracketed portion in the original.
3. Ibid, 174.
4. Ibid. 357.
5. Jean Paul Sartre, *The Words: The Autobiography of Jean-Paul Sartre* (New York: Vintage Books, 1981), 252.

Ghost was the last to go, according to Sartre.

"The retrospective illusion has been smashed to bits: martyrdom, salvation, and immortality are falling to pieces; the edifice is going to rack and ruin: I collared the Holy Ghost in the cellar and threw him out: atheism is a cruel and long-range affair: I think I've carried it through."[6]

Frightening words. . .to say the least. This is what Christ called "the unforgiveable sin." This may be the first autobiography ever published describing in great detail one man's experience with committing the unforgiveable sin. Truly, this man was a child of hell.

"Wherefore I say unto you, All manner of sin and blasphemy shall be forgiven unto men: but the blasphemy against the Holy Ghost shall not be forgiven unto men. And whosoever speaketh a word against the Son of man, it shall be forgiven him: but whosoever speaketh against the Holy Ghost, it shall not be forgiven him, neither in this world, neither in the world to come" (Matt. 12:31,32).

Sartre was a true pioneer or a prototype for the sexual revolution of the 1960s. In his commitment to living a life consistent with his philosophy of self-oriented existentialism, he was unspeakably cruel and treacherous to the one woman who ever loved him and served him (Simone de Beauvoire). As a college professor, he would seduce his female students and he retained multiple mistresses until his death in 1980 at 75 years of age. Some biographers prefer to call him a polygamist.[7]

The breakdown of a Christian worldview must inevitably yield the breakdown of Christian morality. Humanist philosophy will result in humanist ethics and life. Thus, following the philosophies of Descartes, Emerson, and Darwin comes the profligate life of Jean-Paul Sartre and his ilk. The flow of Western life seems to follow the flow of the philosophy that it has been taught, with the West moving irrepressibly towards sexual license and sexual nihilism, social disintegration of family life, homosexuality, abortion, euthanasia, and profligacy. Many people have followed in the trail of leaders such as Sarte. "Ye shall know them

6. Ibid, p. 252, 253
7. Cohen-Solal, 126, 127.

by their fruits."

AN ADVOCATE OF TERRORISM

Several of the prominent humanist philosophers covered thus far are well known for their advocacy of revolution and the de-stabilization of the social order. Jean-Jacques Rousseau and Karl Marx must take responsibility for the bloody political revolutions they inspired. But none of these heartless utopians were as explicit in their endorsement of actual terrorism as Jean-Paul Sartre. Originally advocated in his drug-induced book, *Critique of Dialetical Reason*, Sartre further expanded on the use of violence when he wrote the introduction for a nasty little book by Frantz Faron called *Les damnes de la Terre*. In his opening remarks, Sartre recommends that Africans murder Europeans at will. But then Faron fills the pages of his book with suggestions for a "murderous and decisive struggle," complete with "searing bullets and bloodstained knives."[8] He calls for "absolute violence," and encourages the African to be "ready for violence at all times." In fact, this is the *only way* for the revolutionary to get what he wants, according to Faron. "Violence alone, violence committed by the people, violence organized and educated by its leaders, makes it possible for the masses to understand social truths and gives the key to them."[9] Faron's strategy included arming miscreants and criminals with hand grenades and revolvers to create total chaos in society.[10] Murdering unarmed "settlers," hacking policeman to death, and killing schoolmasters is all part of the agenda. This is chilling stuff, and all too familiar to our present society.

As always, the humanists set out to fix the world's problems with a whole new set of problems. The "solution" always turns out to be more vicious and deadly than the original problem, because they refuse to define man's basic problem as sin against God. Ungodly revolutionaries try to solve the problem of tyranny with more anarchy and tyranny (think Marxism). Historian Paul Johnson suggests that Sartre's contribution to Faron's book turned Sartre into the "academic godfather [for] many terrorist movements which began to oppress society from the late 1960s

---

8. Frantz Faron, *Les damnes de la Terre* (Grove Press: New York, 1963), 37.
Note: This book had an influence on United States President Barack Obama (cf.Barack Obama, *Dreams from My Father*, (New York: Crown Publishers, 1995) 100, 101.
9. Ibid. 147.
10. Ibid. 130.

onwards... By helping Faron to inflame Africa, he contributed to the civil wars and mass murders which have engulfed most of Africa to this day."[11] In the 1970s, Marxist revolutionaries acted on Faron's advice in South Africa, creating a bloodbath in that country that has perpetuated for decades.

An online encyclopedia, *Wikipedia*, lists a handful of terrorist events (worldwide) that took place during the 19th century. It catalogs 369 people killed in ten different events between 1900 and 1949, and 383 people killed between 1950 and 1969 in nine separate events. However, in just the last 40 years, there have been an unprecedented 307 terrorist events resulting in an excess of 22,000 deaths.[12] This represents an increase of almost a hundredfold, yet this list does not include deaths by riots (for an additional 100,000 deaths), and the prolonged bloody revolutions still going on in Africa (for an additional 10,000,000+ deaths).[13] While not all of these deaths are directly linked to communist revolutionary doctrinaire, it would be hard to point to another individual who provided as much intellectual backing for terrorism as Jean-Paul Sartre and Frantz Faron. By their reckless words and popular revolutionary fervor, these men inspired a generation of terrorism and filled the world with bloody carnage.

Not surprisingly, the majority of the violence has occurred in Africa and Southeast Asia The tragic fruit of Sartre's life's work is especially noted in the killing fields of Cambodia and elsewhere throughout Southeast Asia. Johnson elucidates, "The hideous crimes committed in Cambodia from April 1975 onwards, which involved the death of between a fifth and a third of the population, were organized by a group of Francophone middle-class intellectuals known as the Angka Leu ('the Higher Organization'). Of its eight leaders, five were teachers, one a university professor, one a civil servant, and one an economist. All had studied in France in the 1950s, where they had not only belonged to the Communist Party but absorbed Sartre's doctrines of philosophical activism and 'necessary violence.' These mass murderers were his

---

11. Johnson, *Intellectuals*, 246.

12. "List of Terrorist Incidents," *Wikipedia*, Feb. 26, 2013, <http://en.wikipedia.org/wiki/List_of_terrorist_incidents> accessed on Mar. 16, 2013.

13. "List of Wars and Anthropogenic Disasters by Death Toll," *Wikipedia*, Mar. 4, 2013, <http://en.wikipedia.org/wiki/List_of_wars_and_anthropogenic_disasters_by_death_toll> accessed on Mar. 16, 2013.

APOSTATE

ideological children."[14]

BY THEIR FRUITS YE SHALL KNOW THEM.

"My son, if sinners entice thee, consent thou not. If they say, 'Come with us, let us lay wait for blood, let us lurk privily for the innocent without cause: let us swallow them up alive as the grave; and whole, as those that go down into the pit: we shall find all precious substance, we shall fill our houses with spoil: Cast in thy lot among us; let us all have one purse:' my son, walk not thou in the way with them; refrain thy foot from their path: for their feet run to evil, and make haste to shed blood. Surely in vain the net is spread in the sight of any bird. And they lay wait for their own blood; they lurk privily for their own lives" (Proverbs 1:10-18).

"My son, fear thou the LORD and the king: and meddle not with them that are given to change" (Proverbs 24:21).

PHILOSOPHY

Jean-Paul Sartre was a self-described atheist. Darwin preferred the term "agnostic" for himself, Bentham said he liked Jesus over Paul, and Locke didn't want to quibble over Socinianism (Unitarianism). But, by the 20th century no self-respecting intellectual would want to conceal his total apostasy from the Christian faith. After all, atheism was now officially out of the closet. Before we discuss Jean-Paul Sartre's atheism however, we should first review the irreducible definition of God. If God is really God, He must be the ultimate Being, the ultimate source of existence and reality (Exod. 3:14, John 1:1-3); He must be the ultimate source of truth (Ps. 36:9); and He must be the ultimate source of law and ethics (Gen. 2:17). If we deny God as the source of reality, truth, and ethics, we have denied all that makes God, God. And this is precisely what the humanist has done: he has replaced God with himself by ascribing God's attributes to himself. Sartre understood this very well.

"The fool hath said in his heart, 'There is no God.' They are corrupt, they have done abominable works, there is none that doeth good... Have all the workers of iniquity no knowledge? Who eat up my people as they eat

---

14. Johnson, *Intellectuals*, 246.

bread, and call not upon the LORD." (Psalm 14:1,4)

There are two kinds of humanism. The first turns the individual into god, and the second turns the social unit into a god. While men like Rousseau, Marx, and Lenin would have turned the state into god, Sartre sought to turn the individual into god. He was reacting against the totalitarianism of Nazism and communism with his own heresy, which turned out to be just as destructive to the human soul. His was a highly individualized form of existentialism. According to Sartre, "Each human being is seen as absolute master of his soul, if he chooses to follow his path of action and courage."[15] To be free, for Sartre, is to be alone. It is to be constrained only by self and by no other contingency or necessity. Sartre summarizes his philosophy nicely in his play *No Exit* with the aphorism, "Hell is other people." Existentialism is the deification of self. To put all of this deep philosophical jargon into language that a two-year old can understand: existentialism is selfishness. When selfish two-year-olds grow up, they drive around in cars sporting bumper stickers that read, "It IS all about me"—a bumper sticker I spotted recently here in the United States.

If God doesn't exist, how can anything exist? This is a serious philosophical question that Sartre is not afraid to deal with. After all, philosophers are supposed to be in the business of answering the fundamental questions, so Sartre give it his best shot. He writes,

> *"It means that, first of all, man exists, turns up, appears on the scene, and, only afterwards, defines himself. If man, as the existentialist conceives him, is indefinable, it is because at first he is nothing. Only afterward will he be something, and he himself will have made what he will be. Thus, there is no human nature, since there is no God to conceive it. Not only is man what he conceives himself to be, but he is also only what he wills himself to be after this thrust toward existence."[16]*

Sartre's reasoning is not difficult to follow, if you work through it carefully one proposition at a time. At first, man has no nature (or essence)—only existence. He shows up on the scene as an accident in a chance universe. Therefore, he must define his own essence. As he begins to develop a plan and make his "choices," he defines who he is,

15. Jean-Paul Sartre, *Existentialism and Human Emotion*, Chapter 1.
16. Ibid.

APOSTATE

what he is, what he is supposed to do (ethics), and where he is headed (purpose). There is only one small problem with all of this. Sartre begins with assumption of man's existence. How can he possibly assume the premise, "Man exists," without the other important premise, "God exists?" Sartre has still failed to answer the original question. *If God doesn't exist, how can anything exist?* Now you see that Mr. Sartre has not quite earned the title of a "good philosopher."

Sartre's existentialist philosophy is also self-contradicting. He insists that men *should* make authentic choices and thereby establish their essence (or value and purpose). But this essence is of no real meaningful value because his worldview presumes the ultimate purposelessness of reality. Why establish one's own essence, value, and purpose, if reality by definition is purposeless? Sartre's theory reduces to nothing but another random theory in a universe of randomness. Besides, if Sartre is imposing his "values" upon us doesn't he contradict his basic principle that nobody should impose their values on anybody else?

We must therefore, keep asking Sartre about how we can be sure we exist, and how we can define a true meaningful purpose for our existence? But Sartre will still insist that we stop thinking about these issues and just act, no questions asked. Sartre wasn't the only one to suggest this. Since Nietzsche, modern man has given up on asking the fundamental questions. In a last-ditch, pitiful attempt to salvage some sort of philosophy or purpose for life, Sartre holds up self-initiated, authentic action as the ultimate purpose of life. According to Sartre's version of existentialism, when man determines his own opinions, ethics, and actions, he has made himself "God." If, therefore, we can see ourselves as an "absolute" source of truth and ethics by our own self-direction even for a brief moment, we can render ourselves "essence," and we will have established our own existence! This is what Sartre means when he says, "Essence precedes existence." By rendering ourselves essence, we create ourselves. We become the source of our own reality... ergo, "God." If "God" equals the Source of truth and ethics, then He is the Source of reality. Therefore, if man can, independent of all other influence, become the absolute source of his own ethics and truth then he should be the source of his own reality as well. Of course, all of this is futile since no man can separate himself from all outside influence. Man is not god, he cannot predestine reality, and all attempts to seek godhood will be a total failure.

Sartre admits that "everything is possible, if God does not exist."[17] Dostoyevsky shuddered at the notion,[18] but Sartre embraces it. Sartre's "everything" might include intentionally running over old ladies in the street, mass murder, cannibalism, and so forth. But according to Sartre, we need to get comfortable with our freedom first, and then begin to make authentic choices unrestrained by social mores. As with every humanist, his goal is to free himself ethically from the constraints of God's rule of law. Some of the previous humanists never admitted their agenda openly, except perhaps John Dewey and Jeremy Bentham. Yet they were all still committed to complete human autonomy. Sartre writes, "If God does not exist, we find no values or commands to turn to which legitimize our conduct. So, in the bright realm of values, we have no excuse behind us, nor justification before us. We are alone, with no excuses." This smacks of the same agenda that Satan presented Eve in the garden. Nothing has changed much in 6,000 years.

> *"Now the serpent was more subtle than any beast of the field which the Lord God had made. And he said unto the woman, 'Yea, hath God said, 'Ye shall not eat of every tree of the garden?' And the woman said unto the serpent, 'We may eat of the fruit of the trees of the garden: but of the fruit of the tree which is in the midst of the garden, God hath said, 'Ye shall not eat of it, neither shall ye touch it, lest ye die." And the serpent said unto the woman, 'Ye shall not surely die: for God doth know that in the day ye eat thereof, then your eyes shall be opened, and ye shall be as gods, knowing good and evil'"* (Genesis 3:1-5).

THE ALIENATION OF 20TH CENTURY MAN

Everything thus far considered is of less importance compared to the outworking of Jean-Paul Sartre's philosophy upon human relationships in the modern world. *According to Sartre's philosophy, complete human autonomy cannot be achieved with total isolation, and the whole world took the man seriously on this. Without question, Sartre's major contribution to our world was human alienation.* In the last section of this book, we will tell the story

17. Ibid.
18. The Russian author, Fyodor Mikhailovich Dostoyevsky is the original source for this famous statement, "Everything is possible, if God does not exist."

of the powerful cultural revolution that mainsteamed Sartre's ideas in the latter half of the 20th century. However, Jean-Paul Sartre still led the cultural vanguard with his popular books, plays, and persona.

His depiction of modern man in his isolation is particularly well put in his book, *The Nausea*.

> *"I live alone, entirely alone. I never speak to anyone, never; I receive nothing, I give nothing... When you live alone you no longer know what it is to tell something: the plausible disappears at the same time as the fiends. You let events flow past; suddenly you see people pop up who speak and who go away, you plunge into stories without beginning or end: you make a terrible witness. But in compensation, one misses nothing, no improbability or, story too tall to be believed in cafes. . ."[19]*

Modern men and women could identify with these words. Sartre spoke their language and described their lives with a fine precision. In his outrageously popular play *No Exit*, Sartre tells the story of three people locked in a room together for eternity, all of whom have committed some sort of "sexual sin" or "social crime." Their surroundings are reasonably comfortable, but they are eternally set in the presence of each other. Towards the end of the play, one of the characters, Garcin describes the conditions:

> *"So this is hell. I'd never have believed it. You remember all we were told about the torture-chambers, the fire and brimstone, the 'burning marl.' Old wives' tales! There's no need for red-hot pokers. HELL IS—OTHER PEOPLE!"[20]*

Existentialist autonomy will always lead to isolation for this reason: it is impossible for one to be the "ultimate" determinant of his reality or any reality; it is impossible for him to be god (and to determine his own ethics, and exercise his own freedom to do what he wants to do), *while others are competing with him for godhood*. As long as other people are in our lives, we are concerned about how they think about us. We are impacted and influenced by their moral opinions and perspectives. If we are trying

19. Jean-Paul Sartre, *The Nausea*.
20. Jean-Paul Sartre, *No Exit*.

to be god, we cannot tolerate others impinging on this purpose.

The famed playwright Woody Allen captured the existentialist attitudes and perspectives exceptionally well in his plays, including in this segment of *Play It Again Sam*:

WOODY ALLEN (*Standing in an Art Museum*): That's quite a lovely Jackson Pollock, isn't it?

GIRL IN MUSEUM: Yes it is.

WOODY ALLEN: What does it say to you?

GIRL IN MUSEUM: It restates the negativeness of the universe, the hideous lonely emptiness of existence, nothingness, the predicament of man forced to live in a barren, godless eternity, like a tiny flame flickering in an immense void, with nothing but waste, horror, and degradation, forming a useless bleak straightjacket in a black absurd cosmos.

WOODY ALLEN: What are you doing Saturday night?

GIRL IN MUSEUM: Committing suicide.

WOODY ALLEN: What about Friday night?

GIRL IN MUSEUM: *[leaves silently]*[21]

The contrast between characters is important. On the one hand, the girl in the museum admits to the banktuptcy of the humanist position and takes it to its "logical" conclusion - suicide. She is the self-consistent humanist, realizing that there is no purpose for living either on Saturday *or* Friday night, assuming there is no God. Meanwhile, Woody Allen cares little about this nihilist position and desperately clings to the existentialist philosophy. He is only interested in having a little fun on Friday night. He cares little about the girl's plans to commit suicide on Saturday night. As an existentialist, he is only interested in his own well being in the immediacy. Certainly, he cares little for any long term relationships. He has no real interest in the future.

Many people in the modern world would relate to this, because they have become existentialists. Their only purpose for life is that which they establish for themselves in the immediacy. So they live for the next date or hook-up. They live for their next beer, or the next episode of their favorite television program. They have given up on a real purpose for life.

21. Woody Allen, *Play It Again Sam*, Screenplay

SUMMARY OF SARTRE'S THOUGHT

Jean-Paul Sartre admitted that his philosophy walks on the ledge of despair. Although he argued that his existentialism was "less despairing" than Christianity: "It is plain dishonesty for Christians to make no distinction between their own despair and ours and then to call us despairing."[22] Sartre was depressed, but he counted it more depressing to deal with a God who is in charge and holds people to account for sins like rape and adultery. When a man seeks godhood, he cannot stand the idea of a God who curtails his freedom and forces him to deal with his guilt and sinful habits. Proud, autonomous man shudders at the idea of bowing the knee before the living God, admitting his sinful condition, and seeking God's mercy at the cross of Christ. Living in true fellowship with the eternal God sounded so very depressing to Sartre. He rejected all relationships because he didn't want a relationship with his Creator.

Not long after Adam ruined his relationship with God in the garden, his firstborn son, Cain killed human relationships by killing his own brother. Then Cain became a vagabond on the earth and built a city of anonymity where man would be lonely in a crowd. This is the history of man without God.

"And the LORD said unto Cain, Where is Abel thy brother? And he said, I know not: Am I my brother's keeper? And he said, What hast thou done? the voice of thy brother's blood crieth unto me from the ground. And now art thou cursed from the earth, which hath opened her mouth to receive thy brother's blood from thy hand; When thou tillest the ground, it shall not henceforth yield unto thee her strength; a fugitive and a vagabond shalt thou be in the earth. " (Gen. 4:9-12)

I CAN'T GET NO SATISFACTION

When Keith Richards and Mick Jagger released the song "(I Can't Get No) Satisfaction" in 1965, it was a cutting-edge production that retained strong popularity for almost half a century. To this day, *Rolling Stone Magazine* has the song at the Number 2 position on the list of the "greatest songs of all time," (second to Bob Dylan's *Like a Rolling Stone*).[23] VH1 also

---

22. Jean-Paul Sartre, *Existentialism and Human Emotion*, Chapter 1
23. http:// www.rollingstone.com/music/lists/the-500-greatest-songs-of-all-time-20110407

has the song at the top of their list of the "100 Greatest Rock Songs." Commenting on his composition *Satisfaction*, songwriter Mick Jagger elucidated on the theme: "It captures a spirit of the times, which is very important in those kinds of songs... Which was alienation."[24]

Interestingly, the other "great" song of the last two generations was written in the same year as *Satisfaction*. Bob Dylan's *Like a Rolling Stone* captured the same cultural zeitgeist, which explains its enduring popularity and significance to modern music. The theme is the same. . .alienation. *"How does it feel? How does it feel, To be on your own, With no direction home, Like a complete unknown, Like a rolling stone?"*

Jean-Paul Sartre could have written that song, as well as Cain, the first vagabond in the earth (Gen. 4:12,14). Billions of people resonate with this music because this is their life. A life without God is a life without others, because "hell is other people."

INFLUENCE

Jean-Paul Sartre was the *most popular philosopher* of the 20th century. He made philosophy cool for young people who didn't have any idea what he was talking about. During the heady days of the post-war era, Sartre set the cultural tone and paved the way for his philosophy of existentialism through his hugely popular plays. While he could pump out original stuff that sounded pretty good to the university crowd, he was uniquely gifted with the ability to speak to the mass culture through pop media. In France alone, some of his books sold millions of copies. He was also awarded the Nobel Prize for Literature in 1964, although he declined the award.

Jean-Paul Sartre and his "hell-is-other-people" philosophy ruined our world. Today, there are nine times more people living alone (by percentage of total households) as lived alone in 1900.[25] The pro-choice, abortion movement has successfully destroyed the closest of human relations through this self-oriented existentialism. Where abortion was mainly confined to prostitutes in large cities like New York City in the 19th century, this important sacrament of existential humanism is

24. "(I Can't Get No) Satisfaction," *Wikipedia*, Mar. 8, 2013 <http://en.wikipedia.org/wiki/(I_Can't_Get_No)_Satisfaction> accessed on Mar. 16, 2013

25. http://politicalcalculations.blogspot.com/2013/03/single-person-households-in-us-since.html#. UUueMDfSlvC. "Person Statistics: One Person Households (Most Recent) by Country," *Nation-Master*, <http://www.nationmaster.com/graph/peo_one_per_hou-people-one-person-households> accessed on Mar. 16, 2013.

become commonplace via the convenient technology of abortifacient pills, government funding, and professional surgical services available almost everywhere. Some data gatherers estimate over a billion babies have been aborted worldwide in just the last thirty years.[26] Some nations like Russia abort 73% of all babies conceived.[27] What have these existentialist practices done to family relationships over the generations? Can we pretend to compartmentalize human thought and action, in order to avoid the side effects of these tragic decisions? The mass killing of children is only the tip of the iceberg when it comes to the cheapening of human life and destruction of relationship. The love of many has grown stark cold in our day (Matt. 24:12).

Sartre's ideas, among other things, have contributed to the burgeoning divorce rates and the sharp rise in singleness, homosexuality, temporary "shack-ups," and the even more temporary "hook-ups." There were 28 divorces in England in 1858 compared to 153,500 divorces in 2005.[28] That amounts to an increase of 3000 on the annual rate of divorce by total population. The "shack-up" rate has increased at least tenfold since 1970 in this country. The loneliest countries in the world, measured by percentage of people living alone, are the United States (#1), Australia (#2), Sweden (#3), Canada (#4), and Japan (#5).[29] Existentialism is most prevalent in the cities of these countries, where fewer than 10% of urban households are made up of the nuclear family.[30] Wherever family and genuine relational community have largely disappeared, we must conclude that these societies have fully accepted Jean-Paul Sartre's ideologies.

In spite of the fact that 94% of Americans still say that family is important to them, less than half of American households actually consist of a nuclear family.[31]

Why are the modern nations running headlong into unprecedented levels of debt that will bring untold harm to economies for multiple generations? When the economist, John Maynard Keynes was asked if his

26. http://www.numberofabortions.com/.

27. http://www.reuters.com/article/2011/11/08/russia-abortion-idUSL5E7M323R20111108.

28. http://www.guardian.co.uk/news/datablog/2010/jan/28/divorce-rates-marriage-ons; O'Neill, Annie, "Divorce in the UK," *EZine Articles*, Dec. 18, 2007, <http://ezinearticles.com/?Divorce-In-The-UK&id=886801> accessed on Mar. 16, 2013.

29. http://www.nationmaster.com/graph/peo_one_per_hou-people-one-person-households.

30. http://articles.baltimoresun.com/2010-12-18/news/bs-md-census-households-20101217_1_nuclear-families-census-data-young-professionals.

31. http://www.pewsocialtrends.org/2010/11/18/the-decline-of-marriage-and-rise-of-new-families/2/#ii-overview.

fractional reserve banking system (an economic approach that encouraged debt spending) would survive in the long run, Keynes replied, "In the long run, we're all dead."[32] This explains why 80 million retiring baby boomers aborted 80 million babies by way of the abortifacient pills and abortion clinics between 1960 and 2010. This also explains why the population pyramids (worker to retiree ratios) have sunk dramatically in the last three generations.[33] There may be more than a little short-sightedness on the part of Sartre's generation. What will the abortion survivors do to the retiring baby boomers when the social security funds deplete, and the worker to retiree ratio drops below the 1:1 ratio? We have yet to see the horrific fruits of Sartre's existentialism.

Where families used to gather around the fireplace during the long winter evenings, now they gravitate towards individualized and escapistic aesthetic experiences. Until the development of the headphones in the 1960s and 1970s, people would enjoy musical entertainment in community. But something frightening, something surreal, something very sinister has happened to human society in the last 50 years—something we have never seen before in the history of the world. As Mick Jagger put it, people are more alienated than ever before. Family bonds are slowly disappearing, generation by generation. Church communities are shallow, inauthentic, or non-existent. Friendships are formed more by internet banter than face-to-face conversations, producing more stunted, apathetic, short term relationships.

Without question, Jean-Paul Sartre was the idea-man who led both the cultural and the sexual revolutions of the 1960s. The great transformation of our entire social system and the breakdown of the social fabric of the whole Western world occurred under Sartre's watch. Over 50,000 people attended his funeral. To this day, huge segments of popular music, country music, popular literature, and motion pictures retain strong flavorings of Jean-Paul Sartre's existentialism. The unraveling of Christian culture and the entire social fabric of the nation is much to be attributed to this man's work. If the divorce rate is 1000 times what it was in the 19th century, and the illegitimacy rate is 100 times what it was in the 18th century, and the abortion rate is 50 times what it was before Sartre was born, we can only conclude that *something wicked this way came*. Sartre was

---

32. John Maynard Keynes, *A Tract on Monetary Reform*, Chapter 3.
33. http://ww.populationpyramid.com.

a true Nephilim of the highest order.

> *"This know also, that in the last days perilous times shall come. For men shall be lovers of their own selves, covetous, boasters, proud, blasphemers, disobedient to parents, unthankful, unholy, without natural affection, trucebreakers, false accusers, incontinent, fierce, despisers of those that are good, traitors, heady, highminded, lovers of pleasures more than lovers of God; having a form of godliness, but denying the power thereof: from such turn away. For of this sort are they which creep into houses, and lead captive silly women laden with sins, led away with divers lusts, ever learning, and never able to come to the knowledge of the truth"* (2 Tim. 3:1-7).

Part II

THE LITERARY
NEPHILIM

INTRODUCTION

Thanks largely to the liberal arts universities and the humanist education systems, the Christian worldview has lost considerable ground in the West over the last 400 years. Since education is typically centered on literature and reading, we conclude that this is a critical, though oft-neglected battlefield in the war of the worldviews. Therefore, any treatise that intends to grapple with the disintegration of the Western Christian mind and culture must address this field of literature. Before the age of internet and televised mass media, it was the literary geniuses who turned the dry humanist philosophies into paper-printed stories that won the hearts of the masses. When we look for the source of the breakdown of the Christian faith, we must begin with these pioneering apostates.

From our extensive survey of the last four hundred years, it should be clear that this apostasy was a slow and arduous process. It was excruciating for men like Jean-Paul Sartre according to his angst-ridden autobiography in which he described his experience. It is no easy thing to throw off 40 generations of Christian heritage. The powers of darkness had to marshal every social institution, every humanist genius, and every developed nation to the battle. The apostasy had to continue for multiple centuries as there was no way that blatant atheism would sell to the masses in the 16th century. Through the 17th and 18th centuries, the hearts of men steadily turned towards a man-centered epistemology, metaphysic, and ethic. Finally, in the 19th century, men like Nathaniel Hawthorne and Mark Twain could express their new-found humanist faith in sharp tones and stunning clarity by novels and popular literature for mass consumption.

As it turns out, the rise of the powerful modern empires coincided with a growing spirit of rebellion against Christ and His reign. The first empires of the modern age were Spain and France, both of which used the power of the sword to persecute Christian believers in the 1500s and 1600s. Neither empire lasted long. Then England and America quickly retreated from the Christian faith as their respective empires rose to power. Typically, the greatest literature is produced as empires attain the zenith of their power in the city of man. This is what the world usually refers to as "great literature."

There is a reticence among Christians to do battle in the liberal arts classrooms because of the assumption that all "great" literature has to be "good" literature. After all, who wants to assault the towering literary geniuses that make up a humanist classical education? Since Thomas Aquinas, great energies have been expended towards creating synthesis between the City of Man and the City of God. But these days are about over because the institutional synthesis is almost complete, and the hurricane of apostasy already blows at maximum force. Instead of engaging in the war of ideas, Christians were more interested in capitulation and amalgamation. From all accounts, it seems the faithful opposition is reduced to Gideon's 300. The day has arrived for Christians to engage the battle, or there will be no Christians left, an eschatological impossibility. From now on, true Christians will engage the battle of ideas in the academy. The time for giving up ground is over. Now we must fight. We must engage the biblical worldview vigorously in the world of great literature. The greatest wars ever fought in the history of the world are not those fought by sword or by ordnance. The greatest battles are engaged in the realm of ideas.

GREAT LITERATURE

The idea that all "great" literature is good literature is a myth. Writing in his Confessions, Augustine was appalled that parents would pay money to provide their children with a secular, classical education in Homer and other classics.

"O torrent of hell, the sons of men are still cast into you, and they pay fees for learning all these things!. . . These pagans attribute divine attributes to sinful men,

that crimes might not be accounted crimes, and that whoever committed such crimes might appear to imitate the celestial gods."[1]

Augustine also warns of "courtly words" that may hold unwholesome ideas, "Wisdom and folly both are like meats that are wholesome and unwholesome, and courtly or simple words are like town-made or rustic vessels—both kinds of food may be served in either kind of dish."[2] To this, I would simply add that the words, phrases, and syntax used by the great thinkers share more than propositions, but also attitudes, perspectives, carefully constructed systems of thought, and heart trajectories. The great thinkers and writers covered in this survey were truly dangerous men because they believed the wrong things and they taught the wrong ideas. Young, impressionable minds can "cut themselves" on the "great books," and sometimes the wounds get infected. This is usually how we lose our best and brightest young students to the other side, generation after generation. Those Christian children who are not well grounded in a biblical worldview first (that is, in a God-centered way of looking at the world) are easily ruined by worldly philosophy, vain deceit, and bad ethical theories (Col. 2:8).

> *"Beware lest any man spoil you through philosophy and vain deceit, after the tradition of men, after the rudiments of the world, and not after Christ."*

OPTIMISM AND PESSIMISM

That said, what is our general disposition towards the literary classics produced by the great geniuses of our age? Shall we assume the worst or the best of them? Shall we view these influential authors through a lens of optimism or pessimism? This seems to be the operational question that lies beneath the controversy over classical education and the great books produced by the great empires of men. In most cases, Christian universities incline towards viewing these authors favorably for several reasons, legitimate and illegitimate. First, the great empires are more built on faith in men than faith in God. They render more glory to man than to God, and this is the fundamental description of the kingdom of man.

---

1. Augustine, *Confessions,*, Book II.
2. Augustine, *Confessions*, Book V.

In high academia, there is a strong academic hubris that glories in the intellectual accomplishments of men. Within these institutions, men and women imbibe deeply at the trough of "knowledge that puffs up" (1 Cor. 8:1). A fraternity of intellects form, and it would therefore be unseemly to criticize the works of the brotherhood. Hence, the "great" authors are beyond criticism, and they stand in a class of their own. Their novels, plays, and treatises may be fawned over, appreciated, reviewed, and analyzed, but none dare accuse the writers of wicked, rebellious heart motives or render their literature heterodox and dangerous.

Yet, we need to be fair in the assessment of the "great" authors. We still must discern carefully between the good, the bad, and the ugly. There are good Christian men who wish to give proper credit where credit is due. Even the unbelieving humanist is not always self-consistent to his own humanism. This is especially true when these great writers had inherited a thousand years of Christian culture and thinking. Wherever there are remnants of the Christian worldview still operating, due credit needs be given to the kingdom of Jesus Christ. Anything less would amount to gross faithlessness and irreverence for the reign of Christ.

What makes our times different from other eras, including that of the Greeks and the Romans, is the virulent Christian apostasy of the day. This calls for more discernment, not less in our academic pursuits. The old classical pagan world did not work with a rich Christian heritage, and we certainly would not classify Aristotle and Plato as apostates. Because our Western world has entered a period of apostasy, it would be foolish to ignore this factor in the Christian classroom. With very few exceptions, the apostasy that characterized the great philosophers of the 18th and 19th centuries took down the literary masters as well. These men and women enthusiastically embraced the apostatizing ideas of Latitudinarianism, Unitarianism, Transcendentalism, deism, agnosticism, and atheism, and they usually did so in that order. Some migrated towards these progressive ideas during their university experience (e.g. Nathaniel Hawthorne and Robert Louis Stevenson), and others absorbed these ideas in their high school years (e.g. Ernest Hemingway and John Steinbeck). Also, rebellion against parental authority became increasingly common at the turn of the 20th century with men like Ernest Hemingway, Robert Louis Stevenson, and Jean-Paul Sartre.

THE ENGLISH LITERARY REVOLUTION

Christian author Iain Murray summarizes the work of the English literary giants of the 19th century in his book *The Undercover Revolution*. In case after case, Iain Murray points out the apostasy and the tremendous influence these literary men had on the hearts and minds of millions in England.

Raised in a faithful Christian home with the very best of Christian nurture, Robert Louis Stevenson quickly rebelled against his parents upon entrance to Edinburgh University. He formed a club on campus that incorporated the rule, "Ignore everything that our parents taught us."[3] When his father found out about his son's rebellious path, he lamented in a letter, "You have rendered my whole life a failure!" In turn, Robert mocked his father's concern in a letter to a friend: "It was really pathetic to hear my father praying pointedly for me today at family worship and to think the poor man's supplications were addressed to nothing better able to hear and answer than the chandelier."[4] The spirit of rebellion is palpable and acute in these words, heartbreaking to any parent who is still committed to family relationship and generational faith.

It is probable that Stevenson's broken relationship with his father had something to do with his apostasy from the Christian faith. His father poured out his concerns to his son in another letter: "A poor end for all my tenderness. . . I have made all my life to suit you. . . I have worked for you and gone out of my way for you. . . and the end of it is that I find you in opposition to the Lord Jesus Christ. . . I find everything gone. . . I would ten times sooner have seen you lying in your grave than that you should be shaking the faith of other young men."[5]

Robert Louis Stevenson's story is important because it was a paradigmatic example of apostasy for hundreds of millions of young men and young women who came after him. This sort of radical rebellion is somewhat unique to the modern age. Before the humanist renaissance swept through Europe, the old Scottish Culdean church maintained strong generational continuity in the faith. According to ancient records, some of these Culdean churches were led by pastors from the same family

---

3. Iain Murray, *The Undercover Revolution* (Edinburgh: Banner of Truth, 2009), 12.
4. Ibid. 13.
5. Ibid. 24.

line for twenty generations in a row.[6] With the apostasy rate as high as 80-90% today, it is continuity in the faith that is a rare commodity. In Stevenson's day however, his family members would have been stunned by the news that he hated his father and his father's faith after so many generations of covenantal faithfulness.

Stevenson's adventure stories have enthralled millions of readers over the years. As with most of the "greats" of his era, he was careful to cloak his apostasy in his writings so as not to offend those who retained some respect for the Christian heritage. Tragically, he pursued a relationship with a married woman who divorced her husband for him. Towards the end of his life, he summed up his worldview in so many words in a letter to a friend: "The sods cover us, and the worm that never dies, the conscience sleeps well at last. . . but the truth is, we must fight until we die; and when we die there can be no quiet for mankind."[7]

When analyzing worldviews in literature, one must look at two things: baselines and trajectories. Every author starts somewhere; he works off a baseline and an heritage. But his work also represents a trajectory that reflects his heart direction. Of course, it would be unfair and imbalanced to categorize an author's work by a single sentence, a single paragraph or even a single story. Both literary and artistic work will always reveal trajectories. They will point us in some direction for better or for worse. Moreover, to judge a writer's contributions apart from the religious context of his culture would yield an equally flawed assessment. For example, a writer from the 16th century (fresh out of 1,000 years of Christian heritage) who ekes out an isolated profane statement in one of his theatrical scripts may exhibit more apostasy than a post-modern "artist" who dips crosses in urine. Trajectory is everything. Thus, a careful analysis of the body of his work and his life is important to know the direction to which he leads his careless readers. The influence of literary men like Robert Louis Stevenson, Mark Twain, H.G. Wells, George Bernard Shaw, Thomas Hardy, Ernest Hemingway, and others from this era was tremendous; and all of these men were atheists or Christian apostates of some stripe. They led the masses into apostasy. If we believe that God is still real and apostasy still calls for the judgment declared in 2 Peter 2:18-22, then these were very dangerous men. No one can bear more

6. John Jamieson, *An Historical Account of the Ancient Culdees of Iona*, (Edinburgh: Ballantyne and Company, 1811), 32.
7. Robert Louis Stevenson, *Letter to Edmund Gosse*, January 1886.

of the blame for emptying the churches in England in the 20th century than these men. Church attendance in London in 1850 was 60%.[8] After the smoke has cleared some 150 years later, church attendance stands at a bare 5%. This accounts for hundreds of millions of people over several generations. Assuming there is something to this Christian faith, the existence of God, the eternal judgment of God, the necessity of faith in the death and resurrection of Christ, this apostasy in Europe and Ameria is no small thing. What will happen to these men who were responsible for leading so many people away from the Christian faith?

Based upon historical definitions of the Christain faith, there was precious little Christian worldview and orthodoxy to be found in the "great literature" of the day. In 1952, Dr. Wilbur Smith from Westminster Chapel noted the strident apostasy among the literary giants of the previous century. Smith writes:

> "A few months ago, the New York Times issued a fifty-page brochure. . . entitled 'A Century of Books,' in which the editors gathered together reviews, appearing in this distinguished paper from 1851 to 1951, of 113 notable books, some of which continue to have worldwide influence, and a few, influence over millions. In carefully studying these pages, I am again impressed with the anti-Christian or non-Christian position of the majority of these authors. In fact, apart from Hawthorne [who was not a Christian],[9] I could not recognize one writer, man or woman, who could be called a believing Christian; and not one book among all those referred to here was written to extol Christian virtues, to honour the Lord Jesus Christ, or to expound the Word of God. What can be the result of allowing these volumes to determine one's values but a hardening of the hearts of men against the Christian faith?"[10]

In conclusion, we are pessimistic when we read the great writers of the 19th and 20th centuries in spite of the 1,500 years of Christian heritage that may have seeped a little into the nooks and crannies of their literature. We are pessimistic because these were the leading intellectuals who

8. Steve Bruce, "Christianity in Britain, R.I.P." in *Sociology of Religion*, 2001 62:2 191-203.

9. For most of his life, Nathaniel Hawthorne was a half-hearted Unitarian. At the end, he settled for an empty, nihilist worldview. The trajectory of his life demonstrates a virulent form of apostasy as shall be demonstrated later in this book.

10. Murray, 60, 61.

charted the course of apostasy in Europe and America. It is *their trajectory* that bothers us. We can see the trajectory much clearer now as we look back. We can see the gradual rejection of God in their metaphysic, we can see their rebellion against Christian ethics, and we can see their open repudiation of the more committed forms of Christianity (such as that represented by the reformers and the Puritans of the 1500s and 1600s).

Those who cannot make out the trajectories of apostasy in the great literary works of the last 500 years will fail to understand history or read literature rightly. If they cannot see the literary trajectories, they won't be able to explain why Christian churches are selling their properties to the Muslims in 2012 in London. If there is no discernment, no humility and fear of God, and no serious war of ideas waged in the liberal arts classroom, then there will be another generation of apostates in a long line of apostasy.

Fourteen

MACBETH - WHAT'S THE METAPHYSIC?

WILLIAM SHAKESPEARE | 1564-1616 AD

I n our survey of Western literature, we begin with William Shakespeare because he is hugely influential in the literary world during the decline and fall of the Christian West. According to Wikipedia, Shakespeare is "widely regarded as the greatest writer of the English language, and the world's preeminent dramatist," futhermore, "He is the most quoted writer in the English speaking world after the various writers of the Bible."[1] If his literary influence rivals that of the Christian Bible, it would be worthwhile to compare his fundamental ideas to a biblical worldview.

The weighty question of the moment is this; does William Shakespeare buttress the foundations of a great Christian culture at the inception of the British Empire, or does he actually represent the beginning of the end of Christian culture in the West? If authors like John Bunyan and John Milton retained a strong God-centered view of reality in their writings in the 17th century, did William Shakespeare set a similar trajectory

1. http://en.wikipedia.org/wiki/William_Shakespeare%27s_influence

representing a like robust Christian perspective? Or did he waver on key elements of a Christian world and life view? Some authors maintained a Christian trajectory while others initiated a humanist trajectory that would corrupt the entire Western world. Initially, the differences may be slight and hard to recognize except for the most discerning mind. But this is important work for those who want to identify the cracks in the foundations of the West. It was the synthesis of humanism and Christianity; it was too much sand in the concrete that weakened the foundations of Western civilization. As time progressed, the foundation could no longer bear the load of the superstructure empires resting upon it. These are important matters worthy of consideration for those who want build future civilizations. Was William Shakespeare one of the seminal humanists, or was he a sound Christian thinker?

WHO WAS SHAKESPEARE?

There is a great deal of mystery surrounding the identity of William Shakespeare. No such mystery enshrouds any other major literary figure in the history of literature. In most cases, it is fairly easy to trace the writings of a man to his identity, character, and life. But this cannot be said for Shakespeare. Here is what we know.

William Shakespeare was baptized on April 26, 1564. There is no available record of his birth. At 18 years of age, he married Anne Hathaway who was already three months pregnant with their first child. Mystery surrounds his education, his religious background, and his induction into the theater scene in London. We do know that Shakespeare served as a partner in a theater company known as the "King's Men." The partnership built the famous Globe Theater in 1599, and Shakespeare's plays were performed there until it was destroyed in 1644. The theater was only just rebuilt in 1997.

SHAKESPEARE AND MARLOWE

Christopher Marlowe was the only other playwright that came close to the genius of Shakespeare, and the two men worked side-by-side in the same theater group for several years between 1590 and 1593. Because the identity of William Shakespeare (or the author of the classic plays bearing his name) is shrouded in mystery, some have argued persuasively that Christopher Marlowe was the true genius behind the plays attributed to

Shakespeare.[2] What is known for sure is that William Shakespeare was both an actor and a financier for the Globe Theater.

As the reader no doubt has discerned by now, homosexuality seems to accompany the rejection of the Christian order and the rise of humanism. Before humanist thinking came into full blossom in the 19th and 20th centuries, this aberrant form of sexuality was extremely rare in England and America. In 1533, Henry VIII had issued a "buggery" statute assigning the death penalty for sodomy,[3] and this law stayed on the books until 1861. During the 45-year reign of Elizabeth I, there is record of only one prosecution.[4] Given that background, it is highly significant that the London theatrical fraternity was sympathetic to these sorts of sins. While at Cambridge University, Christopher Marlowe revived the controversial works of the Roman poet, Ovid by translating *Amores* into English. For his poetry that glorified adultery and homosexuality, Ovid was banished from Rome by the Emperor Augustus in 8 A.D., but the Christian apostates of the 16th century were more than happy to revive the works. Christopher Marlowe took up the mantle of these pagans, weaving homo-erotic elements into his plays *Hero and Leander*, *Tamburlaine*, and a few others. Well before Walt Whitman and Oscar Wilde popularized homosexuality in the 19th century, Marlowe was an early pioneer and advocate for this behavior in the London theater scene.

From all accounts, Christopher Marlowe was a foul character. He was known for his public blasphemy against the Holy Ghost,[5] and one of his contemporaries claimed of him, "Almost into every company he cometh he persuades men to Atheism." He was accused of homosexuality, and he may have been prosecuted for it had it not been for his untimely murder (or faked death) in 1593.

According to biographer Park Honan, William Shakespeare and Christopher Marlowe "saw each other dozens of times in an evolving friendship between 1590 and 1593."[6] Many questions have surfaced in connection with their relationship. Did this friendship produce moral compromise on Shakespeare's part? Did Marlowe mentor Shakespeare

---

2. Samuel L. Blumenfeld, *Marlowe-Shakespeare Connection: A New Study of the Authorship Question* (Jefferson: McFarland, 2008)

3. "Buggery Act 1533," *Wikipedia*, Feb. 26, 2013 <http://en.wikipedia.org/wiki/Buggery_Act_1533> accessed on Mar. 19, 2013

4. Park Honan, *Christopher Marlowe, Poet or Spy*, (Cambridge: Oxford University Press, 2005), 298.

5. Ibid. 298.

6. Ibid. 187.

APOSTATE

in the theater business? What was Shakespeare doing between 1585 and 1592? Why did Shakespeare's first plays surface just a year before Marlowe's death? Could Marlowe have faked his death in 1593 and continued writing under the pseudonym of William Shakespeare?

Whatever the case, there is clear evidence of cross pollination between the two men's works. For example, Shakespeare included an entire sentence from Marlowe's *Hero and Leander* in his comedy, *As You Like It*, he also included a short tribute to Marlowe's reputed death six years earlier in the same play. Shakespeare used at least twenty-four references from Marlowe's *Tamburlaine* in his *Henry VI* trilogy and in *Richard III*. At the very least, it is clear that Shakespeare respected Marlowe's work and counted him a true compatriot in the craft. This in itself indicates a revolt against the Christian order of the day. Certainly, Shakespeare would have known about Marlowe's homo-erotic references contained in *Hero and Leander* and his other works. He must have been well acquainted with Marlowe's sordid reputation in the Elizabethan world.

"Be not deceived: evil companions corrupt good morals" (1 Cor. 15:33).

Since Shakespeare's day, the theater and the fine arts have turned into seedbeds for homosexual themes and homosexual behavior. Obviously, in the early 17th century, it would have been a huge risk to publicly admit to homosexual inclinations. Thus, it is difficult to determine for sure the sexual proclivities of men like Christopher Marlowe and William Shakespeare. We do know that Shakespeare lived apart from his wife during most of his professional career, and he is famous for leaving her his "second best bed" in his will. Nevertheless, the passions and proclivities of a man's heart are especially recognized in his writings, and this we have with Shakespeare. While he properly condemns homosexuality once in *Troilus and Cressida*, it is strange and perverse that his love-sonnets were written to a man (dedicated to a "Mr. W.H."). The perversity intensifies in Sonnet #20 and #126. In Sonnet 20 Shakespeare vents his discontentment and frustration towards "Nature" or the "Creator" for making the object of his love interests "a man."

And for a woman wert thou first created;
Till Nature, as she wrought thee, fell a-doting,

And by addition me of thee defeated,
By adding one thing to my purpose nothing.
But since she prick'd thee out for women's pleasure,
Mine be thy love and thy love's use their treasure.[7]

Such revolutionary language introduces dangerous gender confusion into the minds of men. It is the discontentment concerning what God has done, and lust for that which God forbids, that constitutes what the Bible calls "evil desires" (Col. 3:5). This is how men like William Shakespeare cracked the door for the sexual revolution in future generations.

THE ENGLISH REFORMATION VS. SHAKESPEARE

Well recognized by historians, both the Humanist Renaissance and the Protestant Reformation were important ideological movements in the last millenium. The first insisted on a man-centered view of reality and ethics, and the latter maintained a God-centered view. Within the ranks of the English reformation, there were no people more committed to this God-centered worldview than the Puritans. While they did vigorously oppose the Italian version of the Humanist Renaissance and the Roman Church, they were equally concerned with the rising humanism in England.

There has been precious little resistance to the "secularization" of society over the years, and so it is important for Christians to recognize it when they see it. Of course, the occupying force of humanists will despise these "narrow-minded bigots" who oppose their agenda with a passion. But Christians should always appreciate the work of those who were true to the faith when others are giving up on it. While they may not have been perfect in their understanding and application of the Bible, the Puritans are worthy of recognition.

In 1606, the Puritan faction in Parliament successfully secured a piece of legislation known as the "Act of 1606," which made it an offense "for any person in an interlude, pageant, or stage play to use jestingly or profanely the name of God, or of Christ Jesus, or the Holy Ghost or the Trinity." This was specifically directed towards what was happening at the Globe Theater under Shakespeare's watch. As a result, at least "three of Shakespeare's quartos show signs of revision to meet the requirement of the Profanity Act, to include omissions of obscenity, the word 'God'

7. William Shakespeare, Sonnet #20

APOSTATE

changed to 'heaven' or 'jove,' etc."[8] Following Shakespeare's death, certain folios of his plays were toned down, removing or modifying religious oaths. One editor counted fifty instances in *Othello* alone where profanities were deleted or modified.[9] All of this may sound a little "puritanical" to the present society, which knows no limits in the rampant violation of the third commandment. Barely one Christian in a hundred is all that concerned about the use of minced oaths and the reverential use of God's Name. This comes largely by way of the widespread misuse of God's name and other forms of profanity commonplace in today's stage plays and electronic forms of theater (television and motion pictures).

> *"Thou shalt not take the name of the LORD thy God in vain; for the LORD will not hold him guiltless that taketh his name in vain." (Exod. 20:7).*

For at least sixty years, the Puritans opposed the work of the Globe Theater until it was demolished in 1644. In an article entitled *"Puritan Hostility to the Theater,"* eminent historian Edmund Morgan summarizes the Puritan concerns with the theater.

1. It provided a poor form of recreation (it was exhausting, dissipating, and rendered the spectators 'effete and effeminate').

2. It was foreign and degenerate.

3. It was a non-productive form of labor especially for the actors.

4. It attracted homosexuals and prostitutes.

5. Its subject matter often addressed adultery and fornication that inspired imitation.

6. It promoted hypocrisy and deceit.

7. It competed with the true church.

8. It brought the saved into the company of the damned.

9. It would stir up the emotions and cloud the reason.

Could some of this be said of the mainstream theater and motion picture industry in our day?

> *"And have no fellowship with the unfruitful works of darkness, but rather*

---

8. Fines and Penalties - Swearing, Act, Punishment, and Legal - JRank Articles http://encyclopedia. jrank.org/articles/pages/683/Fines-and-Penalties.html#ixzz1wz2z0Fl9

9. Shakespeare, William - Forms of Swearing, Damnation, Cursing, Bawdy and Obscenity - JRank Articles http://encyclopedia.jrank.org/articles/pages/807/Shakespeare-William.html#ixzz1wz3b-7ktq

reprove them. For it is a shame even to speak of those things which are done of them in secret. But all things that are reproved are made manifest by the light: for whatsoever doth make manifest is light" (Eph. 5:11-13).

SHAKESPEARE'S METAPHYSIC

The only sure evaluation we can make of Shakespeare's spiritual and philosophical journey must be gained from his writings. The mere fact that Christians and non-Christians argue vigorously for radically differing positions regarding Shakespeare's religious beliefs reveals that his true, fundamental worldview was not openly and obviously Christian. Given his uncertain footing and tendency towards the humanist synthesis, this great literary master could easily deceive a young reader who sits at his feet. Great discernment must be exercised while reading his writings.

William Shakespeare's view of reality, God, the future state, sin, and atonement is hard to pin down by a review of his work. Some of his characters speak of purgatory (Hamlet and Claudio in *Measure for Measure*). Many affirm the existence of heaven and hell. Occasionally, his characters toy with pure materialism and annihilationism as in this well-known speech from *Macbeth*:

> *Life's but a walking shadow; a poor player.*
> *That struts and frets his hour upon the stage,*
> *And then is heard no more: it is a tale*
> *Told by an idiot, full of sound and fury,*
> *Signifying nothing.*

At least one modern Christian thinker, R.J. Rushdoony, recognized synthesis of Christian and pagan perspectives within Shakespeare's writings, "with priority often given to the pagan."[10] *Romeo and Juliet*, for example, are subject to a hostile environment in which a fatal heredity destines them to suicide. This is the main thrust of the prologue to the play:

> *From forth the fatal loins of these two foes*
> *A pair of star-crossed lovers take their life.*

10. R.J. Rushdoony, *Revolt Against Maturity*, (Vallecito: Ross House Books, 1978), 87.

APOSTATE

William Shakespeare was not always consistent on these important metaphysical matters, however. For example, Cassius in *Julius Caesar* places *men* as masters of their own fates. Shakespeare wavers; sometimes man controls his own destiny, and sometimes the "fates" control the man's destiny. At the very least, it is clear that Shakespeare could not commit to the notion that God sovereignly ordains the free actions of men. This will be further explored in my review of *Macbeth* later in this chapter.

Prospero, in *The Tempest*, flirts with the Eastern doctrine of *Maya*, which reduces all reality to illusion:

> *Our revels are now ended, these our actors,*
> *As I foretold you, were all spirits, and*
> *Are melted into air, into thin air;*
> *And, like the baseless fabric of this vision,*
> *The cloud-capp'd towers, the gorgeous palaces,*
> *The solemn temples, the great globe itself,*
> *Yea, all which it inherit, shall dissolve,*
> *And, like this insubstantial pageant faded,*
> *Leave not a rack behind. We are such stuff*
> *As dreams are made on; and our little life*
> *Is rounded with a sleep.*

All of the above-mentioned Shakespeare plays are productions from later in his life (1604-1612), and *The Tempest* was produced a year or two before the playwright retired or died. This work has more pagan overtones than his other plays, especially since the hero of the tale, Prospero, is a worker of magic (albeit white magic). This was edgy for the times in which Shakespeare lived.

Contemporary Christians like to point out the 2,000 biblical references in his plays. But this is to be expected of any 16th century playwright. The reality of God, sin, judgment, and Christ was inescapable for Shakespeare and his constituents, since the Elizabethan world was swimming in a world soaked in a thousand years of Christian heritage. Therefore, the question remains. *Was Shakespeare trying to escape this Christ-eclipsed world?* Did he set a trajectory towards humanism, statism, and materialistic determinism in the deep corridors of his mind?

For the scope of this book, we are not interested in counting the offhand allusions that William Shakespeare or any other literary master made to the Bible. What we are interested in is *the fundamental worldview underlying their stories.* Is God the source of reality, ethics, and truth? Or have they put man and the material universe in place of God? What was the trajectory set by the men who synthesized Christianity and Greek humanism? How might they have paved the way into the humanistic and anti-Christian academic world of the 21st century?

MACBETH

Great minds write great literature for good or for ill. Their artistic expressions flow like a river, washing up on this bank or that bank and forming tributaries here and there. Yet the astute mind will be able to follow the main flow of the ideas and discern the deeper and more fundamental message.

Either the mind will accept the message, or oppose it, swimming hard against the currents. All ideas are not created equal. Some ideas are better than others. Therefore, we must distinguish between that which is truthful and that which is not. Some ideas are utterly corrosive to a right worldview, and some are not. To properly discern the difference, we must ask the basic questions, the big questions of each text we read. It is easy to get caught up in the minutiae, the style of writing, the forms, the idioms, the character development, the details of the story, and so forth. But there are deeper issues at the heart of all good literature, and to neglect the substantial matters or to receive them without critical review is foolhardy. This is where much academic apostasy begins for the Christian liberal arts student. Where there is no critical review, no ferocious argumentation, and no "blood in the classroom," there is only a one-sided war.

The Christians who desire to study the academic work of a fading civilization must fly into the heat of the battle and delve to the heart of the matter with an incorrigible commitment to the truth. We should be asking the heavy questions, such as:

What is the view of reality presented here?

What is the ultimate cause of everything that happens?

What is the view of society described here?

In the social system presented, how important is the political sphere vs. the church and family sphere?

What is the place of the family and the church in the lives of the protagonists?

What is the source of ethics?

What is the source of truth?

Is there any hope for redemption in this story? If so, what is the source of redemption?

These are the questions to consider as we review the "great books." In the case of *Macbeth*, the thoughtful Christian reader must first consider Shakespeare's view of reality because this is the fundamental issue and it also happens to be the core message of the story. What is the ultimate cause of everything that happens? Is man responsible for his sins? Is God sovereign or is there some other ultimate cause that directs the events in this universe?

There are four basic views of reality upon which Shakespeare might develop his stories.

1. Everything happens by chance, and there is no ultimate causal force. Whatever forces that exist in the universe are random and disconnected. The problem with this view is that it relieves men of responsibility for what happens. Ultimate values and moral standards disappear in this view, leaving man with no purpose for life.

2. Everything happens according to the purpose of a determinate force. The Greeks reduced the world to a deterministic (or sometimes indeterminate) worldview. In this view of reality, men are forced to do unspeakably evil acts because they are just pawns in a gigantic chess game, or they play the part of a pinball bouncing around in a gigantic pinball machine. This deterministic way of looking at the universe again relieves a man of any moral responsibility for the "evil" things he does. After all, if he was forced into a certain situation by the "fates," how could he have avoided his fate, and why should he be held responsible for his behavior?

3. Man controls his own destiny, in the ultimate sense. This humanist view, assigning to men the sovereign ability to control the outcome of the universe, was espoused by men like John Dewey. Usually, people with this

humanist view end up reverting back to either one of the first two theories because they quickly figure out that man cannot possibly preordain the outcome of the universe. He cannot control all of the environmental influences upon him in order to determine a certain course of events.

4. In the Christian view, a personal, righteous God is in absolute sovereign control of all of reality. He does not coerce the moral actions of men. They act upon their own free will and according to the desires of their own heart, yet God holds them morally responsible for the choices they make. For example, Acts 2:23 speaks of God predetermining the crucifixion of His Son, which may be the worst crime ever wrought by human hands in the history of the world. According to the same passage, God holds these men responsible for their wicked deed despite the fact that He predetermined that this event would happen from the beginning of the world.

> *"[Christ] being delivered by the determinate counsel and foreknowledge*
> *of God, ye have taken, and by wicked hands have crucified and slain."*
> *(Acts 2:23)*

To give in to the Greek idea of the "fates" is a deadly compromise with the biblical idea of a personal God sovereignly ordering the free actions of men. Yet many seek this compromise because there is something incomprehensible about the biblical explanation. However, there is much we do not understand about God, His nature, and His works. For example, we have no idea how He creates a universe out of nothing, and we have not a clue how He ordains the free actions of men.

SUMMARY OF SHAKESPEARE'S MACBETH

The tragedy opens with Macbeth's military victory over the Norwegian forces, and we hear of the traitorous offenses of the former "Thane of Cawdor," who is soon to be executed. In appreciation for Macbeth's valiant efforts, the King of Scotland confers on him the title of "Thane of Cawdor." Throughout the play, Macbeth interacts with the "three weird sisters," also known as "fates." These beings control the winds and render prophetic pronouncements with authority and accuracy. They predict that Macbeth will become Thane of Cawdor and King of Scotland. To Macbeth's disappointment, they also prophesy that Macbeth's friend,

Banquo, will see the monarchy eventually revert to his descendants. With amazing precision, the weird sisters foretell specific details concerning Macbeth's fate. Sure enough, after murdering King Duncan, Macbeth becomes king. Despite Macbeth's yeoman efforts to oppose the will of the fates by murdering Banquo, he fails to dispense with Banquo's son Fleance who escapes in the confusion of the moment. In the final battle with Macduff, Macbeth takes confidence in the prophecy of the fates that he will not be killed by a man born of a woman. At the last moment, he is disappointed to learn that Macduff was "untimely ripped from his mother's womb," born of a C-section.

ANALYSIS

This tale does not contain a Christian view of reality. Although Shakespeare does not refer to the witches as "fates" directly, he uses the term "the weird (wyrd) sisters." The old English word "wyrd" denotes the old pagan idea of fate, and is transliterated "to come to pass."[11] Most Christian literary critics are ambivalent concerning these characters even though their role is a central part in the play. Some pass them off as "demonic influence" upon Macbeth,[12] but this can hardly be the case. The fates predict Macbeth's rise to power and his fall from power, and both certainly come to pass in the play. Anybody familiar with Greek pagan literature would recognize these to be the *Moirai*, the three fates who were supposed to control the "metaphorical thread of life of every mortal from birth to death."[13] There is still some ambivalence among the characters of the play concerning the ultimate causes behind reality. Throughout the production, the protagonists refer to fortune or the will of man as important causes in the events that take place (Act 1, Scene 2).

The prediction of the fates concerning Banquo's descendants is of historical importance for this stage play. According to historical records, the play was performed for James I of the Stuart line in 1604-1605. These were times in which the right to the throne was a hotly-debated issue, and the Stuarts actually claimed descent from a man named Banquo of early Scottish history. The House of Stuart is thought to have descended

---

11. http://en.wikipedia.org/wiki/Wyrd
http://www.etymonline.com/index.php?term=weird
12. Peter J. Leithart, *Brightest Heaven of Invention*, (Moscow: Canon Press, 1996), 168.
13. http://en.wikipedia.org/wiki/Moirai

from Walter Fitz Alan, the grandson of Fleance (the son of Banquo).[14] In Act IV, Scene 1, the witches prophesy that Banquo's line will produce at least eight generations of kings for Scotland. What then is King James, who comes from the line of Banquo, to think of these fates and their prediction? In what sort of light does Shakespeare present "the fates" to King James? Certainly, if the fates were legitimizing James's right to the throne by their prediction, this would only have encouraged James towards an appreciation of the fates.

Over the centuries, there has been a fair amount of ambivalence among literary critics concerning the "weird sisters." No doubt Shakespeare fully intends this confusion. Instead of affirming God's sovereignty over all of reality (including the free actions of men), he tips his hat to the old pagan metaphysic.

The essential matter for our consideration is this; does Shakespeare still hold Macbeth responsible for his moral failures? On the one hand, Shakespeare appears to deprecate Macbeth's revolutionary and treasonous ways. However, if we examine the matter at the fundamental metaphysical level, we may draw different conclusions. If Macbeth is subject to the fates, then everything that happens to him is beyond his own control. He fights valiantly against the fates by murdering Banquo, but he loses in the end because Fleance survives. Macbeth thinks he can overcome his assailant, Macduff, but alas, the man was born by a C-section and is therefore "destined" to kill Macbeth. If this is the major thrust of the play, if the revelation of Macduff's "untimely ripping" is the climax of the play, then Macbeth is ultimately subject to the power of the fates, and this must relieve his moral responsibility. In this case, the fates happen to direct the ultimate outcome of the story towards what most of Shakespeare's audience would consider just and right (the demise of Macbeth). But this may not always be the way pagan stories play out if the fates rather than God are in charge of the universe.

Of course, Shakespeare still had to reckon with 1,500 years of Christianity in English thought and life. So other Christian themes dot the landscape of his play. He clearly incorporated notions of guilt and judgment, as many good writers do. While God fills the role of judge and shows grace to people like Malcolm (Act 5, Scene 8), the witches take care of the business of foretelling the future and sovereignly ordaining the

14. Henry N. Paul, *Royal Play of Macbeth* (New York: Macmillan, 1950)

outcome of events. Clearly, the fates hold the more fundamental control over reality.

Shakespeare's theory of ethics is also somewhat governed by the biblical idea that there are consequences for sin. He seems to have a sense of judgment and hell. But when his characters verbally cast this and that into hell by using the word "damn," the playwright undermines God's prerogative as the One who assigns men to eternal damnation. This profanity lightens the sense of God's justice.

There is no question that guilt is an overriding theme in the play. In the familiar scene, Lady Macbeth attempts to wash away the bloodguilt with water, but to no avail. No mention is made of the blood of Christ. Not surprisingly, the central position of Jesus Christ as Redeemer and King of history is completely ignored. Macduff finds his atonement by revenge, and redemption for him comes by the power of the sword.

Almost every good author plays with the psychological effects of guilt. It makes for interesting character development, but the mere recognition of guilt does not suggest an endorsement of the biblical doctrines of sin, judgment, and atonement in Christ. All of these truths must rest upon a right conception of God and a right conception of man as responsible to this sovereign God. This foundational truth is missing in Shakespeare's metaphysic, and it is a fatal oversight.

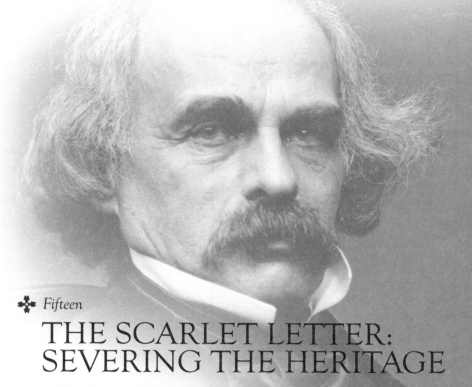

Fifteen

THE SCARLET LETTER: SEVERING THE HERITAGE

NATHANIEL HAWTHORNE | 1804-1864 A.D.

N athaniel Hawthorne was the 19th century American literary giant who did more to shift the American culture away from its national Christian heritage than anybody else. His hatred of the Puritans was deeply personal, relentlessly bitter, and marginally psychotic. Given that the Puritans represented a potent element vitally interested in retaining something of the Christian faith, it was Hawthorne's task to sever this heritage from the memory of the American people. While Americans came to despise this entire class of Christians, their sympathies were simultaneously shifted towards witchcraft, adultery, incest, and other sexual sin. More than anybody else, Nathaniel Hawthorne championed this redirection of our national cultural and moral convictions.

Hawthorne's spite for the Puritans can only be explained by his own religious apostasy and his commitment to a humanist (man-centered) worldview. By any honest measure, the Puritans were very committed Christians. Should a sincere believer perform a careful and honest review of various Christian sects throughout history, they would find the Puritans among the faithful. They were supremely orthodox, spiritually disciplined, and theologically balanced. Their sermons, treatises, biographies, diaries, and prayers contain some of the most God-centered, spiritually-uplifting material ever written. If we set the Hawthorne caricature side by side with the true historical records, there is no comparison. Certainly, any committed Christian should read a selection of the thousands of extant literary works produced by these folk before accepting the word of an apostate.[1] To this day, millions of godly Christians are strengthened by books like *Valley of Vision*, a compendium of Puritan prayers. Often considered the greatest evangelical preacher of the 19th century, Charles Spurgeon is also referred to as "the last of the Puritans." Spurgeon himself heartily endorsed their work, "By all means read the Puritans, they are worth more than all the modern stuff put together."[2] Without exaggeration, the Puritan faith amounted to one of the strongest expressions of Christian orthodoxy in the 17th century.

In spite of their cultural importance and godly influence in America, England, and Scotland, most of the "Christian" West either ignores the Puritans or despises them. Among professing Christians, most are either ignorant of this heritage, or they are embarrassed by it. This cultural disposition is largely a product of Hawthorne's skewed characterizations of this people. Throughout his books, they are presented as harsh, vindictive, and hypocritical killjoys. In the great war of the worldviews, some have said that the winners write the history books. If the Christian worldview has lost some ground since the 18th century, we will have to write our own history books for now. This is the only way the truth will sustain and prevail.

Just as the world was ready and waiting for Darwin and Emerson, this nation was well prepared for Nathaniel Hawthorne's dismissal of the American Christian heritage. Indeed, the Puritans were everything that the apostates of the 18th and 19th centuries hated. How are we to understand a world that finds it so natural to hate a people well known for their godliness and Christian piety?

Hawthorne's own Christian heritage can be traced to his great, great,

---

1. These are available through publishing houses such as Banner of Truth, Reformation Heritage Books, or from various online sources.
2. Charles H. Spurgeon, as quoted in Iain Murray, *The Forgotten Spurgeon* (Carlisle: Banner of Truth, 1966/1998), 184.

great grandfather, William Hathorne, who arrived in 1630 with John Winthrop and the first American colonists. He served as a magistrate in the New England colony. Nathaniel Hawthorne hated this man for his austere dealings with the Quakers, specifically for the whipping of a certain Quaker woman named Anne Coleman. While he attributed this civil action to William Hathorne, historical records indicate that the sentencing of Anne Coleman actually occurred under another magistrate named Richard Waldron, and Hathorne had nothing to do with it.[3]

Nathaniel Hawthorne also disapproved of his great, great grandfather, John Hathorne, because of his involvement in the Salem witch trials. From historical records, it does seem that John Hathorne acted on flimsy, "spectral" evidence for his adjudication of certain cases.[4] Nevertheless, it is clear that Hawthorne was not interested in the details of these proceedings. It was the Puritan pastors that put an end to the trials on the basis of solid biblical reasons. But that wasn't important to Hawthorne.

Nathaniel Hawthorne's personal religious affiliation is hard to construct because it was virtually nonexistent. While his parents' church background was Congregationalist on his father's side and Unitarian on his mother's side, Nathaniel's life was more or less churchless. While at Bowdoin College, the young man made a point to miss evening prayers and public worship on Sundays (even at the risk of having to pay a small fine for his lapses). Hawthorne's writings reveal his rejection of the doctrine of the Trinity and his dismissal of Jesus Christ as Redeemer and King although he does acknowledge "God" here and there throughout his work. He repudiated family worship and Sabbath-keeping,[5] he openly mocked the sermons that spoke of the Judgment of God, and he ridiculed the pastors who had been trained at the more conservative Andover Theological Seminary.[6] Nathaniel's literary influences were multi-faceted. Though he spent some of his early years reading the Puritan John Bunyan, his worldview formed around Rousseau and Montaigne

---

3. Joseph Walton, *Incidents Illustrating the Doctrine and History of the Society of Friends* (Philadelphia, PA: Society of Friends, 1897), 402.

4. We must allow that some of the Puritan magistrates were over-zealous in their civil duties and assigned civil punishments beyond that required by biblical law. Nevertheless, it is important to remember that the governments controlling our socialist nations today are far more intrusive into the lives of the average citizen than what we find in early colonial world.

5. James R. Mellow, *Nathaniel Hawthorne In His Times* (Boston: Houghton Mifflin, 1980), 64.

6. Brenda Wineapple, *Hawthorne, A Life* (New York: Alfred A. Knopf, 2003), 47.
Edwin Haviland Miller, *Salem is My Dwelling Place: A Life of Nathaniel Hawthorne* (Iowa City: University of Iowa Press, 1991), 63.

(another early French skeptic).[7]

Hawthorne married Sophia Peabody, the sister of Elizabeth Peabody, who was a central figure in the Transcendentalist movement in Salem.[8] For his wedding with Sophia, Hawthorne requested the services of a liberal Unitarian minister named James Foreman Clark. The same minister buried him in 1864, and Transcendentalist poet and essayist Ralph Waldo Emerson was among the pallbearers at Hawthorne's funeral. While most of the Transcendentalists and Unitarians in Hawthorne's time represented various stages of apostasy, the whole lot of them made up a fairly close community. The interconnections between Hawthorne and the contemporary liberal Transcendentalists are too many to recount here.

If we were to take the historical records of men like Increase and Cotton Mather seriously, it does appear that New England came under severe spiritual attack during the formation years of the American republic. Regrettably, when Nathaniel Hawthorne recounted these demonic attacks, he did not repudiate Satan's work with clear biblical teaching (James 4:7, Acts 19:19, Gal. 5:20). Instead, he maintained an unhealthy fixation on the demon world throughout his life. As a young writer of 21 years, he wrote a short story called *Alice Doane's Appeal*, excusing witchcraft and ascribing autonomous power to wizardry. As par for the course, he described the Puritan Cotton Mather as "a blood-thirsty man," something akin to "the fiend himself."[9] In his college years at Bowdoin, he would consort with a witch in the town.[10] Later in his life while visiting Florence, Italy, he allowed his wife Sophia to visit a medium and a necromancer.[11] If that wasn't bad enough, his children were caught up in this demonic interplay as well. Sophia's sister (also a medium) insisted that Hawthorne's eldest daughter Una had "the gift of a medium" early on in her life. No doubt as a consequence of her aunt's counsel, the poor girl suffered from mental illness until her dying day.[12] In a letter to his mother from college, Hawthorne suggested that he

7. Ibid. 49.
8. Elizabeth Peabody worked for Transcendentalist philosopher Bronson Alcott, who was a close friend of Transcendentalists Ralph Waldo Emerson and Henry David Thoreau.
9. Nathaniel Hawthorne, *Alice Doane's Appeal*, Source: http://etext.virginia.edu/toc/modeng/public/HawAlic.html.
10. Miller. 70.
11. Ibid. 437.
12. Ibid. 339.

would become a writer but ominously forewarned her that "authors are always poor devils, and therefore Satan may take them." Commenting on this dark suggestion, biographer James Mellow says that this "becomes a persistent theme in Hawthorne's work: the hint that writing involved an almost diabolical form of knowledge, an acquaintance with the darker passions, the hidden sins and guilts of others—that an author was, in a sense, in league with the devil."[13]

> *"There shall not be found among you any one that maketh his son or his daughter to pass through the fire, or that useth divination, or an observer of times, or an enchanter, or a witch, Or a charmer, or a consulter with familiar spirits, or a wizard, or a necromancer. For all that do these things are an abomination unto the LORD: and because of these abominations the LORD thy God doth drive them out from before thee."* (Deut. 18:10-13).

At the root of it, Hawthorne's real sin was his refusal to acknowledge the sin of witchcraft as a true violation of God's law. As a humanist who thinks and acts independently of the law of God, he would accuse the Puritan magistrates of injustice by his own arbitrary humanist "standard." Occasionally, he tried to explain away all supernaturalism with scientific naturalism (which happens to be a demonic lie of another stripe). Woven into his stories is this surreptitious implication that the sin of witchcraft, homosexuality, adultery, or incest (as in the case of Alice Doane) was better than whatever the Puritans were doing during America's early days. This was how humanists turned the moral order on its head, and the liberal thinkers since Hawthorne's day have always been good at this kind of thing. It is a dangerous business.

As a young writer, Nathaniel Hawthorne was driven by a motivation to "achieve my destiny" and build "my monument."[14] He was one of the first literary men to psychologize guilt, separating the idea of sin from the transgression of the law of a transcendent God. He picked at sin as a surgeon picks at diseased flesh. He was also a master at pointing out hypocrisy in the lives of Christians while at the same time quietly excusing the grosser evils of witchcraft and adultery. For example, Hawthorne's

13. Ibid. 26.
14. Ibid. 54.

Young Goodman Brown hesitates to join the devil's errand in the forest, saying, "We have been a race of honest men and good Christians since the days of the martyrs." The devil replies, *"I helped your grandfather, the constable, when he lashed the Quaker woman so smartly through the streets of Salem. And it was I that brought your father a pitch-pine knot, kindled at my own hearth to set fire to an Indian village."* Practically every two-bit atheist and community collegiate skeptic in our day has used this argument to discredit "religion." The argument is usually stated thus: since there are a few Christians who have perverted justice and fought Indian wars (justly or unjustly) in the history of the world, therefore all Christians must be hypocritical fools.

Worst of all, Hawthorne's stories leave his poor, tortured, guilt-ridden protagonists with no hope for any atonement. He ably demonstrates the futility of self-atonement and leaves the reader with one inescapable conclusion: the relief of guilt will only come by the eradication of the concept of sin and the standards of God's law. For Hawthorne, guilt must be handled as Hester deals with it in the *Scarlet Letter.* Whereas Hawthorne stopped just short of explicitly approving of Hester's adultery, it was only 50 years later that Mark Twain recommended serial adultery for women. By refusing to acknowledge *any and all* possibility of atonement, Nathaniel Hawthorne pressed the entire Victorian world towards the only possible solution for humanist man: the elimination of the Lawgiver. If man becomes the source of his own law and God has no moral code to which men must be held accountable, then the problem of guilt is dealt with once and for all.

The progression of these humanist ideas moves quickly. After God is removed as the moral Source, humanist man soon realizes that he must dispense with all absolutes, whether in ethics, truth, or life purpose. Thus, professor Will Provine, PhD from Cornell University wrote recently,

> *"Let me summarize my views on what modern evolutionary biology tells us loud and clear... There are no gods, no purposes, no goal-directed forces of any kind. There is no life after death. When I die, I am absolutely certain that I am going to be dead. That's the end for me. There is no ultimate foundation for ethics, no ultimate meaning to life, and no free*

will for humans, either."[15]

The 19th century Transcendentalists were not prepared for this level of self-consistency. But this was their trajectory.

By the end of his life, Hawthorne began to realize the implications of his ideas. In a letter to Sophia, he identified with the dismal Dimmesdale in *Scarlet Letter* as one whose buried body would blast "the spot of earth which I occupied, while the grass flourished all around." Having cast aside the atoning blood of Christ for his sins, he had abandoned all hope of life and resurrection after death.[16] His final literary work, *Septimius*, is saturated in hopelessness. One would think it was Friedrich Nietzsche or Will Provine writing these words: "We are all linked together in a chain of Death, and feel no remorse for those we cause, nor enmity for that we suffer. And the Purpose? What is Purpose? Who can tell when he has actually formed one?"[17]

Biographer Brenda Wineapple sums up Hawthorne's miserable life with the three things he stood for: "Doubt, Darkness, and the Democratic Party."[18] Self-consistency to humanist ideals will only yield to purposelessness and hopelessness in the end.

> *"But if there be no resurrection of the dead, then is Christ not risen: And if Christ be not risen, then is our preaching vain, and your faith is also vain. Yea, and we are found false witnesses of God; because we have testified of God that he raised up Christ: whom he raised not up, if so be that the dead rise not. For if the dead rise not, then is not Christ raised: And if Christ be not raised, your faith is vain; ye are yet in your sins. Then they also which are fallen asleep in Christ are perished. If in this life only we have hope in Christ, we are of all men most miserable. But now is Christ risen from the dead" (1 Cor. 15:13-17).*

15. "How Would You Reply to This Poll?" *Your Origins Matter*, Jun. 11, 2012 <http://www.youroriginsmatter.com/conversations/view/How+Would+You+Reply+to+This+Poll%3F/27> accessed on Mar. 26, 2013.
16. Mellow. 308.
17. Wineapple. 365.
18. Ibid. 380.

THE SCARLET LETTER

Hawthorne was a true genius, and *The Scarlet Letter* was his *magnum opus*. Published in 1850, this classic work was more than just finely crafted literature. The spiritual effects of the book upon the nation were profound for several reasons. To this day, no other single publication of any genre has been so effective at severing a nation from its Christian heritage. The book is one of the most popular novels still read in full by American high school students.[19] The book works psychologically; it penetrates deeply into the consciousness of millions of people, re-shaping religious perspectives and humanist convictions concerning the Christian faith, the historical church, sexuality, guilt, judgment, atonement, and God's law.

Prior to 1820, most authors could not earn a living by writing novels. There was not much of a market for this genre of literature until the birth of the modern age. Nathaniel Hawthorne was one of the very first popular literary giants, and *The Scarlet Letter* was one of the first mass-produced books published in the United States.[20] The timing for this society-transforming book was impeccable.

Throughout the story, Hawthorne takes the reader up and down the dark corridors of the hearts of unredeemed men. The stories he tells are dismal because he favors those in rebellion to God and church over those who are in covenant relationship with God. Even when the characters find redemption, it is only a pretense—a half-way redemption.

Testifying to his own state of mind while working on the masterpiece, Hawthorne said he wrote it "as if under compulsion." Under what spiritual influence did the writer feel so compelled? He completed this towering literary work in no less than 19 days. Directly upon completion, he wrote to his friend Horatio Bridge, calling the creation, "a positively hell-fired story."[21] Herman Melville wrote a rather disturbing letter to Hawthorne on November 17, 1851, in which he confessed to have written a "wicked book" himself. In a particularly strange portion of the letter, he suggested the same "rushing demon" who had affected Hawthorne in his

19. Kelly, Melissa, "Top Ten Novels for American Literature Classes" *About.com*, <http://712educa-tors.about.com/od/novelsandshortstories/tp/amlitnovels.htm> accessed on Mar. 26, 2013; "Top 100 American Literature Titles," *Perfection Learning*, <http://www.perfectionlearning.com/top%20100-american-lit-titles> accessed on Mar. 26, 2013

20 "The Scarlet Letter," *Wikipedia*, Mar. 17, 2013 <http://en.wikipedia.org/wiki/The_Scarlet_Let-ter> accessed on Mar. 26, 2013

21. Mellow. 303

"solitudes" had also influenced him. Then he questions his own sanity, "My dear Hawthorne, the atmospheric skepticisms steal into me now, and make me doubtful of my sanity in writing you thus. But believe me, I am not mad, most noble Festus."[22]

Was there a powerful spiritual presence in Hawthorne's life and family? What demons may have tortured his mind and inspired his pen? If *The Scarlet Letter* was his magnum opus, why would he confess that the story was conceived or "fired" in the pit of hell? The power of the story is beyond question. The tale bears an influence over the reader that is hard to explain and harder to withstand. In the end, the demons won control over Salem, and Christianity lost its grip in New England. It would seem that spiritual entities with far more power than anything mere humans could muster worked strongly in the hearts and minds of men like Nathaniel Hawthorne and his close friend Ralph Waldo Emerson to lead the apostasy. What did these spiritual powers accomplish through the literary work of the likes of Hawthorne, Melville, and Emerson? History bears out a significant legacy.

When the book was published on March 16, 1850, there was some resistance against it on the part of the Christian church. *The Church Review and Ecclesiastical Register* accused Hawthorne of perpetuating "bad morals."[23] Another religious journal, the *Brownson's Quarterly*, noted that none of the protagonists in the story "really repents of the criminal deed" and concludes that, "It is a story that should not have been told."[24]

What the reader is about to review is a tale fired in hell according to the author's own admission. It is possible that this story has done more harm to the spiritual condition of America than any other single work of fiction. For Christian leaders, teachers, and parents to ignore its content and its influence over the direction of society would be a fatal miscalculation of the highest order. How could anybody understand the historical underpinnings of the worldviews that dominate in schools today without a right assessment of this critical book? Let me say that this study is not for the faint of heart or the undiscerning spirit. It is for those who are ready and willing to do battle in the literary war of the worldviews.

22. Edwin Haviland Miller, *Salem is My Dwelling Place: A Life of Nathaniel Hawthorne* (Iowa City: University of Iowa Press, 1991), 355.
23. Wineapple. 217.
24. Miller. 302.

BRIEF SUMMARY OF THE SCARLET LETTER

The Scarlet Letter tells the story of an adulteress in a pseudo-Puritan colony in Massachusetts. Hester Prynne, unbeknownst to the townsfolk, commits adultery with the young pastor, Dimmesdale. Somehow, the magistrate convicts her of her crime and sentences her to wearing a scarlet "A" embroidered to the bodice of her dress. Her husband, a man named Chillingsworth, returns from a sea voyage. He refuses to make himself known to the rest of the town, but neither does he return to his wife and child. Instead, he chooses to reside with Dimmesdale, the man who had committed adultery with Hester. Chillingsworth finds ways to intensify Dimmesdale's guilt and torture his conscience until Dimmesdale finally reveals his sin to the entire town at the end of the story.

CRITIQUE

From the very first page of the book, Hawthorne presents the Puritans as somber, rigid, hypocritical, graceless, and Christ-less. If you were to read more than two sentences of any Puritan sermon, diary, or treatise, you would find a different theology entirely. These people include constant mention of the Lord Jesus Christ in their writings, something Hawthorne does not dare permit for his Puritans. Those who have read the real Puritans would find Nathaniel Hawthorne's *Scarlet Letter* supremely offensive, even slanderous. Arguably, Nathaniel Hawthorne was the most influential liar in American history. Mark Twain found virtue in lying, but Hawthorne did the most damage by his finely tuned deception.

In the first chapter, Hawthorne accuses the Puritans of excessive severity in civil punishments. He tells of the "undutiful child" that is whipped at the whipping post and the "antinomians" who are chased out of town. Obviously, Hawthorne would not take kindly to Matthew 15:4-6, where Jesus commends the law allowing the death penalty for a young man who curses his father or his mother. Offensive though it may be to antinomians that reject God's law in the Bible, the Puritans did take biblical law seriously. Moreover, Hawthorne mischaracterizes the passage and the Puritans by extending the law to include the "undutiful child." There is a difference between the grown man who curses his father and beats on his mother (as described in Scripture) and the "undutiful child." Historians have yet to identify the "undutiful child" turned over to the civil magistrate in the Puritan colonies. Granted, Jesus Christ and His views on the Old Testament are still mocked by secularists either on the street or in the church. Yet Christians will be careful to fear God enough to avoid mockery and spite for Christ.

As with all apostates, Hawthorne doesn't provide appropriate nuance concerning historical fact, historical context, and biblical truths. His goal is to set a new humanistic ethic and life next to the old Christian order and prove that the new "religion" is better. Of course, he had to place the old order in the worst possible light in order to pull this off. His first propositions are, in a nutshell: God's laws are unjust; the Puritans were evil, unrefined, old-fashioned, and hypocritical; the new order of things is much better.

Hawthorne finds it absurd that the Puritans would limit religious freedom. And it is true that the early colonists preferred that certain denominations such as Quakers, Congregationalists, and Baptists settle their own colonies. When proselytes from certain denominations would attempt to disrupt or to disunify other churches and communities, the magistrate would be forced to act. This makes little sense to the modern mind where there is almost absolute separation of church and state. Yet, Americans still limit religious freedom when it comes to practices like human sacrifice, smoking peyote, and Muslim jihad. Nevertheless, the bounds of religious liberty are never completely obvious. Does a Christian country prosecute human sacrifice, for example? Should the Immigration and Naturalization Service extradite all Muslims from the country or just those who are committed to religious Jihad? Most Americans seldom consider these sorts of nuances, and Hawthorne took full advantage of this ignorance in order to condemn the Puritans for their stance. It does take wisdom to lay out proper boundaries for religious liberties. Over the centuries, the various Christian denominations have learned to live with each other in relative peace. Notwithstanding the earlier sectarian controversies, Congregationalist Puritans like Increase and Cotton Mather attended and supported the ordination of Baptist ministers in Boston.[25] This is something else that Hawthorne would not have liked to admit.

Hawthorne's most successful ploy against the Christian faith came

---

25. Michael G. Hall, *The Last American Puritan: The Life of Increase Mather* (Hanover: Wesleyan University Press, 1988), 347.

APOSTATE

with his attacks on the Puritan view of witchcraft. Admittedly, the Salem "witch trials" did demonstrate certain spiritual weaknesses that existed within the early American colonies. Around this same time frame, European witch hunts had eliminated thousands of supposed witches often using trumped up charges.

Before the age of humanism, Christian countries opposed witchcraft and took biblical passages like Exodus 22:18, 2 Kings 23:24, and Deuteronomy 18:10 seriously. These texts recommend extradition or the death penalty for witchcraft. In an older era, such laws did not seem overly stringent. It is only after some three hundred years of legalized witchcraft, Harry Potter, Ouija Boards, and Nathaniel Hawthorne that the national temperament has changed towards these social and moral abominations. The antipathy towards biblical texts like Exodus 22:18 among many Christians may seem a little odd. Perhaps our culture has been influenced by witches and demons, or by Nathaniel Hawthorne.

We still grant that there were serious problems with the Salem "witch hunt" proceedings because Puritan pastors admitted this to be the case. According to Increase Mather and other witnesses to the Salem witch trials, the court took in "spectral evidence," or evidence based on dreams and visions instead of eyewitnesses. Biblical law requires two or three human witnesses (who themselves are not guilty of committing the same crime) to prove the innocence or guilt of the party. What Hawthorne refuses to acknowledge is that it was the Puritan pastors who put an end to the witch trials at Salem.[26] These are the pastors he mocks in his stories.

The spiritual situation in New England in the late 17th century is worthy of consideration. Could there have been a serious demonic attack upon the colonies at this time in Christian history? In retrospect 300 years later, it appears that something very bad happened at the beginning of the 17th century in this country. Harvard almost instantly turned against Christ and embraced liberal, Latitudinarian thinking. The entire nation then moved towards liberalism, Unitarianism, and Deism within 75 years. Humanist doctrines of socialism, communism, and feminism followed in the 19th century while witchcraft became an accepted norm in American life. (Today, the old Puritan East Church in Salem on the

---

26. Ibid. 261, 262.

corner of Hardy and Essex Streets is a witch museum.)[27] Also, during the 19th century, many cults found their way into the country, and the Christian faith lost significant cultural standing. Suffice it to say that something happened in New England in the 1690s. . . and it had to be something of a spiritual nature.

INTERNAL PROBLEMS WITH THE STORY

There are multiple internal problems in Hawthorne's story that cannot be ignored as we consider this significant American novel that has played such a major role in high school literature classes during the demise of the Christian West. First of all, Hester Prynne is not convicted on the basis of two or three witnesses as would be required by Scripture (Deut. 19:15, 2 Cor. 13:1). In fact, from what we can tell *there are no witnesses at the trial at all*. Even Hester refuses to testify. None of the townspeople are aware of the other party with whom she has committed adultery, and for all they knew, she could have had the child by her husband. Technically, the story should have been over at this point.

Hester's stubborn refusal to implicate Dimmesdale throughout the story is strange. It is possible that she holds some hope for renewing a relationship with him. Whatever the case, she *never* comes across as humble, submissive, or repentant. We see in her behavior the developing persona of the 20th century feminist — a woman without law, completely free to act as she wills. Later in the story, Hester suggests that they run away to Europe together. Dimmesdale almost gives in to her appeal but later chooses to admit his guilt publicly.

As is the case with many of the influential apostates, Hawthorne's agenda and conclusions are ambiguous. His writings are filled with doubts and vagueness. Nevertheless, there can be hardly a question that Hester Prynne is the heroine of the story as that is the way she is interpreted by nearly every literary critic who has reviewed the book. Practically everybody else in the story is either a scoundrel or a victim of scoundrels. The pseudo-Puritans are a misguided, despicable lot. Dimmesdale is a pitiable soul caught up in a misguided, stupid religion. Hester's husband, Chillingsworth, is Hawthorne's villain because he plays on the conscience

---

27. Curley, Jerome, "Then & Now: History Within History—The Salem Witch Museum," *Salem Patch*, Oct. 11, 2012 <http://salem.patch.com/articles/then-now-history-within-history-the-salem-witch-museum> accessed on Mar. 26, 2013

of Dimmesdale, convicting him of his sin and manipulating him towards a public confession. Evidently, Hawthorne does not like the conscience or people who stir up the conscience. Hester's daughter Pearl is Rousseau's wild child — uncontrollable, rebellious, and free. She returns to Europe and gets civilized (whatever that means). While it is clear that Hawthorne dislikes the Puritans, he presents Hester in the best possible light. She steadfastly opposes orthodox doctrine, she cares for the poor, and she acts as the female prophetess for women in the new age.

THEOLOGICAL PROBLEMS IN THE SCARLET LETTER

Now the most serious problems with the book are theological. What makes this "classic" one of the most harmful books of the 19th century is its depiction of Christian theology. Hawthorne presents the worst possible Christian theological milieu in his hell-forged story. He sets the readers up for an anti-biblical, humanist solution by creating a false dilemma in the lives of the protagonists. His is a cruel Christian world because it is based upon a cruel Christian soteriology (doctrine of salvation). In chapter three, the Reverend Wilson preaches a Gospel of damnation and repentance, carefully avoiding any mention of things like faith, grace, and Christ. It is this very separation of faith and repentance that has done immeasurable damage to the church over the succeeding 150 years. Now, most churches prefer to preach a faith without repentance, which may be a knee-jerk reaction to Hawthorne's imbalanced pseudo-Puritans. In reality, one would have had to look long and hard to find even a single instance of a Puritan church that preached repentance without faith. *The Westminster Confession of Faith* (referred to in Chapter 8 of *Scarlet Letter*) was careful never to separate justification from sanctification. In fact, the confession requires the preaching of faith and repentance together in accordance with Paul's example in Acts 20:21.[28] Evidently, Hawthorne's Puritans failed to read their own Confession—strange Puritans indeed!

Perhaps the most dreadful characterization of this crippled theology comes in Chapter 20 of the book where the Christian Bible is described as the "Hebrew" Scriptures. Imagine a Christian Bible without the New Testament! This is the height of the caricature. Hawthorne attempts to

---

28. Westminster Larger Catechism, Question 77, *Westminster Confession of Faith*, Chapter XV, Section I

present a Bible without Christ because it is a Bible without the New Testament. What he may not know is that Christ insisted that the Old Testament spoke of Himself (Luke 24:27). Even if Hawthorne's real agenda was a total repudiation of the Old Testament law with its inconvenient ethical code, he would still have contradicted what Christ said about the law during His ministry.

> "Think not that I am come to destroy the law, or the prophets: I am not come to destroy, but to fulfil. For verily I say unto you, Till heaven and earth pass, one jot or one tittle shall in no wise pass from the law, till all be fulfilled. Whosoever therefore shall break one of these least commandments, and shall teach men so, he shall be called the least in the kingdom of heaven: but whosoever shall do and teach them, the same shall be called great in the kingdom of heaven" (Matt. 5:17-19).

Years ago, when I set out to study *The Scarlet Letter* for the first time, I did a computer word search of the text for the words "Christ" and "Jesus." I remember the eerie, sinking feeling that settled in my stomach as I came to realize that Hawthorne could only configure a Christ-less Christianity! He makes constant references to penitence and atonement, but it is self-atonement. Dimmesdale's "A" seared into his chest is one of the most vivid pictures of self-atonement in all of literary history. At the very climax of the story (in Chapter 23), Hester insists that they have been redeemed by all the suffering they have gone through. In this painfully twisted scene, Dimmesdale tells everybody that God shows mercy by making people suffer for their sins, and this is how he is saved from being "lost forever." Of course, all of this makes a mockery of the atoning death of Jesus Christ.

There are two gospels presented by Hawthorne in the story, both counterfeits. On the one hand, the gospel of Hawthorne's pseudo-Puritans is law without grace, and repentance without faith in Jesus Christ. According to this pseudo-gospel, one must self-atone by wearing a "scarlet letter" or by some other form of self-immolation. There may have been some fear of God amongst this odd bunch, but hardly a love for God and certainly not a willingness to keep His laws.

Then, set against the pseudo-Puritan gospel is the gospel of Hester and Hawthorne, which should be very familiar to most Americans. This gospel teaches love without law. It is a human definition of love, and from what we can tell, God is not the object of that love. It is a love that eludes definition. Adulterers love their neighbor's wives, homosexuals love their friends, and cannibals love their victims — they taste good. Hawthorne's gospel rejects *both* repentance and faith. Effectively, it is a gospel without atonement because there is no law broken. This element of the pseudo-gospel is less obvious, but a careful reader will identify this gross autonomy in Hester's words and behavior.

Hawthorne leaves us with an empty gospel. Set against these pseudo-gospels is the gospel of Jesus Christ. This true gospel relies entirely on Christ's sacrifice for our sins and His resurrection from the dead. If we repent *and* turn to Christ in faith for salvation, we will be saved (Luke 13:3, 5; Acts 3:19; Acts 16:31; Rom. 10:9).

Chapter 18 could have been written by the "Angel of Light" himself. It is the most daring chapter of all, especially for a 19th century author. Don't forget that Hawthorne is writing in the face of over a thousand years of Christian social and moral structures which are not easily toppled. Nevertheless, this is a chapter that preaches the "gospel" of modern humanism loud and clear. It rushes into the soul like a "Flood of Sunshine," which happens to be the title of the chapter. For a brief moment, Dimmesdale is released from the "dark world" of Puritanism into that Flood of Sunshine. He becomes a "loving and cheerful man" for a few minutes as he runs back into the arms of the adulteress. Hester gives him the gospel of autonomy, suggesting that they run away to the continent together. Briefly, Dimmesdale experiences great freedom and a release of his burden of guilt. According to Hawthorne, Hester has "habituated herself to a latitude of speculation." She even recommends that they go outside of the settlement of the Christians and into the open wilderness with the natives where they will be "happy." Thus, Hester's freedom from guilt is associated with freedom from the demands of God's law.

In the same chapter, Hawthorne himself tries to excuse their "sin" as a sin of passion, as opposed to the "worse" sins of principle or purpose. Ergo: they really didn't mean to do it, and they violated no principle. They just got a little too emotional, a little too excited, and they didn't let their better judgment dictate. Towards the conclusion of the scene in the forest, Hawthorne insists that the two adulterers are meant to be together forever, eternally conjoined. He defines love outside of the bounds of the law of God. Surely Rudyard Kipling described modern man accurately as the one "who started by loving his neighbor, and ended by loving his wife." By now you will recognize this to be plain and simple humanism, rooted in the ethical autonomy of the ancient Greeks.

Throughout the story, Hester refuses to submit to the laws of the state and the church concerning her adultery. She even imagines herself embracing the pagan ways of the Indians who couldn't care less about the marriage covenant.[29] Hester comes to the point where she loses all respect for Christian laws and the Christian faith. Meanwhile, Mr. Dimmesdale finds it more difficult to escape the "prison" of Christianity. His faith in the new-found religion of humanism is not nearly as strong as Hester's. Even as he decides to pursue this adulterous relationship further with Hester, he tosses one more "Will you forgive me for this too?" up into the heavens.

Importantly, this chapter presents the brightest moment in the whole wretched tale. It is a most hopeful and joyful moment because there is a pseudo-joy that comes to a man or a woman who throws off the old moral order. For the last 150 years, the entire Western world has worked hard to fully realize this chapter. Indeed, the gospel of Hawthorne has yielded fruit—bad fruit, but fruit.

Some Christians point to Dimmesdale's public confession in the last chapter as proof that the story ends well. But the confession itself is presented as "self-atonement" in its shame and humiliation. There is no answer to be found in Christ, and Dimmesdale dies a miserable man. The reader cannot help but feel an emptiness and sadness in this poor man's demise.

There should be very little debate on the major moral thrust of the story because the author plainly gives it to us—three times (Chapter 24): "Be true. Be true. Be true." This becomes the highest ethic for the humanist. There is nothing here about obeying God, believing in Christ, and loving God with heart, soul, mind, and strength. The humanist ethic is simply, "Don't hide who you really are. Be yourself. Be true to yourself. If you are a cannibal or a murderer or adulterer, just admit the fact. Don't pretend to be somebody that you are not." However, Jesus Christ begs to

---

29. When Lewis and Clark set out across America and came upon Indian tribes, they found that it was not unusual for the natives to sell their wives (or even rent them) to the white men.

differ with this wild human autonomy. Clearly, the highest ethic for the Christian is to love God and keep His commandments (John 14:15, 1 John 5:2). It is to glorify God and enjoy Him forever (1 Cor. 10:31).

The conclusion of the story does retain some intentional vagaries that are concerning to the Christian reader. If the author has an opportunity to recant or to adjust his trajectory, it would be at the end of the story. But Hawthorne leaves us hanging, and we are even more concerned. After a hiatus in Europe, Hester returns to the town and dons the "scarlet letter" again. But now the townsfolk look upon the symbol with "awe and reverence." What does this mean? If the "scarlet letter" represents adultery, one should never look upon sin with awe and reverence. Or if the "scarlet letter" represents self-atonement, it is a false atonement, and this reverence would only detract from the glory due the cross of Christ. Adultery is a shameful thing and ought not to be viewed with anything but horror and reproach. Once more, Nathaniel Hawthorne launches a full frontal attack on the law of God.

In her waning years, Hester becomes a prophetess of sorts, providing counsel to those who come to her with "unyielded, rebellious hearts." From the beginning to the end of the story, she is the archetypal woman rebel of the 19th century. She bows to nobody. She opposes the old order with everything that is in her.

This woman rebel is vividly reincarnated 60 years later in the form of Margaret Sanger, Margaret Mead, and other feminists. Eventually, the independent woman is looking for "sex before marriage, and a job after marriage," to use Gloria Steinem's familiar words. In order to advance sexual independence for women, the floodgates opened to abortion on demand and the abortifacient pill (producing about a billion dead babies worldwide since 1980).

To the women that seek her counsel, Hester tells of some new truth that will come in the future. Nothing more about this truth is revealed, except that it is a truth that Hester will find more to her liking. This "truth" cannot be the final revelation of God in Jesus Christ because Hawthorne has already rejected 1800 years of Christ. Therefore, this new truth must be something like a "new" humanist truth such as what we find in the *Humanist Manifesto*. Most likely this new truth will look a great deal like the same old lie told in the garden: "You shall be as gods [determining] good and evil" (Genesis 3:5-8).

CONCLUSION

Hawthorne still half-heartedly recognizes some remnants of a Christian view of reality. Throughout, his characters offer some lip service to God as Creator and Providential Sustainer. Also, he revels in his depiction of human guilt, but he doesn't quite know what to do with it. Sigmund Freud has yet to explain it away completely for the liberated humanist of the 20th century.

Hawthorne's view of Satan is a little difficult to discern. It is clear from Hester's interaction with the witch, Mistress Hibbins, that the author wants to deny the supernatural, explaining these powers as something mechanical and scientific (confined to the material universe). At one point, he describes Mistress Hibbins as "insane," not demon-possessed. Clearly, he prefers Hester's autonomy over Mistress Hibbin's weirdness. Hawthorne is moving towards humanism in his 19th century thinking as he attempts to separate what Hester is doing from the "mythical world of witchcraft." The Bible disagrees on this point, stating that "Rebellion is as the sin of witchcraft" (1 Sam. 15:23). Whether or not Hawthorne intends this to be the case, Hester and Hibbins are effectively of the same mind.

Of course, Hawthorne does interact with the Christian ideas of God, religion, providence, mercy, guilt, and atonement in his book because he must work from the baseline of a Christian heritage. However, the mere mention of these things does not imply that the author conveys *the right perspective concerning them.* What really matters is *how* he treats these subjects. It is important also to take note of what is missing from his message. There is no Christ, no Holy Spirit, no Trinity, no respect for God's law, and no effectual atonement. Hawthorne is abandoning the Christian faith and taking the world with him.

Nathaniel Hawthorne tosses the Christian reader into a false dilemma by first creating a straw-man of Christianity hardly recognizable by any true disciple of Christ. Either Hawthorne deliberately misrepresents the Christian gospel, or he misunderstands it because the gospel of Christ is centered on the atoning work of Jesus Christ on the cross.

As the age of apostasy progressed, it is interesting that the Christian gospel came under all-out assault right here. It was the cross that was the most offensive element to the modern humanists. A good many of the 19th century writers did retain some respect for the doctrines of the providence of God and the sovereignty of God. But they had to obfuscate the cross of Christ even though it is by the power of the cross that the powers of darkness are crushed. The demons cannot tolerate the message of the cross!

The Scarlet Letter is a no-holds-barred attack on the Seventh Commandment. It is Hawthorne's best shot at stripping back a social moré that had been in place for 1500 years. If he were alive today, no doubt he would be delighted to learn that adultery is now commonplace in most Western societies. There are now websites dedicated to helping people commit adultery, and the social stigma is virtually gone.[30] The divorce rate has increased by orders of magnitude in England and America since the 1830s. Most households are led by single women like Hester Prynne, and fatherlessness is everywhere. What a crowning achievement for Nathaniel Hawthorne's vision.

> *"He that despised Moses' law died without mercy under two or three witnesses: Of how much sorer punishment, suppose ye, shall he be thought worthy, who hath trodden under foot the Son of God, and hath counted the blood of the covenant, wherewith he was sanctified, an unholy thing, and hath done despite unto the Spirit of grace?" (Heb. 10:28,29).*

30. Croyden, Helen, "Adultery Dating Websites: Three 'Happily Married' Men Explain Why They Go Online Looking for Affairs" *Mirror News*, Aug. 2, 2012, <http://www.mirror.co.uk/news/re-al-life-stories/adultery-dating-websites-three-happily-1202044> accessed on Mar. 25, 2013

Sixteen

HUCKLEBERRY FINN: REJECTING THE FAITH

MARK TWAIN | 1835-1910 A.D.

B orn in Florida, Missouri on November 30, 1835, Samuel Langhorne Clemens (Mark Twain[1]) would come to popularize the American independent spirit. Just a few months after he was born, the first wagon trains left Independence, Missouri to settle the Western frontier. Out of this new breed of independent Americans there came a great deal of family-disintegrating feminism, murderous violence, libertarianism, divorce, strange cults, and weak Christian churches. To this day, the highest divorce rates in America are found in the Western states.[2] Mark Twain either played off of this social milieu or contributed to it.

Mark Twain's mother raised him in the Presbyterian Church, where

---

1. Clemens' pen name came from the men running the riverboats. As they approached the depth of two fathoms, the ship mates would cry, "Mark twain!" Clemens worked as a riverboat captain in his early 20's.
2. "Divorce in the United States: Divorce Rate by State" *Wikipedia*, Mar. 26, 2013 <http://en.wikipedia.org/wiki/Divorce_in_the_United_States#Divorce_rate_by_state> accessed on Mar. 26, 2013

APOSTATE

he remained until 1858 (when he was 23 years old). For the rest of his life he would refer to himself off-and-on as a Presbyterian. What he called his "Presbyterian conscience" would continue to nag him for the rest of his life, giving him no end of angst. Mark Twain's apostasy may have been encouraged by his father, who called himself a deist.

Mark Twain's first antipathy was towards "organized religion." It was not unusual for the 19th century apostates to save their most acidic salvos for the organized church, while eking out a little faint praise for Jesus and God just in case He exists. For example, Jeremy Bentham vented strongly against organized religion and the Apostle Paul but stopped short of publicly confessing his atheist faith. As it turns out, Jesus would not have been impressed by these attacks on His church, with which He is intimately connected. He would say, "Love Me, love My friends, love My church" (John 13:34, 35; 1 John 4:20,21). However, when it comes to the church of Christ, somehow the apostate mind becomes a straw-man factory. Given enough time, an unbelieving, malicious mind will characterize every church and every Christian as the great enemy of all that is rational, good, and authentic. To this day, millions of Americans express nothing but contempt for the organized church, though they still half-heartedly acknowledge a "God" or a "Savior."

For most of his life, Mark Twain cloaked his atheism in humor, dubitable statements, and mockery at the more dysfunctional elements of 19th century Christianity. With the years, his apostasy only became increasingly self-conscious, serious, and foreboding. By the end of his life, he may have been the most famous writer in the world. He was a great leader in a rapidly-expanding literary world, and he was an apostate of apostates. In 1906, he chose to include a chapter in his autobiography that revealed his complete break with the faith. He warned his publisher William Dean Howells up front, "Tomorrow I mean to dictate a chapter which will get my heirs and assigns burnt alive if they venture to print it this side of 2006 A.D."[3] In this bone-chilling chapter, Mark Twain clearly communicated his unmitigated hatred for Christians, the Bible, and God. For example, he called the Bible "the most damnatory biography that exists in print anywhere." He said, "It makes Nero an angel of light and leading, by contrast." He also referred to God as "repulsive,"

3. Michael Shelden, *Mark Twain: Man in White* (New York: Random House, 2010), 76.

"vindictive," and "malignant.[4] Ultimately, he conceded that death is "the only unpoisoned gift earth ever had for them—and they vanish from a world where they were of no consequence; where they achieved nothing; where they were a mistake and a failure and a foolishness. . ."[5] Finally the apostate of the modern era has arrived at the self-consistent position of hopeless nihilism and epistemological bankruptcy. You will remember that Nietzsche fought desperately to avoid such a predicament in his thinking, but the modern man finds resistance futile.

I must relate one last horrible event in Mark Twain's life that completed his singularly spectacular apostasy from the Christian faith. In 1909, only a year before he died, he transcribed what he called a message from Satan himself entitled *Letters from the Earth*. He fully understood the extent to which these writings would sully his public image should they be published. Concerning *Letters*, Twain told his friend, Elizabeth Wallace, "This book will never be published. In fact it couldn't be because it would be a felony."[6]

In these letters from Satan to the archangels, Mark Twain held nothing back. Among other assorted blasphemies, he called the Bible a compendium of "blood-drenched history... and a wealth of obscenity; and upwards of a thousand lies."[7] The book is self-consciously evil. The immoral, the irreverent, the blasphemous, or demonic, it is all fair game in this hell-forged tome. He even exhorted women to "the high privileges of unlimited adultery."[8] Harper and Brothers tried to publish the work in 1939, but the project was nixed by Twain's daughter Clara. Eventually, the book was published in 1962.[9] By this time, the sexual revolution was in full swing, and Mark Twain's brave, progressive views were well in step with the wider culture. Without question, he was a powerful influencer and a pioneer for the anti-Christian, anti-morality, anti-family agenda that dominates our world today. As a popular writer, he met his market. The Marquis de Sade was 200 years ahead with his moral perversions. But Mark Twain was the man of his age, the leader of the revolution, and an apostate of the Nephilim class.

---

4. Ibid. 77.
5. Mark Twain, *Autobiography of Mark Twain*, vol 1, (Los Angeles: University of California Press, 2010), 325.
6. Shelden, 383.
7. Mark Twain, *Letters from the Earth* (New York: Perennial Library, 1974), 20.
8. Ibid.
9. Shelden, 384.

He may have "gently" mocked Christian traditions in *Tom Sawyer* and *Huckleberry Finn* as some biographers put it, but Americans weren't ready for *Letters from the Earth* until the nation had grown up on *Huckleberry Finn*. Would Americans have wanted to believe that Mark Twain was a full-fledged apostate in 1909? As one biographer observed, Mark Twain "secretly compiled the texts that would fully declare his apostasy after his death."[10]

While exaggerating the power of Satan and rendering him omnipotence is antithetical to a Christian worldview, it would also be dangerous to minimize his power. If Christians do not recognize the work of Satan in men like Mark Twain, they will most likely be deceived by men. . .like Mark Twain. As Christians, we are not frightened, but we must take the evil words and works of an evil man seriously. If God takes it seriously, and if God's judgment will take it seriously, then we must take it seriously. Few Christian literature teachers and students know how to reprove "the unfruitful works of darkness" because they do not categorize them as "the unfruitful works of darkness" (Eph. 5:11). They fail to recognize the antithesis when they see it.

Mark Twain hated Christian missionaries especially. He supported the communist Nikolai Tchaikovsky, and publicly endorsed fund-raising campaigns for the Russian communist revolutions.[11] He told the New York World, "I sympathize with these Russian revolutionaries, and in common with some other people, I hope that they will succeed." As it turns out, they did succeed—by slaughtering of tens of millions of innocent people in Russia, not to mention the other communist pogroms in China, Vietnam, and Cambodia. It was the most thorough going persecution of the Christian church since the Roman days. No doubt Mark Twain would have been pleased with the success of the revolutions. [12] Before she died, his mother expressed regrets that he had lived beyond his childhood years.[13]

Mark Twain serves as a prototype for other literary apostates who took the world by storm in the 20th century. Doubtless, Ernest Hemingway and John Steinbeck wouldn't have minded the moniker. The tradition continues with men like Frank Schaeffer, who shocked the world in the

10. Ron Powers, *Mark Twain: A Life* (New York: Simon and Schuster, 2005), 31.
11. Ibid. 462, 463.
12. Twain, *Autobiography*, vol 1, 158.
13. Ibid, vol 1, 216.

early years of the 21st century with his vitriolic criticism of his parents' Christian faith and culture. After breaking ranks with the Christian reforming efforts of his father, the Christian-apologist Francis Schaeffer, Frank became one of the most outstanding apostates of the modern age. His books detailing his father's sins, his mother's sexuality, and his hatred for the "blasphemous God-of-the-Bible" market well with the growing audience of atheists, agnostics, apostates, and generally profane readers. Schaeffer takes Mark Twain's apostasy to a new level.[14]

In short, if you believe that God is real and Satan is real, then Mark Twain was a dangerous man. He may have been a talented writer, and he may have enthused hundreds of millions of people around the world, but he set a bad trajectory for himself and his readers during the great apostasy of the Western world. Mark Twain hated God, and he led the masses into apostasy. The apostate philosophers (covered in the first part of this book) wrote for the academics, but Mark Twain wrote for the masses, for the high school students, and for the ordinary citizens of America. It was the masses, the high school students, and the ordinary citizens who themselves would abandon the orthodox faith in the 19th and 20th centuries.

> *"Ye are of your father the devil, and the lusts of your father ye will do. He was a murderer from the beginning, and abode not in the truth, because there is no truth in him. When he speaketh a lie, he speaketh of his own: for he is a liar, and the father of it. And because I tell you the truth, ye believe Me not. Which of you convinceth Me of sin? And if I say the truth, why do ye not believe Me? He that is of God heareth God's words: ye therefore hear them not, because ye are not of God." (John 8:44-47).*

THE INCREDIBLE IMPACT OF ADVENTURES OF HUCKLEBERRY FINN

Mark Twain was the quintessential American author; he was arguably the most popular writer this country has ever produced. His book *Adventures of Huckleberry Finn* shows up on almost every list of the most important books of the last 200 years. Goodreads.com rates *Huckleberry*

---

14. Frank Schaeffer, *Sex, Mom, and God* (Philadelphia: Perseus Books, 2011), 29, 33, 83.

Finn as the second most important American novel of all time (second to Harper Lee's *To Kill a Mockingbird*). Wikipedia.com lists two 19th century novels in the list of "Great American Novels," and *Adventures of Huckleberry Finn* is included (along with Melville's *Moby Dick*). Recently, 125 of the most prominent modern authors provided lists of their favorite ten books of all time. The two American novels that made the top ten list were Fitzgerald's *The Great Gatsby* and Twain's *Adventures of Huckleberry Finn*.[15] It would be fair to say that no other American novel has had more influence on modern writers than this book. To understand what happened to the faith in the West, students of literature and history must understand something of the impact of Huckleberry Finn.

Adventures of Huckleberry Finn is an American classic. Ernest Hemingway said of this work that "all modern American literature stems from this one book." H.L. Mencken wrote on the discovery of this novel as "the most stupendous event of my whole life." This novel has won the hearts of millions of Americans... towards Mark Twain's strident agnosticism. It is impossible to miss the Huck's worldview if you're looking for it. Sadly, the book was written for adults and children alike, many of whom morphed into Mark Twain's worldview without even knowing it.

Mark Twain takes advantage of the uncritical mind and the biblically illiterate Christian. He knows how to construct complex ethical scenarios in order to tie the unwary Christian reader up in knots. The main character in the story, Huckleberry Finn, is presented as the likable, footloose and free, practical-minded American who is confused and turned off by the Christian caricatures he meets along the way. Virtually all of the characters in the story have their roots half buried in 1500 years of Western Christianity. Even the hucksters know enough Christianity to hold a revival service. But the Christians are all characterized with varying shades of hypocrisy and ignorance, and by the end of the tale, the overall taste for the Christian faith has pretty well soured.

Whereas Hawthorne mocked a certain form of Christianity, Mark Twain unashamedly bashes every single symbol and sacrament of the faith. His protagonist sees no need to atone for his guilt, whereas Hawthorne's Dimmesdale and Hester Prynne continued to exert the futile motions of self-atonement all the way to the end.

15. Lev Grossman, "The Ten Greatest Books of All Time," *Time Entertainment*, Jan. 15, 2007, <http://www.time.com/time/arts/article/0,8599,1578073,00.html> accessed on Mar. 26, 2013

SLAVERY

Mark Twain's first attack on the Christian faith is formidable. It is an historical, social, and moral argument, and it has won many converts over the years. It must be answered by thoughtful Christian apologists. When the Northern Unitarians won the war against the Southern Presbyterians and Baptists, the more "conservative" Southern churches were seen to have taken the "lower moral ground." The progressive humanists won the propaganda war in the 19th century, and they took advantage of an American public that was unwilling to think critically and biblically about these issues. Some of the Southern churches had tolerated slavery and attempted a biblical defense for it. They argued that the Apostle Paul did not categorically treat slavery as a sin in his letter to Philemon.

On the one hand, Paul does not condemn Philemon for owning slaves, and he is willing to return Onesimus, an escaped slave, to his master. However, this does not amount to a categorical approval of slavery. While he does sends Onesimus back, he also entreats Philemon to accept the young man "not now as a servant," but as a brother (Phil. 16). No doubt, this is not enough for the revolutionary spirit of the 19th century humanists. Paul did not endorse slave revolts in the Roman Empire. Instead, he chose a peaceful, brotherly approach to end the chattel slave problem one household at a time.

The roots of Southern slavery are important as well. What Mark Twain fails to mention is that Southern slavery was born out of the English and Spanish apostasy. The American church was always stronger in the North at the beginning of the nation's colonization. While the Puritans and Pilgrims were forming strong and healthy family economies in the North, the South was building plantations and feeding English mercantilism. It wasn't until the later 1700s that the evangelical gospel reached the South through George Whitfield, Samuel Davies, and others. At this point, however, the Southern economy was already steeped in a slave-based system.

WHAT THE BIBLE SAYS ABOUT SLAVERY

The question of slavery deserves an answer from biblical Christians. Regardless of nationality, skin color, or denominational background, Bible-believing Christians ought not to be ashamed of the Scriptures. They ought to be able to give an answer on this argument that has been used so effectively to dismantle the Christian faith in this country.

If we have rejected man's reason and still hold to Scripture as our epistemological and ethical authority, we cannot compromise on this point. First of all, without this ethical authority, we have no possibility of any ethical absolutes at all. We must argue our case for ethics on the basis of Scripture and nothing else. Thankfully, the Bible does have a great deal to say about slavery, and all of the data must be taken into account. Disingenuous, ignorant, and malicious opponents to the Christian faith will do their best to the undermine the faith by a mishandling of the Bible. They may favor one text over another or misinterpret certain texts. What follows is a fair handling of the corpus of biblical data concerning slavery in brief.

1. Kidnapping and enslaving another person is a capital crime in the Bible.

"And he that steals a man, and sells him, or if he is found in his hand, he shall surely be put to death" (Exod. 21:16).

This would have been enough to condemn the slave trade that ravaged Africa in the 18th and 19th centuries.

2. Sometimes, a nation may punish criminals (either those who violate the laws of the land or those who invade the country) by imposed slave labor. Even this form of slavery was subject to regulation by Old Testament law (Exod. 21:2-4).

This may come across as repulsive to the humanist, who has been carefully indoctrinated in the hopelessly defective ethical approach taken by the 19th century progressives and social gospel do-gooders. After their brave new experiment with humanist solutions, we can see the chaos that has ensued. The massive prison systems they have erected are not biblical, and they have proven themselves to be even more restrictive, cruel, and costly than slavery. They fragment the family, saddle the taxpayer with costs, and associate criminals with criminals in an unhealthy community. Besides this, it is an unbiblical form of punishment as defined by God's laws. Moreover, a fairly high percentage of those incarcerated are doing time for crimes that do not meet the biblical definition of crimes (although they probably meet the biblical definition of a sin).

This country has the highest incarceration rate in the world at 716 per 100,000 people.[16] Moreover, the incarceration rate for black men is seven times that of the rest of the population. The statistics are grim. . .one in ten young black men are in prison. "One in three African-American boys born in 2001 stands a lifetime risk of going to jail, according to the American Leadership Forum. In 2007, one in every 15 black children had a parent in prison." [17] In case one is tempted to think that criminal tendencies are determined by "skin color," there are plenty of examples of Africans living in other time periods and other places which would never substantiate this. While men are responsible for the sins they commit, much of the crime in America is a product of our social planning, our education, our welfare programs, our culture, our churches, our politics, and our economics. These are consequences of the humanist, socialist experiment of the last 150 years.

3. The Bible stands opposed to slavery in the same way that it opposes divorce and debt (another form of servitude) (1 Cor. 7:21-23, Rom. 13:8). Yet, Scripture is realistic. The life of slavery, debt, and divorce may be counter to God's design, but these things are inevitable in a sinful world. Shall Christians be content to live under these less-than-optimum conditions? The answer is multi dimensional. On the one hand, we reject the idea of a utopia or perfection on earth, and we will not attempt to achieve it by burning down banks, creating revolution, and refusing to pay off our loans. Paul does not advocate slave rebellions in 1 Corinthians 7:21-23. If one is called as a servant, Paul says he should be content in that state. However, if the opportunity for freedom presents itself, he should "use it rather." This applies to freedom from big government tyranny, debt, and any other forms of unnecessary servitude. If Jesus Christ proclaims a perpetual year of jubilee (Luke 4:16-21), then it is our responsibility to pursue this vision. We seek maximum freedom from the unnecessary servitude of men. As Jesus said, "If the Son will make you free, you will be free indeed!"

Paul concludes with, "You are bought with a price, be not the servant

16. http://en.wikipedia.org/wiki/List_of_countries_by_incarceration_rate
17. http://www.guardian.co.uk/commentisfree/2012/jan/15/jail-reflects-collapse-black-communities-us

of men." Evidently, Christ's blood pays for more than just the release from the bondage of sin and death. He delivers us from bondage to local fiefdoms and tyrannical governments as well. This is because slavery is a consequence of sin. America's founders understood this lesson well when men like Benjamin Franklin or William Penn would write, "Men who will not rule themselves will be ruled by tyrants." Without personal morality and self-government, men will always revert to some measure of servitude. If men and women will be delivered from sin, tyrannical inclinations, and failure to self-govern, this can only happen by the salvation provided in Jesus Christ.

> *"Thou shalt call His name Jesus, for He shall save His people from their sins" (Matt. 1:21).*

The kind of slavery we experience today is much larger in sheer numbers than that which Mark Twain accused the Southern churches of promoting. Throughout history, we have seen human society moving from decentralized fiefdoms (as in the slave plantations of the South) to large, centralized tyrannies. Governments control over 50% of the Gross National Income in most modern nations today, which means that most people have far less freedom now than they did in previous centuries. There is now six times as much government in their lives (when measured by government spending as a percentage of the GNI). There is about seven times more debt to banks (as a percentage of the GNI). There is also at least six times more "corporate" slavery - where corporations govern people's lives in coordination with powerful governments and their regulatory agencies. Although he may not recognize it, the average man is tied down by a thousand "Lilliputians." He becomes increasingly irrelevant to his family because the state owns his children and provides his wife with her own "benefits" package. As of the beginning of the 21st century, the majority of Americans receive aid from the government in the form of welfare or social security.[18] As humbling as it may be to admit, those on welfare are hardly different from the slaves on the plantations in the 18th and 19th centuries. Their needs are supplied by faceless masters, and their minds are manipulated and formed by government-

---

18. Annalyn Kurtz, "Majority of Americans Have Received Government Aid," *CNN Money*, Dec. 18, 2012 <http://money.cnn.com/2012/12/18/news/economy/government-entitlement-aid/index.html> accessed on Mar. 26, 2013

funded education. Sometimes they are forced to work, but often they try to avoid work. After several generations of this chattel slavery, the family is decimated, and record numbers are confined to another "plantation" called prisons.

These are the sad results of Mark Twain's glorious humanist vision. He blamed the sins of his nation upon "the system" and the "Christian faith," but he failed to properly understand the root problem with human nature. The problem is the heart. Unless the blood of Jesus Christ cleanses a nation—including its slave-master politicians, its prison inmates, its educators, and its families—that nation will endlessly oscillate from one form of slavery to another.

4. Christ's jubilee discontinues the cross-generational slavery of Leviticus 25:44-46. Thus, permanent slavery is unacceptable for *any* Christian society (1 Cor. 7:21-23). It is must therefore be the goal of every Christian leader to seek *more* freedom from governments, from banks, from corporations, and from bond-slavery to fiefdoms. This cannot happen by revolution. It must come about by regeneration of the hearts and lives of the masters and servants that hear the Word of God and the Resurrection message of Christ preached in the churches.

5. According to biblical law, no person may return an escaped slave to his master (Deut. 23:15,16). Since *Adventures of Huckleberry Finn* is centered around an escaped slave, this principle is critical to the story.

Mark Twain used slavery as a ruse to undermine the Christian faith, refusing to condemn the Southern form of slavery by biblical law. Meanwhile, the Southern socio-economic system prior to the Civil War similarly failed to submit to biblical law on several accounts. They refused to acknowledge Christ and His Jubilee and completely ignored 1 Cor. 7:21-23. Also, Southern slavery did not provide a legal foundation for slave marriages, which would have protected the families of the slaves. From the beginning, the black family in America was disadvantaged by the legal system. For example, the enslaved man could not pursue charges if somebody committed adultery with his wife. Moreover, the master could split up the family at will, and in such cases the child custody would always fall with the mother. These were bad seeds to plant for the future generations of precious children raised on these plantations. All of this violated the principle of God's law. Exodus 21:3ff clearly permits a married man reduced to indentured slavery to take his wife and children with him. Sadly, the same violations of God's law continue in our day unabated. Humanist slave-based systems in the form of prisons and welfare programs still divide up families and unravel the social unit. Both prisons and welfare systems are to blame for the ongoing disruption of families in America (to include African-Americans).

The church must take something of the blame for the injustices (the violations of God's law) committed by the nation in the 19th and 20th centuries. On all sides of the slavery debate, there was very little application of God's law after the turn of the 18th century. For some reason, the Bible was reduced to an "evangelical" use, and Christ's commission was hardly employed (Matt. 28:18-20). As churches teach the death and resurrection of Christ, they are supposed to teach their people to "observe all things whatsoever Christ has commanded." This involves passages like Matthew 5:17-19 and Matthew 15:4, 5. While it is true the New England Puritans were somewhat better rooted in a biblical worldview and biblical ethics, this was soon to disappear in 1700s and 1800s. There was little preaching on the laws of God after the first Great Awakening. Revivals were all about "getting people saved" in one-time emotional experiences, and there was little discipleship in the vein of Matthew 28:18-20.

Nevertheless, Mark Twain wasn't interested in discovering what the Bible really said about slavery or anything else. At heart, he was a humanist. It was already a decided fact in his mind. So he took advantage of a weakened faith, created more straw men, and proceeded to take it apart piece by piece, all the while presenting his "better ethical system" to the world. All humanists are moralists at heart. They loudly claim that their own cheap moral agendas will produce more good in the world than the old Christian order. Of course, just the opposite happens.

In *Huckleberry Finn*, Mark Twain puts Huck solidly between the horns of a dilemma. Either he must support slavery or oppose the Christian God and go to hell. At first, Huck thinks he should turn over his escaped slave friend, Jim, to the authorities; but then he decides against it (Chapter 31). In this pivotal scene from the book, Twain depicts the American-Christian God as some pro-slavery villain who would have Huck surrender his friendship for the cause of slavery. The utter disgust

Mark Twain held for the Christian God is inescapable.

HUCKLEBERRY FINN

Mark Twain endears us to the hero of the story, Huckleberry Finn, mainly by his use of humor. Of course, Huck's commitment to help Jim with his escape from slavery wins the hearts of the readers. As Huck adamantly rejects thin-coated, hypocritical Christianity, the reader will almost inevitably want to take his side. By the end of the story, we get the message loud and clear: Huck is a good old boy, and Christians are stupid. As is typical with the individualized American religion, Huck makes up his religion as he goes along. His religion is sometimes dualistic (he believes in a good god and a bad god) and sometimes agnostic. As the story plays out, Huck is particularly given to the sins of cursing, blasphemy, dishonor of parents, cross-dressing, stealing, and lying.

Perhaps the most appalling part of Huck's character is his readiness to break God's law without regret. His forthright disobedience of God's law, his apparent lack of conscience, and his audacious rebellion against God was impressive to 19th century readers. This was how our nation lost its respect for God's law and God's judgment. Of course, the stars of today's world break God's law with abandon, but before any of these celebrities showed up there was Huck Finn. People emulate their heroes. When the humanist cultural power centers manufactures heroes that exemplify godless, immoral lifestyles, hundreds of millions of people will follow them. Huck is such a hero. Today, the cultural machine cranks out the new heroes every year or two, including some familiar names as Michael Jackson, Eminem, Hannah Montana, Katy Perry, Carrie Underwood, and Taylor Swift. Some of these stars start out with a little respect for Christianity, but they quickly demonstrate their true commitments. They began selling teens on homosexuality, serial fornicating hook-ups, and other assorted iniquities. These cultural icons dominate the minds and hearts of the masses. They are the hero gods of the current age and their influence is impressive.

Within the first couple pages of the book, Huck mocks the idea of God's judgment and the Christian doctine of hell when he tells Miss Watson that he wishes he was in hell. No wonder H.L. Mencken and Ernest Hemingway were so appreciative of this groundbreaking work. To put this in historical perspective, neither Shakespeare nor Hawthorne openly mocked the idea of God's judgment. Hester Prynne was less concerned about God's judgment than Lady Macbeth, but she wasn't going to mock it in 1850. But by the 1890s, the Western world was well prepared to rid themselves of this fear of God business - that is, the beginning of wisdom (Proverbs 1:7; 9:8). The fear of God was quickly fading from the American mind.

From Chapter 28, the story turns downright grim. Here Huck shrugs off Mary Jane's prayers, comparing prayers for him to something like praying for Judas Iscariot. Then in Chapter 31, Huck makes the fateful commitment to remain wicked and "go to hell." All in all, this makes for a rather unhappy story, when we realize that we are actually visiting with "the Man in the Iron Cage."[19] At this point, the story is no longer entertaining. We cannot fellowship with the character, but shall we pity him? Shall we weep over him? Certainly it is hard to laugh while he works his merry way through the gates of hell. At the least, we hope that the readers of this dreadful story will not identify with Huckleberry Binn in his skepticism. Alas, that is typically not the case in American high schools and colleges.

Of course, Huck must deal a little with his conscience in this story. He dislikes his conscience because he thinks it is irrational. "Whether you do right or wrong, it still attacks you," he complains. In the end, Huck settles for pragmatism as the best ethical course. He says, "I don't care about the morality of it" (Chapter 36). Both Huck and Tom agree that the ends will justify all means to accomplish the goals they have in mind. For these boys, the means usually involve a fair amount of stealing and lying. Despite a little guilt, Huck refuses to find redemption in Christ. As in *The Scarlet Letter*, we find that the Person of Christ is conspicuously missing from this story, though it repeatedly mentions Christians, the Bible, God, heaven, and hell. In the end, Huck is redeemed by abandoning his conscience (as well as any "traditional" or biblical morality) altogether. Thus he is free to make up his morals as he goes along.

The other characters in the story take on different "religious" perspectives. Tom Sawyer believes the Bible is a bunch of fairy tales (Chapter 3). Mary Jane is the most genuine believer in the story, though still misguided in Huck's perspective (Chapter 28). Uncle Silas and Aunt

---

19. Refer to the character in John Bunyan's *Pilgrim's Progress*, who was convinced he was going to hell, and could not be persuaded otherwise.

Sally are well-meaning Christians who support slavery and de-humanize the African-American with their language by referring to him as something less than human (Chapter 32). Huck's father is an unbeliever, an abusive drunk, and a scofflaw. Huck's friend, Jim, practises a religion that mixes pagan animism and Christianity. But the Christian family that best represents the historical American family is the Grangerford family (Chapters 17 and 18). Huck meets this family on his way down the Mississippi river. They are presented as church members. Their home library consists of the Bible, Pilgrim's Progress, and a Hymnal. This "nice" Christian family attends church on Sunday morning, and then they murder people on Sunday afternoon. Despite the fact that the old matriarch spends most of the day reading the Bible, this family engages in murderous activities on a regular basis. If Mark Twain truly believes the Bible is a repository of a "blood-drenched history" and a "wealth of obscenity," then the Grangerford family activities were truly inspired by these Scriptures. I guess this was all very consistent to the apostate mind of Mark Twain.

Fittingly, the story ends with: "Yours truly, Huck Finn." There is a dark irony contained in these last words. Throughout the story, Huck has proven himself to be the consummate liar, and he justifies his lying. He makes up new stories for just about every single person he meets. By the end of the account, there is no way to know whether Huck has just pulled the wool over the eyes of the reader as well as everybody else in the story. Of course, the story is fictional but what about the story behind the story? At the beginning of the novel, Mark Twain opens with these words, "This book was made by Mark Twain, and he told the truth, mainly." But if the story justifies lying for the protagonist, what can we say for the author? What about the worldview behind the fictional story? What about the mockery of Christianity or the agnosticism of Huck? *Was all this true, mainly?* Or does Mark Twain prevaricate, equivocate, fabricate, and calumniate as much as Huck lies? Mark Twain may have been a great writer, but he was also an expert liar. Pilate asked a very important, fundamental question at the trial of Lord Jesus Christ. "What is truth?" Mark Twain abandoned the only possible source for an absolute truth— divine revelation. Without the truth of God's Word, we are forever lost in a snowstorm in Antarctica when it comes to discerning what is true and what is false. When Mark Twain gave up this truth, all he could do was play with lies. That is what he did... and he was good at it.

> *"Now the Spirit speaketh expressly, that in the latter times some shall depart from the faith, giving heed to seducing spirits, and doctrines of devils; speaking lies in hypocrisy; having their conscience seared with a hot iron." (1 Tim. 4:1,2).*

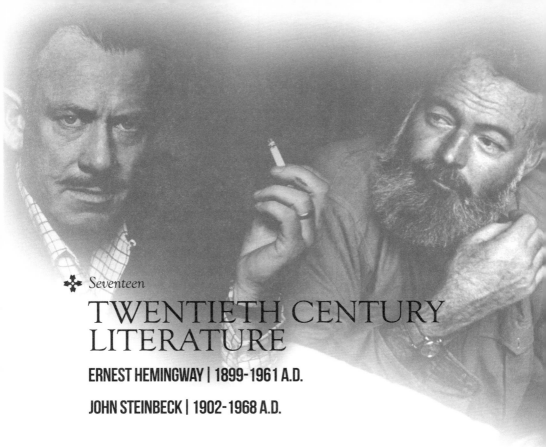

Seventeen

TWENTIETH CENTURY LITERATURE

ERNEST HEMINGWAY | 1899-1961 A.D.

JOHN STEINBECK | 1902-1968 A.D.

T he next and final stage in the decline of Western civilization comes in the 20th century. By the 1930s, the humanists and progressives (epistemologically-self-conscious humanists) had gained almost complete control over the major universities, John Dewey's public school system, and the mainline churches. There were a few dusty old theologians still holding desperately to historical orthodoxy—men like J. Gresham Machen who broke from the Northern Presbyterian Church in the 1930s to form a new denomination, a marginalized Orthodox Presbyterian Church. It wasn't that every writer and thinker in England and America was corrupted by the ideas of the Renaissance and the Enlightenment, but at this point, the victors had been laureled and the anthems were playing. The winners—the intellectual elite, the avant-garde, the cultural leaders—were the apostates. They were self-consciously anti-Christian if "Christian" had anything to do with the faith taught by the Apostles, Polycarp, the Didache, Augustine, Martin Luther, and John

Calvin. Church attendance was cultural, not religious. For the most part, the mainline denominations had little to do with advocating a Christian worldview.

As the 20th century progressed, the sun finally did set on the English empire, and another world power with a strong centralized government took its place - The United States. She was the last in the series of Western empires or powerful states. This country provided the cultural, social, and economic energy to propel the entire Western world through a good part of the 20th century. Great empires always call for great literary work, and America provided that literature by way of Nathaniel Hawthorne, Mark Twain, Ernest Hemingway, and John Steinbeck. As Mark Twain passed from the scene and Hemingway matured into adulthood, America was coming to full strength as the most powerful and the most prosperous nation the world had ever seen. These leading literary figures incarnated the worldview of this rising nation in their literature. They defined the curriculum, the universities, and the national culture. At the height of the nation's glory, as these authors reached the apex of their own pursuit of fame, they planted the seeds of destruction.

Modern literature represents an increasingly aggressive opposition to God and His law-order. Through the 20th century and well into the 21st century, their godless ideas filtered into the wider culture. Initially however, the target market was the literate and the educated world. If a civilization will collapse, it is the pillars of the social order that must come down first. As should be expected, recent surveys indicate that 87% of college professors call themselves "liberal," 70% support homosexuality, and 80% support abortion on demand. Not surprisingly, the Literature Department and the Religious Studies Department represent *the most liberal* elements of the universities according to these surveys.[1] The universities produce the acidic solvents necessary for the dissolution of the pillars of society - the future political, business, and academic leadership. Eventually, the super structure comes down, but only after the corrosive ideas work their way into the mass culture (which is the subject of the next chapter). For now, a right interpretation of the literature of the 1940s and 1950s is key to recognizing the destructive ideas that are infecting the popular culture in the 21st century.

---

1. http://www.washingtonpost.com/wp-dyn/articles/A8427-2005Mar28.html (Downloaded March 26, 2013). College Faculties A Most Liberal Lot, Study Finds, By Howard Kurtz.

It is hard to recommend any of the literature produced in the 20th century for the Christian literature student. Most of the "best" literature used in high school and college classrooms is virulently anti-Christian, nihilistic, suicidal, and hopeless. It is perverse on the face of it - the language is defiling. If the readers come too close, they will find themselves in fellowship with the "unfruitful works of darkness" (Eph. 5:11). This introduces a catch-22 of sorts. On the one hand, well-crafted literature requires close communion in order to understand the content and fully appreciate its emotional tones and its several layers of thought. As it turns out, the devil is a good writer, and ungodly men often produce excellent literature in form. How then does the literature student properly engage the material without this close fellowship? It is appropriate for the "men of Issachar" to strive to "understand the times" and do battle with those ideas that corrupt the world (1 Chron. 12:32, 2 Cor. 10:4,5). On the other hand, the Christian reader must keep the ideas at arm's length, so as not to commune with the unfruitful works of darkness, or meditate long and hard on things that are *not* true, *not* lovely, and *not* pure (Phil. 4:8).

Moreover, it is also very difficult to identify the *most significant* American and English writers of the 20th century. There were only minor differences betwen them in terms of their worldview perspective and influence. The "greats," F. Scott Fitzgerald, John Steinbeck, Ernest Hemingway, and J.D. Salinger were all committed to set a destructive course in their writings. The literary expression was fragmented, chaotic, and directionless. *When* they communicated clearly, they wrote of suicide, isolation, drunkenness, apostasy, fornication, mental illness, and profanity. All of them did a fine job depicting life without God in a post-Christian world. When they attempted to write of redemption, their scribblings were half-hearted and ill-fated. There were a few exceptions of course. Occasionally, a Christian peeled away from the destructive course to set a different trajectory,[2] but Christians don't win Nobel Prizes from apostate institutions.

In this survey, we are tracking the trajectory of an entire civilization. We are following the flow of the river of Western civilization all the way downstream and over the Niagara Falls into oblivion. While we are thankful for the occasional diverting stream that was provided by Christian thinkers and writers, the mission of this book is to chronicle the decline

2. T.S. Eliot, C.S. Lewis, and J.R.R. Tolkien may serve as examples.

APOSTATE

of the main course of the "river" of the Western world. It is important that our children and grandchildren understand what happened in the 19th and 20th centuries to bring about the collapse of a civilization.

PAVING THE WAY FOR CULTURAL SUICIDE
ERNEST HEMINGWAY (1899-1961)

Thus far in the developing saga of humanism, we have come across apostates of all stripes, including Roman Catholics, Lutherans, Anglicans, Congregationalists, and Presbyterians. In this "cross-denominational" apostasy, all of the apostates featured up to this point belonged to sects of Christianity with roots in Western Europe. Throughout the 19th century, however, America developed a new breed of Christianity that was highly individualized, relatively conservative in doctrine, aggressively evangelistic, and barely ecclesiastical. They called themselves "evangelicals," and much of the movement had its roots in the evangelistic campaigns of Charles Finney and Dwight L. Moody. While some of those who were converted in revival services did hang on for dear life to the faith, apostasy came easily for their children. The generational roots never ran very deep in this sect of the Christian faith.

The famous 20th century American author Ernest Hemingway, was born into one of these evangelical Christian families on July 21, 1899. His maternal grandfather was a friend of Dwight L. Moody and a graduate of Wheaton College, the evangelical "mothership" of a new breed of Christian colleges. Ernest's father's brother served as a medical missionary.

His was a typical raising in evangelicalism. Ernest's parents stocked his shelves with G.A. Henty tales. His father took him to a dinosaur dig, reminding his son that God had created the world in six days. Hemingway's sister later recalled, "We had morning family prayers accompanied by a Bible reading and a hymn or two."[3] His family conscientiously applied the rod of discipline and corrected foul language in their home by washing the children's mouth with soap. These were familiar experiences for many evangelical children raised in American homes during the first half of the 20th century.

When Ernest was eight years old, his father wrote him a tender note:

3. Madeleine Hemingway Miller, *Ernie* (Holt: Thunder Bay Press, 1975), 92.

"Your Daddy loves you and prays that you may be spared many years to praise God and help your parents and sister and others about you." On his 16th birthday, his father wrote similarly encouraging words: "I am so pleased and proud you have grown to be such a fine big manly fellow and will trust your development will continue symmetrical and in harmony with our highest Christian ideals... I want you to represent all that is good and noble and brave and courteous in Manhood, and fear God and respect women."[4] Alas, his father's vision was not to be.

While still in his teen years, Ernest Hemingway produced several shockingly pornographic stories, pouring out a torrent of foul language previously unheard of in American literature.[5] He was a true pioneer in sexually decadent expression from the beginning of his writing career. His apostasy is quite different than what we find with Charles Darwin, Nathaniel Hemingway, or even John Dewey. His rebellion comes across as radical, pathological, even dangerous or sinister. As far as biographers can discern, he never felt any pangs of guilt whatsoever about his twisted thoughts and expressions, no second thoughts. This apostate plotted his course early in his life and never looked back. At 18 years old, he was done with church although he still insisted to his mother that he was a "good Christian."[6] His life henceforth was filled with fornication, adultery, and divorce. He toyed with homosexuality. Throughout his lifetime, he routinely took God's name in vain and seemed to specialize in abusing the name of Jesus Christ. Most of the agnostics and atheists of the 19th century were never so daring as to employ the kind of abusive and blasphemous language commonly used in the 20th century. By this time, the brave Nephilim were pretty well convinced that God was nothing to be concerned with, or He would never act on His warnings.

> *"Thou shalt not take the name of the Lord thy God in vain, for the Lord will not hold him guiltless that taketh His name in vain" (Exodus 20:10).*

Another unique characteristic of Hemingway's rebellion is found in his patricidal rebellion. This took the modern apostasy to a whole new

4. James R. Mellow, *Hemingway, A Life Without Consequences* (New York: Houghlin Mifflin, 1992), 12.
5. Ibid. 53.
6. Ibid. 47.

level. He hated his father. On one occasion as a young man, he leveled a gun at his father and sighted the weapon on his head. He came just short of pulling the trigger.[7] At 21 years old, he crossed another line and cursed his mother.[8] Based upon her comments recorded in various letters and diary entries, it is clear that she was appalled by her son's behavior. She was concerned that he was corrupting the other youth with "general lawlessness" and "deceit,"[9] which, judging from the nature of his writing, at the time, was a reasonably accurate accusation. His parents called him "cruel," "abusive," and "threatening." Here was a true Matthew 15:4 case materializing.

> "But [Jesus] answered and said unto them, 'Why do ye also transgress the commandment of God by your tradition? For God commanded, saying, Honour thy father and mother: and, He that curseth father or mother, let him die the death'" (Matt.15:3, 4).

Whether or not the civil punishment is warranted, the general principle must not be missed. Jesus Christ takes the Fifth Commandment very seriously, and He strongly underscores the egregiousness of Hemingway's crimes. When a young man takes it this far, he walks over a very big line, and the repercussions upon society will be significant.

In her letters to him, Ernest's mother issued strong warnings: "Unless you, my son, Ernest come to yourself, cease your lazy loafing and pleasure seeking—borrowing with no thought of returning... stop trading on your handsome face, to fool little gullible girls, and neglecting your duties to God and your Savior, Jesus Christ—unless, in other words, you come into your manhood, there is nothing before you but bankruptcy: you have over drawn."[10] She referred to his writings as "filth." To the end of her life, she never ceased imploring him: "I have never lost hope for you, nor ceased to pray that the Great Awakening will come to you, before this life closes."[11]

However, his relationship with his mother never repaired; it just seemed to get worse. As a 50 year old man (in 1949), he referred to his

7. Ibid. 40.
8. Ibid.119.
9. Ibid. 119.
10. Ibid. 120.
11. Ibid. 546.

mother as a female dog and publicly stated, "I hate her guts."[12] When she died, he refused to attend her funeral. Could Hemingway have been the exemplar for the Matthew 15:4 scenario described by Christ? Here was a violent, angry man who cursed his father and mother, and then joined the Nephilim class of the literary giants.

The damage that a man of this social stature can do is extensive. For any child born into a family, the most fundamental relationship from the beginning will be the parent-child relationship. When all respect for parents is eliminated, and the Fifth Commandment is violated without restraint, the social repurcussions are usually devastating as is pointed out in Proverbs 30:11-14:

> "There is a generation that curseth their father, and doth not bless their mother. There is a generation that are pure in their own eyes, and yet is not washed from their filthiness. There is a generation, O how lofty are their eyes! and their eyelids are lifted up. There is a generation, whose teeth are as swords, and their jaw teeth as knives, to devour the poor from off the earth, and the needy from among men."

Ernest Hemingway received something of a Christian heritage and character but used it to foul ends. He stands at the head of a long line of apostate "celebrities" that produce the popular literature and popular music of the day, who continue in the same vein.[13] Over the last one hundred years, millions of children raised in similar Christian homes have peeled off into apostasy, and Hemingway was the prototypical apostate that they followed. Recently, the Southern Baptist denomination reports that a full 88% of children raised in Christian families leave the church as soon as they leave the home.[14] Ernest Hemingway showed them how.

Breaking the Fifth Commandment is the heart and soul of a cultural and social revolution, and it is usually the requisite ingredient for bloody, political revolutions as well. It is the undoing of a civilization. The only thing that keeps social systems together is the honor of parents and grandparents. Even pagan societies understood this principle. Without

12. Ibid. 565.
13. Chapter 18 will provide many examples of this popular apostasy.
14. Jon Walker, "Family Life Council Says It's Time to Bring Family Back to Life," *2002 SBC Annual Meeting,* Jun. 12, 2002, <http://www.sbcannualmeeting.net/sbc02/newsroom/newspage. asp?ID=261> accessed on Mar. 28, 2013

some respect for the good traditions and cultural expressions passed on from previous generations, societies disintegrate and civilizations die out. Since Hemingway and Sartre, this respect has all but dissipated. From hence comes the rock rebels of the 1960s and 1970s, Eminem's "rape rap" (2000s), the drug culture (1960s), the dating culture (1950s-1960s), the shack-ups (1970s-1990s), the hook-ups (2000s-2020s), fatherlessness (1980s-2020s), the huge rise in homosexuality (1980s-2020s), 80 million abortions (1960s-2020s), and the 80 million elderly soon to be euthanized (2020s-2050s).

These are the seeds of teenage rebellion, now common in modern life. Teenage culture was still "in utero" between 1880 and 1946. According to sociologists who have studied modern teen culture, the "new adolescent" came of age on October 12, 1943 when 30,000 frenzied girls swarmed into Times Square in New York to meet their new pop idol, Frank Sinatra.[15] Father-daughter and father-son relationships hardly play a part in modern society and culture. The modern world has experienced a social revolution unlike anything seen over 5,900 years, and the parent-child relationship lies at the root of it. Always, the social revolution yields cultural revolution - they are intimately connected. Generally, the youth today are expected to reject whatever decent cultural expressions were conserved by their parents. With each generation, the youth must revolt against the previous generation in moral standards, music standards, dress standards, and language.

Hemingway's generation represented a shift from the previous apostasy of the 18th and 19th centuries. With John Locke, Charles Darwin, or Nathaniel Hawthorne, we find a gradual move away from the Christian world and life view while they did retain some remnants of Christian culture and morality. However, the 20th century brought about the large-scale political, cultural, social, and moral revolutions that had already taken place in the hearts of Karl Marx, Jeremy Bentham, John Dewey, and Charles Darwin. Thus, the apostasy is more sudden and radical. The apostasy has metastasized.

These cultural revolutions cannot build up a civilization. Quite the contrary, they are finishing off Western civilization. Already, the cultural and moral revolutions have destroyed much of what little Christian capital and character is left in the West. At this point, there is hardly

---

15. Jon Savage, *Teenage: The Creation of Youth Culture* (New York: Viking, 2007), 442.

any faith left from which to apostatize. Humanist man is coming into his own. He is discovering his self-consistencies and expressing them in pop culture. He doesn't see a need to borrow from Christian foundations anymore. Now he will reject *all* absolutes, *all* Christian morality, and *all* Christian social moorings. Finally, he will abandon all possibility for a transcendent purpose in life and society. That is when modern man loses the will to carry on his civilizations. In this way the rotting epistemological foundations will always ruin the empires upon which they are built.

HEMINGWAY'S WRITINGS

As would be expected from any apostate locked in Bunyan's iron cage,[16] Ernest Hemingway's stories are hopeless. They reflect a metaphysic that disallows all meaning and purpose to life and death. One modern writer, Russell Banks, defines a Hemingway protagonist as a "sort of existential hero" who reflects the "romantic alienation that [Hemingway himself] seemed to be emblematic of and that he manifested in his style as well." The modern hero is a vagabond, alone in the cold, empty world of post-modern existentialism. The modern hero is lonely because he killed relationship. This was Cain.

Professor Ganesan Balakrishnan, PhD, sums up Hemingway's writings in this way:

> *"Hemingway, in his novels and short stories, presents human life as a perpetual struggle which ends only in death. It is of no avail to fight this battle, where man is reduced to a pathetic figure by forces both within and without. However, what matters is the way man faces the crisis and endures the pain inflicted upon him by the hostile powers that be, be it his own physical limitation or the hostility of society or the indifference of unfeeling nature."*[17]

Hemingway's work represents a crossing over of the "line of despair"[18] for the modern humanist. During the age of Descartes and Locke, man was still optimistic in his attempts to define himself, his reality, his truth, and his ethics on his own terms. By the 20th century, popular literary

16. John Bunyan's *Pilgrim's Progress*
17. http://www.literature-study-online.com/essays/hemingway.html
18. The "line of despair" is a phrase used by the eminent 20th century Christian philosopher and historian, Francis Schaeffer.

figures like Hemingway and Steinbeck had capitulated to humanist pessimism and suicidal nihilism. On Sunday morning, July 2, 1961, Ernest Hemingway slipped two cartridges into his twelve-gauge Boss Shotgun and ended his own life by suicide. Thirty-five years later, on July 1, 1996, his granddaughter Marguaux Hemingway committed suicide in Santa Monica, California. She was "the fifth person in four generations of her family to commit suicide."[19]

Hemingway was a critical player in this chronicle of the decline of the West because he lived and died consistently to his worldview. He lived a dissipated, godless life, and then he committed suicide at the end.

"I the LORD thy God am a jealous God, visiting the iniquity of the fathers upon the children unto the third and fourth generation of them that hate me" (Exod. 20:5).

ERNEST HEMMINGWAY - THE OLD MAN AND THE SEA

The Old Man and the Sea won Hemingway the 1953 Pulitzer Prize for Fiction and it probably clinched him the Nobel Prize in 1954, as it was cited for special recognition by the Nobel Academy. It was also the last novel published in his lifetime. The story is set in Cuba, representing something of the old Christian order inherited from Spain. In Hemingway's world the Christian heritage had all-but faded, however he could not escape that reality entirely.

The Old Man and the Sea is the story of an old fisherman who is enthralled with the notoriety and ability of Joe DiMaggio, a famous baseball player. The old man wants to make a name for himself even as DiMaggio made a name for himself in baseball. After a long, unsuccessful interval in his fishing enterprise, he launches out into the deep water and hooks the biggest marlin of his life. Over a period of five long days he fights the marlin, secures him to the boat, and works his way back to land. The old fisherman is a stubborn man, and we are told he once engaged in an arm-wrestling match for 24-hours straight. Of course, the story speaks about

19. "Coroner Says Death of Actress Was Suicide," August 21, 1996, *The New York Times* <http:// www.nytimes.com/1996/08/21/us/coroner-says-death-of-actress-was-suicide.html> accessed May 14, 2012

more than the "character" of the man. His humanist ideology is clearly explained when the fisherman claims that man is not made for defeat. He says, "A man can be destroyed, but not defeated." That is, a man lives his life to the fullest when he fights to the bloody end. According to Hemingway's hero, the purpose of life is to attempt to strive for mastery over the environmental forces that surround the man, despite the fact that such efforts always prove to be a lost cause. Man always dies in the end.

All of this completely contradicts a biblical teleology. From 1 Corinthians 10:31 and other texts, we know that we are here to glorify God and enjoy Him forever. We do not seek our own fame and our kingdoms; rather we are here to seek the kingdom of God and His righteousness (Matt. 6:33).

For the Christian however, battle is not an unfamiliar motif. We wrestle with enduring courage, but we do not battle against brute forces and impersonal causes. Our opponent is not the material universe - it is not flesh and blood (Eph. 6:12). We are in a spiritual battle against the world, the flesh, and the devil. There is more to life than the natural, physical world. There is the supernatural and the spiritual. Therefore, the stakes are much higher for us than for the old fisherman, as we battle in God's arena. It is a glorious battle and there is eternal value for the combatants who take the side of the Kingdom. The battle is intensely meaningful because there is a personal God in sovereign control of the universe, and the outcome is determined in a secondary sense by our performance in the battle. Our strength comes from God, and yet we struggle with all of our might out of sheer love for God in the conflict. Though our faces drip with blood and our hands are chafed to the bone, there is joy in the battle and hope in our hearts as we fix our eyes on the day of consummation when the battle will be won. Then our great Captain will greet us at the gates of the heavenly Kingdom with the words, "Well done, thou good and faithful servant!" This is what renders the Christian life true meaning and eternal purpose. What a contrast to the empty nihilism contained in the worldview of a man who committed suicide!

Throughout the story, the old fisherman identifies with stars and lions. Of course, these are the most powerful forces in the universe, and the fisherman imagines himself "killing the stars." This story may be the most vivid representation of Nietzsche's "Will to Power" to be found in modern literature. Despite the fisherman's references to luck and fortune throughout the tale, he is caught between indeterminate brute forces and his futile desire to control these forces. Hemingway's metaphysic cannot help but admit to a meaningless universe filled with indeterminate forces. Somehow he wants to believe there is still value in fighting these forces, but in the end he has to admit that all is meaningless and futile.

Hemingway's worldview is self-contradictory. As with Nietzsche, he struggles to identify a fragment of a purpose in life. Desperately, he wants to find honor and value in the struggle against the forces of the material universe. He wants to argue for a purpose in life, but his universe is indeterminate and material. There is no possibility of purpose in a purposeless universe.

Atheism is a "given" in this tale. Hemingway doesn't bother taking the time to mock the God of the Bible as Mark Twain did a generation earlier. He doesn't feel the need to toy with guilt as Hawthorne would. He mentions sin once, but quickly dispenses with it. Towards the end of the story, the younger man (the old fisherman's protégé), commits to disobeying his parents at the old man's insistence. But it is of little consequence in the narrative. What is more significant is that the young man leaves his parents' world to subscribe to the worldview advocated by the fisherman.

Unlike Nathaniel Hawthorne or William Shakespeare, Hemingway makes no allowance for God's providence, God's judgment, human guilt, or the eternality of the soul. God is dead, as far as he is concerned.

It is also abundantly clear that Hemingway has no confidence in the resurrection. For the Christian, the resurrection of Christ and the future resurrection of the body is essential to the faith. But for Hemingway death is the end, and hope plays no part in his life motivation. This is the message he sent home, when he sent a shotgun slug through his own brain. Among the fisherman's musings, we learn that everything dies, including the stars and the moon. A person is only matter in motion that changes form from time to time (when that person dies.) Also, Hemingway's worldview pits the individual against everything else in the world. It is a worldview without God, and a world without other people.

In terms of his writing method, Hemingway's stories come across as if they are written in a trance. The words ring hollow and monotonous, and the reader feels as if all the characters in the story are hermetically sealed up in their own little jar. Of course, this accommodates the alienation of post-modern man. When man rejects God, he rejects reality. If God isn't real, nothing is real. As a real, live Christian reads post-modern literature, he will find himself fighting the author's form every inch of the way. For the Christian's reality includes the ultimate reality and that is God Himself. This author and the characters in his story may be fading into a dream for now, but we will not allow this to destroy our conception of true reality.

JOHN STEINBECK (1902-1968)

John Steinbeck did not commit suicide, as Hemingway did, but he was the first of the great Nephilim to murder his own child. His life bore striking similarities to Hemingway's in many regards. As with most of the rest of the philosophers and literary men, he was born into a family with a strong Christian heritage. His grandfather was a deeply devout Christian (a Lutheran), and his grandfather's brother was martyred for the faith while serving as a missionary in Palestine.[20] As far as we know, John's parents were faithful members of the church in Salinas, California their whole lives. His mother encouraged him to be involved in the church, but from the beginning he resisted her appeals.[21] As a college student, he was a drunk and a sexual libertine.[22] Biographer Jay Parini writes, "He seems to have made a conscious point of straying from the narrow path his parents had laid down for him."[23] Teen rebellion was already the defining spirit of the 20th century and both Hemingway and Steinbeck were out in front of the crowd.

By his 18th year, John Steinbeck's hatred for the Christian faith was manifest to all who knew him. On one particularly momentous occasion, he rudely interrupted a Christmas church service, announcing to those with him that the message was a "lot of [manure]." Then he screamed at the congregation, calling them a bunch of hypocrites and stomped out of the church.[24] Later in his 20s, John attempted to rape and murder a

20. Jay Parini, *John Steinbeck: A Biography* (New York: Henry Holt, 1995), 6.
21. Ibid. 12.
22. Ibid. 24, 25.
23. Ibid. 25.
24. Ibid. 29.

young girl named Polly Smith while he was drunk.[25]

John Steinbeck took his apostasy seriously. It was his task to lead the Western world into adultery, divorce, and abortion. Shortly after the publication of *Grapes of Wrath*, 33 years before the American nation approved convenience abortion by a Supreme Court decision, this mighty cultural leader forced his wife Carol to abort their first child.[26] She never recovered from the tragic event, and remained sterile for the rest of her life. Meanwhile John conducted his affairs and eventually divorced poor afflicted Carol for another woman. His new marriage was interrupted with more affairs and another divorce.

John Steinbeck appears to be the first of the cultural and philosophical leaders who deliberately aborted a child. While Jean-Jacques Rousseau did not quite kill his children, and Karl Marx's children committed suicide, there are still some common threads. For example, Rousseau dispensed with his children because he was concerned that he could not "achieve the tranquility of mind necessary for my work my garret filled with domestic cares and the noise of children." Steinbeck aired similar concerns. According to Biographer Parini, "Steinbeck was afraid that fatherhood would interfere with his writing."[27]

This single abortion may not sound all that significant after a third of all American babies conceived since 1960 have been aborted through surgical abortions, day-after pills, and the abortifacient birth control pills. Nevertheless, societies really do act as corporeal units and their visionary cultural leaders are important. That is what makes these stories so significant. Granted, John Steinbeck was not the only leader in the cultural revolution, but he was an important leader. Should a lone prostitute abort a child in a slum in New York City, the consequences no doubt are tragic. But this can hardly be compared to the social repercussions that come about when a major cultural leader (whose work influences millions of people), steps over the same line. One man's actions are important. They impact more people than we can imagine.

Since 1960, the accessibility of abortion and the pill exploded. Over a billion babies have been aborted worldwide in the last sixty years. With birth rates for 59 countries around the world falling under replacement

25. Ibid. 73.
26. Ibid. 227.
27. Ibid. 227.

levels (about half the globe), [28] we are looking at the largest worldwide demographic shift since the Genesis Flood. This is Nephilim work. Of course, Jean-Paul Sartre takes responsibility for the pro-choice, existentialist philosophy that undergirds much of it. But what about Ernest Hemingway[29], John Steinbeck, Margaret Sanger, Havelock Ellis, and Margaret Mead? These were the cultural leaders that made the headlines in the 1930s, 1940s, and 1950s. If there is anything we have learned in these biographical analyses, it is that the lives of these men are as important as their writings. One person's choice to abort a child may effect the lives of millions, even billions, especially if he bears the influence of the Nephilim class.

> *Why standest thou afar off, O LORD? why hidest thou thyself in times of trouble? The wicked in his pride doth persecute the poor: let them be taken in the devices that they have imagined. For the wicked boasteth of his heart's desire, and blesseth the covetous, whom the LORD abhorreth. The wicked, through the pride of his countenance, will not seek after God: God is not in all his thoughts. His ways are always grievous; Thy judgments are far above out of his sight: as for all his enemies, he puffeth at them. He hath said in his heart, I shall not be moved: for I shall never be in adversity. His mouth is full of cursing and deceit and fraud: under his tongue is mischief and vanity... Arise, O LORD; O God, lift up Thine hand: forget not the humble. Wherefore doth the wicked contemn God? he hath said in his heart, Thou wilt not require it. Thou hast seen it; for Thou beholdest mischief and spite, to requite it with Thy hand: the poor committeth himself unto Thee; thou art the helper of the fatherless. Break thou the arm of the wicked and the evil man: seek out his wickedness till thou find none. The LORD is King for ever and ever: the heathen are perished out of his land. LORD, thou hast heard the desire of the humble: thou wilt prepare their heart, thou wilt cause thine ear to hear: To judge the fatherless and the oppressed, that the man of the earth may no more oppress"* (Psalm 10).

---

28. http://www.lifenews.com/2009/06/29/int-1248/ Documentary Demographic Bomb Follows Demographic Winter Population Expose.
29. Ernest Hemingway commends abortion in his short story, *Hills Like White Elephants.*

HUMANIST EXTRAORDINAIRE

In 1962, Steinbeck gave a speech in the presence of the King of Sweden in which he very succinctly summarized the humanist worldview. He said, "Man himself has become our greatest hazard and our only hope. So that today, John the Apostle may well be paraphrased: In the end is the word, and the word is man, and the word is with man."[30] This is blasphemy of the highest form, but self-consciously humanist thinking. It is Nietzsche all over again, setting himself against Christ. John Steinbeck understood his competition. He understood the historical reality of Jesus Christ who spoke the final Word and rules history from the right hand of the Father. He knew he was setting himself against Christ. *John Steinbeck is apostate, quintessence.*

> *"The kings of the earth set themselves, and the rulers take counsel together, against the Lord, and against His anointed, saying, 'Let us break their bands asunder, and cast away their cords from us.' He that sitteth in the heavens shall laugh: the Lord shall have them in derision"(Psalm 2:2-4).*

JOHN STEINBECK'S *OF MICE AND MEN*

John Steinbeck's *Of Mice and Men* may be the clearest and most consistent incarnation of the destructive ideas of the age. It was a toxic little book of significant cultural impact - it landed the author the Nobel Prize for Literature in 1962.

By this time in Steinbeck's life, he had given up on any possibility for there being meaning in his random, chance-created universe. He was the epistemologically self-conscious modern man. Incredibly, when John Steinbeck describes a senseless murder in his story, the author is entirely dispassionate about it. The murder was senseless because in Steinbeck's view everything is senseless! According to biographer, Panini, "No divine interaction will change the lives of these characters for the better, and no redeeming grace may be found in their demise."[31]

---

30. Elaine Steinbeck and Robert Wallsten, ed., *Steinbeck: A life in Letters* (New York: VIking, 1975), 897-898.
31. Parini, *John Steinbeck*, 185.

THE STORY

Briefly, the story goes like this: Two men without roots and without families wander into a ranch in Soledad, California, searching for work (presumably in the 1930s). They are friends, but only in a superficial, empty sort of way. One of the men is a foul, God-hating wretch, who abuses God's name hundreds of times throughout the short story. His name is George. The other is slightly mentally retarded. His name is Lennie.

Lennie has a strange proclivity to running his hands over the surfaces of dead mice and women's clothes and hair. This gets him in trouble with George and others. Just prior to the events told in this story, the two men were forced to leave some other ranch 300 miles north because of Lennie's disgusting habits.

There are relationship strains between all of the characters in the story, almost without exception. The ranch hands constantly avail themselves of whore houses. The boss's son is married to a whorish, Proverbs 7 type of woman, who is constantly seeking the attention of other men. The boss's son is also extremely combative and pugnacious, even dangerous. Almost everybody takes God's name in vain, and curses everything and everyone around them. There are no meaningful relationships in the story, whatsoever.

The only true companionship of any consequence is the friendship between an old man and his old dog. But the old dog is diseased and stinky. So the boss's son "helpfully" takes the dog out back and shoots him. This, of course, ends the companionship.

For the first half of the book, George constantly reminds Lennie of the importance of staying out of trouble. He is tired of losing jobs because of Lennie's indiscretions. Their relationship is very strained because of this. But they "need each other." It is hard to say why George needs Lennie, except that Lennie is a human being and he may be George's last friend. Off and on throughout the story, George mentions his dream of settling down on his own little farm (with Lennie), where he can raise rabbits.

Regrettably, the boss's son's wife (the whorish woman) gets a little too friendly with Lennie. In response to her sexual advances, the mentally-unstable fellow gets angry and kills her. Later he explains the reason for his anger. He did not want George to think less of him for his inappropriate

    APOSTATE

contact with the woman, and risk losing George's friendship. But when George finds out about the killing, he shoots his friend Lennie in the head and that puts this miserable story out of its misery.

ANALYSIS

The most shocking aspect of this book to the Christian mind is the unrelenting abuse of God's name. It comes in almost every single sentence in the story. At times, the foul language comes off as the central message. Thus, apostasy and rebellion against God is palpable in the 20th century. Shakespeare at least pretended to fear God in his oaths, and Nathaniel Hawthorne and Mark Twain were reticent to include bald-faced vulgarities in their writings for fear of the backlash that would have come from the reading public. But this is most certainly *not the case* with the 20th century humanist "classics." It is interesting that the author and the characters in *Of Mice and Men* do their best to ignore the reality of God, yet they mention Him constantly. They ignore God except to insult Him at every opportunity. They are eager to let their audience know that they do not fear God and neither do any of the characters in the stories. They know about this Christian God and they hate him, and they want the world to know this. So they perfect the art of impiety and godlessness. What might we find in history to compare with the virulence of 20th century apostasy? If Josephus is accurate in his depiction of the impiety in Jerusalem in 70 A.D., perhaps we have something similar here. Truly with these Nephilim, "There is no fear of God before their eyes" (Rom. 3:18).

As 20th century man escapes the reality of God, He severs relationship with his fellow man. After Adam sinned against God and cut off his relationship with Him, Cain killed his brother and John Steinbeck killed his child. Then they became vagabonds on the earth (Gen. 4:14-16), wandering around somewhere "east of Eden." These three verses sum up the writings of John Steinbeck. They describe the plight of post-modern man. He is lonely in the big city. He terminates his relationships with his family and church and community. He wanders from city to city, and generation by generation, his family relationships grow weaker and weaker. What little friendship is left in the world is destroyed when somebody shoots the old man's dog, and when George kills his only friend in the world. Life outside of God's order is supremely lonely.

Steinbeck wins Nobel Prizes when he describes the barrenness, the emptiness, the loneliness, and the death of the modern world, where there are many people and very few meaningful relationships. *Of Mice and Men* has spoken to the hearts of millions, if not billions of people in our world. As the back of my copy of the book reads, "This beautiful, timeless novel speaks of... the painful search for self!" The brave existentialist is hopelessly self-oriented in his choices, and he sentences himself to a life of loneliness and the death of a culture. As Jean-Paul Sartre put it, "Hell is other people."

> "And Cain said unto the LORD, My punishment is greater than I can bear. Behold, Thou hast driven me out this day from the face of the earth; and from thy face shall I be hid; and I shall be a fugitive and a vagabond in the earth; and it shall come to pass, that every one that findeth me shall slay me. And the LORD said unto him, Therefore whosoever slayeth Cain, vengeance shall be taken on him sevenfold. And the LORD set a mark upon Cain, lest any finding him should kill him. And Cain went out from the presence of the LORD, and dwelt in the land of Nod, on the east of Eden" (Gen. 4:13-16).

Part III

THE CULTURAL
NEPHILIM

✣ *Eighteen*
PANDORA'S MACHINE

Before laying out the final episode in this terrible saga of the fall of Western civilization, I need to issue a cautionary note. For some, this will be the most frightening chapter yet because it strikes close to home. It will demonstrate how the devastation reaches into practically every village, every neighborhood, every church community, and every family in the Western world. Yes, we have arrived at the 21st century apostasy, and it is everywhere. The social, cultural, economic, and political repercussions are severe, but the storm is not over yet. In the unlikely case that some of my readers may have failed to recognize what is happening, this short review of the last fifty years will come as a dreadful shock. Something wicked this way came. It appears as if somebody must have opened Pandora's Box.[1]

It is somewhat unnerving to watch the social and moral fabric of our

---

1. Ironically, the largest online radio station in the world is called "Pandora Radio," now with 80 million subscribers.

nations unraveling so quickly. At this point, however, the reader should have an adequate understanding of the historical background for what happened in the 20th century. Civilizations cannot change direction overnight. There was much preparatory work that had to be done in previous centuries in order to bring about the destruction of Western civilization. The herculean work of the powerful philosophers from previous centuries was effective in turning this ship of our institutions and civilizations. They forged the humanist ideas that produced the social and cultural consequences we are experiencing today. These philosophers exerted tremendous influence over the minds and lives of billions of people around the globe.

But how could a few philosophical highbrows pack such a punch? How did they gain so much influence for their destructive ideas? Ultimately, these civilizations come down for the same reason that Assyria, Babylon, Persia, and Rome came down. God brings them down. This is the plain testimony of Isaiah, when he prophesies Persia's destruction of Babylon.

> *"Remember the former things of old: for I am God, and there is none else; I am God, and there is none like me, declaring the end from the beginning, and from ancient times the things that are not yet done, saying, My counsel shall stand, and I will do all my pleasure: Calling a ravenous bird from the east, the man that executeth my counsel from a far country: yea, I have spoken it, I will also bring it to pass; I have purposed it, I will also do it." (Is 46:9-11).*

God may use powerful evil forces and influential men to accomplish His will in the destruction of large empires that exalt themselves in their pride. If there are malevolent spirits working, these also are well under the sovereign hand of God (Job 1:12).

From our vantage point, it is clear that the humanist philosophers of the 18th and 19th centuries exerted huge influence on the world. However, their ideas did not reach the rank and file immediately. If the masses were going to live out the worldview of Sartre and Nietzsche; if this worldview would corrupt morality, marriage, family life, and faith in the mainstream, something more had to happen. The universities had well adapted the ideas into the curriculum, and John Dewey had worked hard to secularize the K-12 public schools. But this was not enough to capture the hearts of the masses. Let's face it, the average kid doesn't read Friedrich Nietzsche, John-Paul Sartre, and Ernest Hemingway for fun or for meaningful comprehension. This new breed of cultural leaders took upon themselves the task of incorporating man-centered philosophies into mass media for public consumption.

DEVELOPING MASS CULTURAL UNIFORMITY

Without centralized systems, it would be nigh impossible for these ideas to permeate the warp and woof of a civilization. Thus, centralized contol mechanisms in the political state, the educational programs, and the mass culture are important. The instinct to centralize power is nothing new. Since the Tower of Babel, natural man is inclined to "build a tower and make a name for themselves" (Gen. 11:4).

Right away, the 20th century political leaders went to work using powerful civil governments to bring about a humanist utopia structured according to the ideas of Karl Marx, Jean-Jacques Rousseau, John Dewey, and Charles Darwin. As it turns out, many of the political leaders lived out their apostasy. For example, Kim Il Jung, the madman that formed the most oppressive, anti-Christian communist state in the world today was raised in a devout Christian family. His father served as an elder and his maternal grandfather as a pastor in the Korean Presbyterian Church.[2] Another communist leader, Josef Stalin may have been the man responsible for more deaths of innocent people than anybody else. Raised by a single mother who worked her fingers to the bone to get her son through a seminary in Georgia, Stalin eventually rejected the Christian faith entirely, along with his mother's aspirations. She hoped he would become a bishop in the Orthodox Church.[3] Apostasy can have dangerous social implications.

However, there is a limit to what political leaders can do to mainstream the humanist ideas. After forty years of forced abortions and infanticide, the communist government of China barely reduced the birth rate down to 1.6. In contrast, South Korea didn't need to use political means to reduce the birth rate. Simply by incorporating Western ideas of existentialism and materialism into their country by other cultural

2. "Kim Il Sung," *Wickipedia*, Mar. 25, 2013, <http://en.wikipedia.org/wiki/Kim_Il-sung> accessed on Mar. 28, 2013
3. "Ketevan Geladze," *Wikipedia*, Mar. 21, 2013, <http://en.wikipedia.org/wiki/Ketevan_Geladze> accessed on Mar. 28, 2013

APOSTATE

means, this country reduced its birth rate to 1.2 in just as many years.[4] As it turns out, it takes more than politics to infiltrate a civilization with dangerous and corrupting ideas.

That is where the cultural machines take over. Since 1900, unprecedented technological and sociological changes produced a new medium of communication by various electronic forms. Powerful television and radio "networks" enabled a huge amount of power centralization in the communication of ideas - this is something the world had never seen before. To form uniformity of thought among the masses, these networks needed only to control the distribution of music, news, and story-telling by film and television. While there were a few alternative sources and small "Christian" networks here and there, the mass flow was always controlled by a handful of networks heavily regulated and limited by the Fedearal Communications Commission. It wasn't long before the cultural trajectory was fairly uniform. Whether a young man lived in Chicago, Illinois, or Winner, North Dakota, he would have access to the same music, the same movies, the same television programs, and the same worldview. Aiding this cultural machine were the large age-segregated public schools, teen culture, peer groups, the urbanization of society, and a willing public. The timing was right for this new media, because the breakdown of the family and the socialization of education also meant the breakdown of literacy. Fewer people could read Nietzsche's big words with any comprehension, but now they didn't have to.

The media replaced the church and the family as the major source of information transfer, worldview education, and cultural formation. For thousands of years, it was the pastors and fathers in villages and homes that formed the culture. Farmer boys like Almanzo Wilder and pioneer girls like Laura Ingalls Wilder sat with their parents around the fireplace during the long winter evenings, and danced about the living room as "Pa" played the fiddle and sang his folk songs. All of that changed with the advent of electronic media. Now every kid has his own iPod and television set, and he is plugged into "the Matrix."

The church hardly leads the culture anymore. If a youth pastor steps out in front of his youth group on his first day at work and finds that all the kids have bones in their noses, what will he do? If he will properly

4. "Low South Korean Birth Rate Raises Fears" "Download Mar. 25, 2013 http://www.ft.com/cms/s/0/3be6ec40-4dd4-11e2-9e71-00144feab49a.html#axzz2Owxvv3yK

contextualize in the culture and relate to the youth, he will have to find a bone to shove through his nose as well. There are machines in Nashville and Hollywood that direct the mass culture and administer the cultural revolutions.

As mentioned in the previous chapter, a new teenage social identity appeared in the 1930s and 1940s through the large junior high schools and senior high schools. Laura Ingalls and her sisters would never have rushed into Times Square in New York City to fall at the feet of teen-star Frank Sinatra. It's hard to imagine President John Adam's daughters screaming for hours in an Elvis Presley concert, as the star danced around creating sexual tension in the crowd. They were raised in a different social context.

Somewhere in the last century, the most influential and popular cultural icons moved out of the church and into the hands of Nashville's music moguls. The cultural leadership transferred from Johann Sebastian Bach (1700) to Eminem and his rape rap (2000). The most popular song in the nation in the 1880s was *My Grandfather's Clock*, a song that honored the memory of a grandfather. Nowadays, Eminem refers to his mother as a "female dog," and Katy Perry encourages 13 year old girls towards lesbianism. For those who missed it, that is total cultural and social revolution in a nutshell.

It wasn't just the work of Eminem and Katy Perry. This massive revolution came about largely by the leadership of the Beatles. The British Invasion began with their hit song, *I Want to Hold Your Hand*. It seemed pretty innocuous at first. But by 1968 they were asking, *Why Don't We Do It in the Road?* In effect, the Beatles served as the pastoral leaders of the 1960s, and they led the sexual revolution.

DISCERNING THE GENERAL TRENDS

In retrospect, it didn't take all that long to see the moral, cultural, and social implications of Nietzsche, Sartre, Bentham, and Dewey worked into the broader society. The general trends of mass culture in recent history are not really all that hard to follow. For example, Bobby Darin's *Mack the Knife* came off as a little edgy in 1959. The song celebrated rape, murder, and thievery in a cloaked way, taking the popular audience "Beyond Good and Evil" with Friedrich Nietzsche. The song netted Bobby Darin a #1 on Billboard's Hot 100 and a Grammy Award for Best

Album.[5]

A few decades later (in 1996), Marilyn Manson's *Antichrist Superstar* reached #3 on Billboard's 200 List. Never mind the fact that Manson publicly endorsed Satanism in an interview: "I incorporate satanic philosophy, more times subtly than others. It gets across the philosophy without the name 'Satanism.' After people get close to me, I let them know my affiliation with the church [of Satan]."[6] He still received the MTV Nomination for Best Hard Rock Video in 1996 and 1997. This superstar has sold 25 million records thus far, a hundred times more distribution than Nietzsche ever saw with his books.

Maybe Frank Sinatra came across as a little daring with *Strangers in the Night* in 1966, a chart-topper that left his listeners wondering if they were going to fornicate "before the night was through." But that was nothing compared to the dime-a-dozen songs that glorify lesbianism, homosexuality, and the fornicating one-night stands that rolled off the pop and country charts in the 2010s.

STILL APOSTASY

In true fashion to the previous generation of Nephilim, these cultural leaders still represent the same old apostasy. The personal lives of the popular singers reflect the same legacy left by the philosophic and literary geniuses covered previously in this book. Take for example the "edgy" Katy Perry who started out as the daughter of a Christian pastor in Santa Barbara, California. By her own admission, she grew tired of singing *Amazing Grace*, so she jumped onto the pop machine where she led millions of teenyboppers towards accepting lesbianism with her hit song *I Kissed a Girl*.[7]

Shock-rocker Marilyn Manson (Brian Warner), was also raised in a Christian home, and went on to produce a highly destructive form during his music career.[8] Incidentally, his violent, demonic music has inspired quite a few teenage murderers to act out their basest desires from the 1970s to the 2010s. For example, a young man named Matthew Murray

5. http://en.wikipedia.org/wiki/Mack_the_Knife
6. "The Black Flame," Volume 6, Numbers 1 & 2, <www.churchofsatan.com> accessed on Mar. 28, 2013
7. Julia Wang, ed., "Celebrity Central: Katy Perry: Biography," *People*, <http://www.people.com/people/katy_perry/biography/0,,,00.html> accessed on Mar. 28, 2013
8. "Marilyn Manson," *Wickipedia.org*, Mar. 26, 2013, <http://en.wikipedia.org/wiki/Marilyn_Manson> accessed on Mar. 28, 3013

went on a murdering spree in Colorado in 2005. Himself raised by devout Christian homeschooling parents, this young man was particularly inspired in his rebellion and violence by the music of Marilyn Manson.[9] Another young man obsessed with Marilyn Manson's music, Kip Kinkle, killed his parents and shot up his school on May 21, 1998.[10] The cultural destruction takes on many forms, but these represent some of the more egregious elements. This may be the first time in history in which so many young people are influenced to engage in gross immorality by the fantasy world of violent games, internet pornography, motion pictures, and music.

The most recent mega-star, "Lady Gaga" was raised in a Catholic home and educated in Catholic schools. She now promotes her Christ-blasphemy and sexual nihilism on stages all over the world. Her recent album promoting homosexuality, *Born This Way*, reached the top chart position in every major Western nation that charts music, and she has sold almost 100 million albums and singles thus far.[11] Jeremy Bentham's philosophy is now mainstream.

The "machine" cranks out new stars every year, targeting younger children all the time, which solidifies its control over the minds of successive generations. Young Miley Cyrus was raised and baptized in the Southern Baptist Church.[12] She played the part of "Hannah Montana" in her early teens, winning the hearts of millions of little girls. More recently, her handlers have moved her towards soft-porn spreads in Vanity Fair Magazine and stripper-style pole dances in her rock concerts. Another example is the hugely-popular Carrie Underwood, who started her career singing *Jesus Take the Wheel*. It was admittedly a weak Christian theme, and within a few years she was endorsing homosexuality and singing songs that would have made prostitutes blush back in the 1920s.[13]

As always, the apostates must lead the world in the work of cultural devolution. They are the ones most capable of destroying civilizations

9. "Reports: Gunman Posted Anti-Christian Warnings" *CNN.com*, Dec. 11, 2007, <http://www.cnn.com/2007/US/12/11/shooter.youth/> accessed on Mar. 28, 2013

10. Phil Chalmers, *Inside the Mind of a Teen Killer* (Nashville: Thomas Nelson, 2009), 64.

11. "Lady Gaga Discography," *Wikipedia*, Mar. 25, 2013 <http://en.wikipedia.org/wiki/Lady_Gaga_discography> accessed on Mar. 28, 2013

12. Sessmus, Kevin, "Miley Cyrus: 'I Know Who I Am Now,'" *Parade*, Mar. 21, 2010 <http://www.parade.com/celebrity/2010/03/miley-cyrus.html> accessed on Mar. 28, 2013

13. Fox, Hilary, "Carrie Underwood's Gay Marriage Support Prompts Backlash From Fans," *HuffPost Gay Voices*, Jun., 20, 2013 <http://www.huffingtonpost.com/2012/06/20/carrie-underwood-gay-marriage-backlash-london_n_1612498.html> accessed on Mar. 28, 2013

nationally and internationally. These celebrities are the cultural Nephilim, and they are leading today's apostasy. They sell hundreds of millions of albums, and their music pipes into the brains of billions of people through iPods and iPhones. Certainly, the Nephilim did not have this level of control over the populace in the rural areas and the urban areas in the 1840s when Karl Marx was writing his demon-inspired plays and poems. But now the machine is mass-producing Jeremy Bentham, Friedrich Nietzsche, Jean-Paul Sartre, and Ralph Waldo Emerson in bite-sized pieces for the consumption of the masses. Occasionally, the machine throws in some "Christian" lyrics that get a few unwary Christian listeners back on track towards Nietzsche's nihilism.

MASS-PRODUCING SARTRE AND NIETZSCHE

In the early 1900s, there was no pop-music machine and there were no superstars that controlled the hearts and minds of billions of people through music and media. But by the 1960s, the centralized network of radio and television stations was in place. The family farm was a thing of the past, and fathers had disappeared into large corporate systems. Already, two generations had passed through John Dewey's socialized public schools. It was a perfect storm.

Immediately, the dangerous ideas of the great philosophers from the 19th century surface everywhere in the "cool" music produced in the 1960s. As mentioned previously, Bob Dylan and Mick Jagger effectively captured Sartre's alienation of man in the two most enduring rock songs of all time. The John Lennon-Paul McCartney song, *A Day in the Life* is recognized as "the greatest Beatles song" and as "the greatest song ever written."[14] The composition introduced a mass audience to escapism and nihilism, with a gratuitous reference to the recreational use of drugs.

According to the pop music chart records, the most popular song of all time is Frank Sinatra's *My Way*. Recorded in 1966, it was on the charts for 75 weeks. This song was one of the clearest representations of Sartre's existentialism ever produced in mass culture—man will define his own existence by his own determinate choices. The song also contained a sort of public confession of apostasy. According to these lyrics, the autonomous man desires. . .*"To say the things he truly feels, and not the words*

---

14. "A Day in the Life," (cf. *Recognition and Reception* Section). http://en.wikipedia.org/wiki/A_Day_in_the_Life

of one who kneels." The song clearly represented the raw humanism of
John Dewey who signed *Humanist Manifesto I*, and refused to bow the
knee to God (in fear, humility, and reverence).

When Debbie Boone sang "It can't be wrong, when it feels so right"
in the wildly popular song, *You Light Up My Life*, she captured the hearts
of millions of Americans. "It became the most successful single of the
1970s in the United States, and set a new Hot 100 record for longest
reign at No. 1."[15] Jeremy Bentham would have been pleased. Incidentally,
the songwriter for Debbie Boone's song, a man named Joe Brooks
committed suicide in June of 2009 while he was on trial for 91 counts of
sexual assault, etc. Apparently, he tried to live consistently to the message
of his song.[16] The song revealed the heart of the 1970s sexual rebellion,
and the songwriter's demise makes for a fitting picture of what happens
to a generation who embraces the wrong cultural ethic.

THE INFLUENCE OF THE CULTURAL GIANTS

The Cultural Nephilim nurture the hearts of billions of people around
the globe through the powerful medium of music (and sometimes the
visual medium). Their religious trajectory and worldview commitments
are expertly woven into musical forms, and gradually bring the world into
conformity with their thinking.

As measured by album sales, the Beatles take their place at the top of
the pyramid as the most influential musicians in history. . .They were
far and away the single most important worldwide influence in the last
century. This band more or less formed the Zeitgeist of the modern world;
their total album sales is estimated to be somewhere between 1 billion
and 2 billion.[17] That is far more mass appeal than Ralph Waldo Emerson
attracted in his day. The Beatles had an immediate, international impact
that has lasted for fifty years. They formed the cultural trajectory for
the world, exceeding the influence of any other musician, philosopher,
writer, movie producer, or preacher in the modern age. If their ideas

15. "You Light Up My Life (the song)" http://en.wikipedia.org/wiki/You_Light_Up_My_
Life_%28song%29

16. Kappstatter, Bob; Grace, Melissa; and Kennedy, Helen; "'You Light up My Life' Songwriter
Joseph Brooks, Accused Rapist, Commits Suicide: Cops," *NY Daily News*, May 22, 2011 <http://
www.nydailynews.com/new-york/light-life-songwriter-joseph-brooks-accused-rapist-commits-sui-
cide-cops-article-1.143293> accessed on Mar. 28, 2013

17. "List of Best-Selling Music Artists," *Wickipedia*, Mar. 28, 2013 <http://en.wikipedia.org/wiki/
List_of_best-selling_music_artists> accessed on Mar. 28, 2013

APOSTATE

formed the spirit of age, it would helpful to know something of their lives and ultimate epistemological commitments.

The band members were all raised in Roman Catholic or Protestant homes, but they professed Agnosticism, Atheism, Humanism, or Hinduism later on in their lives. The band's organizer, John Lennon, was probably the most influential songwriter of modern times. Conceived out of wedlock, young John was raised an Anglican by his uncle and aunt in the 1940s and 1950s. Biographical sources indicate that Lennon attended Sunday School as a child, he joined the Bible Class, and sang in the choir. He was confirmed at 15 years old, apparently of his own volition.[18] But he was of the breed of Nephilim. More than any other person, this man led the popular culture of the 1960s and 1970s into rebellion against God. In 1966, Lennon was quoted by Maurice Cleave in a magazine article saying, "Christianity will go. It will vanish and shrink. I needn't argue about that; I'm right and I'll be proved right. We're more popular than Jesus now; I don't know which will go first—rock 'n' roll or Christianity." Several years later (on May 18th, 1968), he told the other members of the band that he was the reincarnation of Jesus Christ.[19]

Lennon's testimony is familiar. Nietzsche said something similar before he went insane. Also, John Dewey maintained the same view in his essay on Darwin. In the 1960s, Lennon takes the prophetic role as he assesses the progress of two hundred years of advancing humanism in the form of Bentham, Emerson, Marx, Darwin, and Dewey. Certainly, Lennon was feeling something of the euphoria of victory over the old Christian order. In some respects, it was hard to argue with him. Forty years after his statement, it may be even harder to argue with his assertion that Christianity is shrinking, but that some of us can see the shape of a hand and the handwriting on the wall. While Nietzsche lived, his blasphemy against Christ was cloaked in mystery and only accessible to a few academics and cultural elites. But as the apostasy came to full maturity in 20th century, the most popular singers and writers thought nothing of making such bold and public statements to the news media for international consumption. In press conferences later, Lennon confirmed that he believed in the "God in all of us," which amounts to

18. "Religious Beliefs of the Beatles," *Wickipedia*, Feb. 27, 2013 <http://en.wikipedia.org/wiki/Religious_beliefs_of_the_Beatles> accessed on Mar. 28, 2013
19. "More Popular Than Jesus," *Wickipedia*, Mar. 18, 2013 <http://en.wikipedia.org/wiki/More_popular_than_Jesus> accessed on Mar. 28, 2013

an Eastern Pantheism or an Emersonian Transcendentalism.[20]

Recent surveys put John Lennon's song *Imagine* at the top of the list of the most popular songs of all time (rated #3 by Rolling Stone, and rated #1 by Squidoo.com). This song became the "Apostle's Creed" of the modern apostasy in the West since it came out in 1971.

> *Imagine there's no heaven*
> *It's easy if you try*
> *No hell below us*
> *Above us only sky*
> *Imagine all the people living for today*
>
> *Imagine no possessions*
> *I wonder if you can*
> *No need for greed or hunger*
> *A brotherhood of man*
> *Imagine all the people sharing all the world*
> *You, you may say*
> *I'm a dreamer, but I'm not the only one*
> *I hope some day you'll join us*
> *And the world will live as one.*

This is how John Lennon marketed the egalitarian philosophy and atheism of Karl Marx, as well as the existentialism of Jean-Paul Sartre who taught us all to "live for today." John Lennon's creed also appeared in his 1970 release called *God*, in which he explicitly confessed that he did not believe in the Bible, but rather, "I just believe in me." If you weed through all of the profanities contained in Lennon's foul little composition, *Serve Yourself*, you will find the most explicit existentialist confession of autonomy ever to show up in popular music: "You're gonna have to serve yourself and that's all there is to it."

The Beatles gave way to Michael Jackson in the 1980s who became known as the "King of Pop." His top-selling album *Thriller* sold 65 million copies, a world record. The album celebrated "the thrill of evil" expressed in sexuality. Reminiscent of *Mack the Knife*, Jackson ended his song with

---

20. "Religious Beliefs of the Beatles," *Wickipedia*, Feb. 27, 2013 <http://en.wikipedia.org/wiki/Religious_beliefs_of_The_Beatles> accessed on Mar. 28, 2013

"No mere mortal can resist the evil of the thriller." Ethical ambiguity is inescapable in another number on the album that repeats the lyric, "It doesn't matter who's wrong or right," about 15 times. His follow-up album, titled *Bad,* again confused good and evil in the Nietzschean tradition. Michael Jackson was a lapsed Jehovah's Witness, but became a Muslim by the end of his life (a sad commentary on both the Christian apostasy as well as the bankruptcy of humanism).

The fourth most popular musician of all time (by music sales) after The Beatles, Elvis Presley, and Michael Jackson is Madonna (Madonna Louise Ciccone). She was raised in a devout Catholic family that sent their children to Roman Catholic schools in the Detroit area. Throughout her career, she promoted pre-marital sex, homosexuality, sadomasochism, and feminist sexual domination. Her albums, concerts, and music videos are filled with innuendoes that mock Christian themes, ergo: *Like a Virgin, The Immaculate Collection,* etc. These albums sold hundreds of millions of copies, and dominated the Top-40 airwaves and MTV and VH1 music video playlists for decades. In 2003, she publicly promoted lesbianism with Britney Spears, another rising star in the decadent culture of the day. Also raised by a devout Christian mother, Spears was another model candidate for the cultural "machine" that paved hundreds of highways towards apostasy, cultural debauchery, and social disintegration.

The fifth most popular musician of all time by album sales, is the Brit, Elton John: a professed homosexual since he exited the closet in 1975. After Jeremy Bentham, Walt Whitman, and Ernest Hemingway, a major cultural leader needed to open the doors wide for the widespread public acceptance of the sin in the 1990s. After Elton John, many other musicians (Freddy Mercury, George Michael, Boy George, etc.) came "out of the closet." This was the consummation of Jeremy Bentham's vision for England and the Western world.

If album sales-volume is any indication of the impact of the cultural Nephilim, then the heavy metal pioneers from England, the Led Zeppelin band, left a mark not soon to be forgotten. With over 250 million albums sold, this band takes the sixth place in the pantheon of the "greats." Among the philosopher humanists of previous centuries, a few actually acknowledged admiration for Satan (eg. Mark Twain, Karl Marx, etc.). The Nephilim of the popular culture were no different. For some reason, the heavy metal genre seemed to attract the more epistemologically self-conscious demon worshipers. The Led Zeppelin band was a true pioneer in this cultural trend. Of course, part of the demonic nature is confusion and contradictions. Shock rock wasn't supposed to take itself seriously, or perhaps it didn't know if it was taking itself seriously. After all, there was no point in trying to glorify Satan if they were calling into question the existence of Satan and God and the supernatural. The business of apostasy is obfuscation, always trading one lie for another.

Nevertheless, Led Zeppelin's guitarist Jimmy Page was well-known for his appreciation of Aleister Crowley, the famous Satanist who Page referred to as the "misunderstood genius of the 20th century."[21] In the band's most popular song, *Stairway to Heaven*, reference is made to Crowley's poem "May Queen." For their compilation (called *Led Zeppelin III*) the band placed the phrase "Do What Thou Wilt" in the lacquer of the album itself.[22] This was Aleister Crowley's well-known moniker, and it directly reflected the autonomy of Jean-Paul Sartre.

The hard rock culture that adored Led Zeppelin gladly accepted the accusation that the members of the Led Zeppelin band were akin to the pre-flood giants: the God-hating, murderous Nephilim. For example, Mick Wall's biography on Led Zeppelin is entitled, *When Giants Walked the Earth*. Quoting a music correspondent, William Burroughs, he writes, "Rock stars may be compared to priests. . .[the concert] bears some resemblance to the trance music found in Morocco. . .concerned with the evocation and control of spiritual forces. . .For this magic to succeed, it must tap the sources of magical energy, and this can be dangerous."[23] Author Mick Wall cannot disagree with the "fundamentalist Christian" argument that *Stairway to Heaven* is the "evocation of Aleister Crowley's bold Luciferian teachings."[24] Mick Wall writes that Jimmy Page's friend Kenneth Anger "described 'Stairway to Heaven' as Zeppelin's 'most Luciferian song,' . .including. . .quest for spiritual rebirth. . .pagan imagery. . .May Queens. . ." According to Jimmy Page, the lyrics for this

---

21. "Boleskine House," *Wickipedia*, Mar. 2, 2013, <http://en.wikipedia.org/wiki/Boleskine_House> accessed on Mar. 28, 2014. Note: Alleister Crowley (1875-1947) was raised by devout Christian parents, his father a pastor in the Plymouth Brethren denomination. He quickly apostatized in his college years, and became an early promoter of decadent sexuality, recreational drug use, and witchcraft. In his writings, Crowley associates himself with "the Beast" and opposes Jesus Christ in the most blasphemous terms.

22. "Led Zeppelin III," *Wickipedia*, Mar. 23, 2013 <http://en.wikipedia.org/wiki/Led_Zeppelin_III> accessed on Mar. 28, 2013

23. Mick Wall, *A Biography of Led Zeppelin: When Giants Walked the Earth* (London: Orion Books Ltd, 2008), 327.

24. Ibid. 264.

gigantic song came quickly. "It was like someone was guiding his hand."[25] Page bought an occult bookstore and Aleister Crowley's house, which was believed to have been habited by demons. On a visit with Jimmy Page at his home, another rock star, David Bowie, became convinced the place was "overrun with satanic demons whom Crowley's disciples had summoned straight from hell. . ."[26] Eventually, the band's infatuation with Satanism caught up with them, and what they perceived to be demonic attacks contributed to the dissolution of the band in the 1980s.

All of the above only certifies the spiritual nature of the forces that captured the hearts and minds of hundreds of millions of people. What other cultural forces held so much sway over the masses in the 1970s, 1980s, and 1990s? Christian singer Michael W. Smith topped out at 13 million in record sales, a paltry number compared to the billions sold by the modern-day Nephilim. George Beverly Shea continued to sing the old hymns at Billy Graham crusades in the 1970s, but the remnant of Christian culture could not compete at the level of these Nephilim during the years that "the giants walked the earth."

Through the 1990s and 2000s, popular music becomes increasingly more difficult to understand. It is chaotic, disjointed, and meaningless. For example, Nirvana's *Smells Like Teen Spirit* was the second most popular song of the 1990s. According to Wikipedia, "The lyrics to 'Smells Like Teen Spirit' were often difficult for listeners to decipher, both due to their nonsensicality and because of Cobain's slurred, guttural singing voice." Band organizer and former member of band *Fecal Matter*, Kurt Cobain, committed suicide in 1994. Culture always moves in ebbs and flows, but now post-modern man is coming to self-consciousness of his meaninglessness. He is more sure of his "non-existence." He is committing epistemological suicide.

This cultural suicide is now well beyond the avant-garde. It is spreading into the masses. Lady Gaga represents a cross-over from sexual decadence to sexual nihilism.[27] The cultural wasteland is international. When a South Korean popular singer captured almost a billion downloads for a completely vacuous song called "Gangnam Style," he may have set world records. But he was not impressed. The song was intended to mock the

25. Ibid. 245.
26. Ibid. 329.
27. Camilia Pagila, "Lady Gaga and the Death of Sex," *The Sunday Times*, Sept. 12, 2010<http:// www.thesundaytimes.co.uk/sto/public/magazine/article389697.ece> accessed on Mar. 28, 2013

same people who listened to it. Songwriter and performer, Psy (Park Jaesang) comments, "Human society is so hollow, and even while filming I felt pathetic."[28] He is right. Almost every popular song now celebrates decadence, but mocks the celebration in the very same breath. The use of a vile word denoting an act of violent rape, is ubiquitous on the top-40 charts in the present day. All of these things are indications that our mainstream social and cultural systems are perpetually transitioning from decadence to suicide. There is nowhere else to go—except repentance, of course, which was unthinkable for Jean-Paul Sartre and Friedrich Nietzsche.

We are at the very end of an era. Elvis is dead. John Lennon is dead. Michael Jackson is dead. Elton John is almost senile. Where does popular culture go next? After decadence and self-immolation, then what? It is hard to imagine that the mass culture will stay on the present course for much longer. Splintering is inevitable. Something will be salvaged, but only for those with the prescience and the will to begin a new civilization.

THE MEDIUM IS THE MESSAGE

The isolation of modern man has not abated in the least over the last century. If anything, it has accelerated since the advent of the internet. Access to online pornography (sexuality without any relationship whatsoever) is a thousand times more prevalent than it was 30 years ago. And the most popular entertainment media is no longer music or movies—there were 270 million computer games sold in 2008. Young people relate more by short, meaningless text messages than by phone or person-to-person.

Jean-Paul Sartre's world is everywhere. It is surreal, escapist, and isolationistic. Postmodern man seeks escape ramps from the highway of reality, and there are 10,000 ramps available. Increasingly, young men are losing a vision for life and a vision for the future. They play computer games while "Rome" burns. As with the fall of Rome in the 5th century, the masses seek bread and games, but they do not have what it takes to save the empire. As Neil Postman says modern man is "entertaining himself to death." All of this has only accelerated since Postman wrote

28. Max Fisher, "Gangnam Style, Dissected: The Subversive Message Behind South Korea's Music Sensation," *The Atlantic*, Aug. 23, 2012 <http://www.theatlantic.com/international/archive/2012/08/gangnam-style-dissected-the-subversive-message-within-south-koreas-music-video-sensation/261462/> accessed on Mar. 28, 2013

his book in the 1980s.

IS THE CHURCH ACCOMMODATING THE APOSTASY?

What has the church done during the recent cultural landslide? Generally, the Christian church has made many pitiful attempts to borrow the medium created by the mass culture - to express the church's own message. They call it "contextualization." If the world offers a nihilistic form of expression, the church gladly employs it. Should the world use a finger gesture to demonstrate gross disrespect (in a cultural form), how long would it take before youth pastors tried to incorporate the gesture in the "praise and worship?" Similarly, the world has already created music forms that convey gross irreverence and destructive attitudes, and the Christian church is quick to borrow these forms. What they do not realize is that these cultural forms are strong symbols, and they represent associations that reinforce certain ideas in the minds of the people. Generally, the music mediums created in the present day are strongly attached to the dishonor of parents and an irreverence towards God. When these forms are taken into the church to accommodate songs about "Jesus," they drag the world's connotations with them. Thus synthesis prevails, teenage rebellion continues, cynicism and irreverence is the new normal, and the church witnesses higher rates of apostasy among its youth. As long as the church tries to contextualize with a culture that is fast moving towards the Niagara Falls, it will be practically powerless to impact that culture,.

If culture can be described as worldview externalized, Christians should first get the right worldview down well. Then they can effectively communicate their worldview by way of culture—through music, movies, dress, language, etc. They must understand the antithesis, and the points at which the Christian worldview opposes the other worldviews (many of which are presented in this book). Then, they must set a good trajectory in terms of how they will live out these ideas in every area of life. This will transform the culture.

As long as our people are immersed in the cultural devices represented by the other worldview(s), their thinking and living will never conform to the Word of God.

"I beseech you therefore, brethren, by the mercies of God, that ye present your bodies a living sacrifice, holy, acceptable unto God, which is your reasonable service. And be not conformed to this world: but be ye transformed by the renewing of your mind, that ye may prove what is that good, and acceptable, and perfect, will of God" (Rom. 12:1,2).

The abandonment of the biblical ethical structure results in the weakening of the faith. More frequently, we are seeing protestant reformed and evangelical clergymen endorse homosexual marriage and civil unions.[29] As they perceive themselves to be irrelevant in an increasingly hostile, anti-Christian culture, Christian leaders feel pressed to water-down the ethical statements of God's law in order to retain some "relevance" in the conversation. For example, Christian legal organizations reduce themselves to fighting for rights for transvestites in the public schools in complete disregard for Deuteronomy 22:5. Pseudo-Christian music bands freely employ the "F" word, yet land positive reviews in Christian magazines for their "Christ-haunted lyrics."[30] (Note: Ephesians 4:29 does touch on this issue of corrupt communication.) Desperately, Christians grasp for relevance and impact in a dissolute culture, but to no avail. Does a "Christian actor" make "an impact for Jesus" when he is cast in the most popular comedy on television, even though the "filthy show" endears the themes of bestiality and sexual orgies?[31]

Without a firm grasp of Old and New Testament law, Christians will slowly adopt the pagan ways of the apostasy, whether it be homosexuality, vampirism, witchcraft, body-mutilation, or the hundreds of forms of idolatry found in the society around us. The hard-and-fast separation of grace and law in the evangelical message is slowly undermining the Christian faith by disallowing the Word of God to speak to worldview issues. While a distinction between grace and law, and faith and works,

29. Dr. Michael Horton, "Should We Oppose Same-Sex Marriage?" *FreeRepublic.com* May 11, 2012 <http://www.freerepublic.com/focus/f-religion/2919093/posts> accessed on Mar. 28, 2013; and Lavers, Michael K., "Ted Haggard: Same-Sex Marriage Should Be Allowed by the State," *Washington Blade*, Oct. 25, 2012, <http://www.washingtonblade.com/2012/10/25/ted-haggard-same-sex-marriage-should-be-allowed-by-the-state/> accessed on Mar. 28, 2013

30. Kevin P. Emmert, "Mumford and the Son," *Christianity Today*, Sept. 25, 2012 <http://www.christianitytoday.com/ct/2012/september-web-only/mumford-and-the-son.html> accessed on Mar. 28, 2013

31. Lonnell Johnson, "Angus T. Jones Offers Apology for Two and a Half Men Comments," *Examiner.com*, Nov. 30, 2012 <http://www.examiner.com/article/angus-t-jones-offers-apology-for-two-and-a-half-men-comments> accessed on Mar. 28, 2013; and "PTC Summary: *Two and a Half Men*," *Parents Television Council*, <http://www.parentstv.org/ptc/shows/main.asp?shwid=1771> accessed on Mar. 28, 2013

APOSTATE

is retained in Christian orthodoxy (for salvation from the penalty of sin) a robust unity of Christian life and liturgy is essential (James 2:26). The laws of God are the ethics of God. Now is not the time to compromise on Christian ethics just to make Jeremy Bentham happy. If there will be faith and civilization after the post-modern storm blows over, it will be found with those who have held with white knuckles to the hope of the Resurrection of Christ, and the ethics found in the Word of God.

> "Here is the patience of the saints: here are they that keep the commandments of God, and the faith of Jesus" (Rev. 14:12).

Nineteen

GARDENS IN THE ASHES

The 2012 election results stunned the conservative and Christian coterie in America. It was a reality check for the old "Christian Coalition" and "Moral Majority." They should have known better. For one thing, it was the first time that the leading presidential candidates associated themselves closely with Mormonism,[1] Mohammedanism,[2] and Marxism,[3] all worldviews that are antithetical to a Christian way of thinking. Previous presidential races featured Roman Catholics, divorcees, and liberal Protestants, but this was different. Both candidates in 2012

1. Stack, Peggy Fletcher, "Before Politics, Mitt Romney Was a Mormon Bishop," *USA Today*, Mar. 28, 2012 <http://usatoday30.usatoday.com/news/religion/story/2012-03-28/mitt-romney-mormon-bishop/53836844/1> accessed on Mar. 29, 2013

2. Pipes, Daniel, "PIPES: 'Barry Was a Muslim,'" *The Washington Times*, Sept. 10, 2012 <http://www.washingtontimes.com/news/2012/sep/10/barry-was-muslim/> accessed on Mar. 29, 2013

3. Paulson, Scott, "Opinion: Obama: I Actually Believe in Redistribution," *CBS Boston*, Sept. 20, 2012 <http://boston.cbslocal.com/2012/09/20/obama-i-actually-believe-in-redistribution/> accessed on Mar. 29, 2013

supported homosexual involvement in the Boy Scouts organization,[4] and when the votes were cast, America went for the candidate most likely to support infanticide,[5] Marxism, and homosexuality.[6] If there had been any uncertainty concerning the cultural direction of the nation prior to the 2012 elections, this was the defining moment. Americans rejected outright the pro-life cause, Christian values, and conservative fiscal ideas. Finally, Christian leaders were forced to admit that they had lost the cultural war, and there would be very little to salvage in the political sphere. Southern Baptist leader Al Mohler explained, "Our message was rejected by millions of Americans who went to the polls and voted according to a contrary worldview."[7] In an opinion piece, Conservative leader, William Bennett announced that, "Republicans lost the culture war."[8]

Given the historical context provided in this book, it should be obvious that these developments fit into the philosophical, literary, educational, and cultural trends set down over 200 years. How can we expect young conservatives to take a position against gay marriage when country singer Carrie Underwood endorses it? According to Pew Research, the millennial generation is far more liberal on the issues of homosexuality, socialism, and evolution than the baby boom generation and the silent generation.[9] Of course, they receive their ideals from mass culture. Also 90% of the populace are trained to think by public school teachers taught by professors, who were taught by John Dewey and Jeremy Bentham and their ilk. What the conservatives have finally learned is that there is no use fighting these battles in the polls, unless they are first fought in the schools and culture—and ultimately, in the family. Without the restoration of the family as the guardian of biblical values over the

4. Dwyer, Devin, and Compton, Ann, "President Obama, Mitt Romney Agree: Gay Boy Scouts OK," ABC News, Political Punch, Aug. 8, 2012 <http://abcnews.go.com/blogs/politics/2012/08/president-obama-mitt-romney-agree-gay-boy-scouts-ok/> accessed on Mar. 29, 2013

5. "Obama Born Alive Controversy," Conservapedia.com, Jul. 28, 2012 <http://www.conservapedia.com/Obama_born_alive_controversy> accessed on Mar. 29, 2013

6. Hananel, Sam, "Obama's Gay Appointees Smash Record," Huff Post Politics, Oct. 26, 2012, <http://www.huffingtonpost.com/2010/10/26/obamas-gay-appointees-sma_n_773898.html> accessed on Mar. 29, 2013

7. Hagerty, Barbara Bradley, "Albert Mohler: 2012 Election an 'Evangelical Disaster,'" WFPL News, Nov. 8, 2012, <http://wfpl.org/post/albert-mohler-2012-election-evangelical-disaster> accessed on Mar. 29, 2013

8. William J. Bennett, "Republicans Lost the Culture War," http://www.cnn.com/2012/11/14/opinion/bennett-gop-election

9. "2012 American Values Survey," Pew Research Survey for the People and the Press, <http://www.people-press.org/2012/06/04/partisan-polarization-surges-in-bush-obama-years/01_pp_12-05-25_values_slideshow/> accessed on Mar. 29, 2013

generations, there won't be a faith in years to come.

The picture I have painted in this book is not a pleasant one, I know. For anyone who still calls himself a Christian or sympathizes with the Christian faith, this apostasy is bad news. Every genuine Christian is disappointed by the effects of the blasphemous ideas of these powerful apostates. The rapid adoption, the enthusiastic reception, and the ease by which the ideas were incorporated into the warp and the woof of the Western world is stunning.

Given that it took over 400 years for the Roman Empire to fall after Nero's reign, it seems that the worldwide demographic shifts, the social erosion, and the economic ruin brought about by the modern existentialist worldview is coming about relatively quickly. The modern humanist empire is falling faster than Rome. When Augustus strengthened the nuclear family by illegalizing adultery and exiling Ovid, he may have extended the life of the empire. But most of the western governments are going the opposite direction. State after state, and nation after nation legalizes adultery, promotes no-fault divorce, and legitimizes civil unions for homosexuals. Meanwhile, international programs funded by the United States and the United Nations have worked hard to assure that Western ideas thoroughly predominate in Asia, Africa, and South America. The United Nations Population Control Program provided awards to Mexican television producers who introduced the themes of fornication, adultery, abortion, and birth control to Mexico by way of soap operas.[10] Since 1997, sixteen countries have encouraged abortion by "liberalizing" their abortion laws (including Cambodia, Columbia, Ethiopia, Iran, Portugal, Switzerland, and Thailand).[11] Nations like South Korea, China, and Japan are experiencing their own severe birth implosions thanks to the existentialist and humanist worldviews exported from the West into these Asian countries.

Hopefully, this book has adequately described the reasons for the social, political, cultural, and academic breakdown of the Western world. At the very least, I hope that those who have read this book will be able to explain to future generations what happened to Western civilization.

10. "Sabido Methodology - Background," *Population Media Center*, <http://www.populationmedia. org/what/sabido-method/> accessed on Mar. 29, 2013
11. Carmin, Lauren, "Abortion Laws Liberalized in 16 Countries Since 1998," *Guttmacher Institute Media Center*, Oct. 27, 2008, <http://www.guttmacher.org/media/nr/2008/10/27/index.html> accessed on Mar. 29, 2013

Now, what about the future?

JESUS CHRIST IS STILL A FACTOR

An astounding amount of energy was expended by the modern Nephilim against Jesus Christ. A few of them openly admitted their anti-Christ agendas (Friedrich Nietzsche, Mark Twain, and Karl Marx). All of them worked hard to undermine the authority of the revelation of Jesus Christ in the Bible. By the 20th century, John Dewey, Jean-Paul Sartre, and John Lennon truly felt that they had the upper hand in the conflict with Christ. And it may have appeared that way in 20th century England. However, notwithstanding his other unorthodox positions, John Locke did get something right. He understood the importance of Acts 2:32-35, though he failed to grasp a right perspective of the nature of Christ.

> *This Jesus hath God raised up, whereof we all are witnesses. Therefore being by the right hand of God exalted, and having received of the Father the promise of the Holy Ghost, he hath shed forth this, which ye now see and hear. For David is not ascended into the heavens: but he saith himself, The Lord said unto my Lord, Sit thou on my right hand, until I make thy foes thy footstool (Acts 2:32-35).*

It is an indisputable fact. The Lord Jesus Christ is risen from the dead, and He is reigning as sovereign Lord on the right hand of the Father, until all of His enemies are under His footstool. For the Christian, this is the historical fact by which all other previous and future events are to be understood. It is the most important historical fact of all. Marx and Nietzsche hated this historical reality, and they fought it with all that they had within them. When the enemy takes ground, strips down the churches, compromises orthodoxy, opposes righteousness, and destroys Christian culture, this serves as a test of faith to the servants of Christ who are still standing in the battlefield. Were Nietzsche, Dewey, and John Lennon correct in forecasting the end of the faith, after 2,000 years of the fixed and the final? Now is the time for stalwart faith! Now is the time to act on the assumption that Jesus Christ is on the throne. Now is the time to challenge the kings of the earth to kiss the Son, lest they perish from the way (Psalm 2).

History will prove Nietzsche wrong. Within a few more decades

Wikipedia and other academic sources will abandon the "Common Era" and revert back to the A.D. designation. However the future is viewed, there is no avoiding one stubborn, historical fact—*Jesus Christ has risen from the dead, and His kingdom will never fail.* Faithless men will put together eschatological scenarios that ignore this fact. Faithless men will minimize the antithesis or compromise with it. Faithless men will give too much credence to the antithesis and not enough to Christ. Contrary to John Lennon's premature pronouncements, this is not the end of the Christian influence in the world. It is only the beginning.

DON'T APOSTATIZE

After we have witnessed the fruits of apostasy in the lives and work of the philosophical and cultural leaders of this book, the message should be clear. *Don't apostatize from the faith.* Even if the reader is not a Christian, I exhort him not to adopt the apostate ideas that came out of the Christian West. When Muslims, Buddhists, Hindus, or Animists take on humanist ideas, they do so to the detriment of their own families and nations. Above all, follow Christ.

The forces that press the Western world towards apostasy are intense. The false prophets, or the most influential philosophers are the best the devil could produce, "to seduce, *if it were* possible, even the elect" (Mark 13:22). Nevertheless, the last words of Christ ring strong and true 1,950 years later for those who refuse to leave this faith. "And he that overcometh, and keepeth my works unto the end, to him will I give power over the nations" (Rev. 2:9). There is a faith that endures, (Heb. 10:38,39; Luke 8:13), and it rests upon the grace of God and it is rooted in the Word of God.

Western apostasy is based in human rationalism and individualism, as Emerson taught. Each man becomes his own "pope" and makes up his own religion as he goes along. With the proliferation of denominations and cults that have sprung up since the 1820s, the church has given far too much credence to Emerson's American religion, and many churches have only proven to be halfway down the road to apostasy themselves. Much of this is connected to the Emersonian revolutionary impulse to cut off the past.

To avoid apostasy, it is essential that we are first rooted in the truth of Scripture. Secondly, we should take care to deeply root ourselves in the historical Christian church. If we read anything more than the Bible, I recommend a thorough study of the apostolic fathers who wrote between A.D. 80 and A.D. 150. These men were discipled by the Apostles themselves. From their writings, we look for the unity of thought, the major emphases, and the scope of the material. These primitive saints may not have been exceedingly precise in their doctrinal definitions, but the reader can certainly ascertain the range of thought contained in their writings on the more difficult "mysteries," such as the sacraments and church order. Those who are steeped in early church history will be more balanced in their handling of doctrinal disagreements in the present. Modern day believers should also be familiar with the creeds and confessions of the historic church, especially those written during periods of reformation. These documents constitute summaries of the major battles fought against heterodoxy through the centuries.

Disunity among the brethren is as reprehensible as compromise with the antithesis. Yet another indication of the weakening of the faith is seen among professing Christians whose fellowships devolve into circular firing squads. Therefore, it is vital for the continuance of the faith that every Christian correctly discern the antithesis of the day and address it with the biblical thesis. That has been the objective of this book. By compiling a succinct sum of the writings of the powerful men who professed to hate the Christian religion, we have defined the enemy. Now, we must subscribe to what God's Word says in clear opposition to the words of Sartre, Nietzsche, Marx, Darwin, Dewey, Rousseau, and Emerson. It should not be difficult to define the ideas that are antithetical to Christ. Where the antithesis is not understood, and the thesis from God's Word is not taught in the churches, we will expect imminent apostasy. Every Christian pastor or teacher who will hang onto a relevant faith in the 21st century will most certainly teach the antithesis with clarity, drawing sharp contrasts between the centrality of man and the centrality of God— in epistemology, metaphysics, ethics, worship, and life. They will answer the antithesis with the thesis that is only to be found in the Word of God. And as they define the biblical position against the position of their enemy, they form the major battle lines between the Christian church and the anti-Christian, compromised church. At the time of this writing, the apostasy is in full swing. The antithesis reveals itself in stark colors and it is easier to identify now than ever before. Those who are uncomfortable with taking sides in the conflict and opposing the antithesis will dissolve into the apostasy of the ages. But I hope those Christians who are left will fight against these false ideas with every ounce of their strength, at every battle front, in every institution of modern life, and in every Christian home in the Western world.

Unless God brings about a major reformation of faith in the Western world, millions upon millions will probably leave the Christian church over the next generation. These are the initial results we have seen from surveys conducted by Pew Research, Barna Research, and Answers in Genesis.[12] The fire will burn. Some ministries will yield the gold, silver, and precious stones that will sustain them through the raging apostasy of the day (1 Cor. 3:11,12). Where men will stand by faith and preach strongly against the antithesis of the day, calling for repentance in mind and life, there will be something solid left upon which the church may be built in the future.

BUILDING ON NEW FOUNDATIONS

For now, the course is set towards the unraveling of Western civilization, and a worldwide readjustment is practically inevitable. But the good news is that the "great" philosophers are all dead. We have already seen the political, social, cultural, and economic ramifications of their ideas worked out into everyday life, and it will be only more obvious in the next forty years. Their bad ideas will prove themselves to be nothing but bad ideas. Descartes, Bentham, Marx, and Dewey had their shot at it. The tsunami waves of humanism have rolled over Europe and North America, and they have done their damage. We could not be more optimistic at the possibilities. The mighty waves have spent their force. Not many years hence, the waves will recede and we will have our opportunity to rebuild once more. It is time to stake out a piece of territory in the mud, and rebuild the walls on better foundations. Much of this will be pioneering work. We will need to rebuild our educational systems, our churches, our families, our economic systems, our charitable systems, and our political systems.

DECENTRALIZATION IS INEVITABLE

12. Jon Meacham, "The End of Christian America," *The Daily Beast*, Apr. 3, 2009, <http://www.thedailybeast.com/newsweek/2009/04/03/the-end-of-christian-america.html>

Every time that man has set out to "make a name for himself" by centralizing power, God has brought the towers down. This is the legacy of Babel, Egypt, and Rome. After centralization comes decentralization. Already, the cultural monopoly maintained by Hollywood and Nashville is starting to crack. Mainstream print media and television now compete with a million websites put together by a million basement operations. Thousands of young film makers are independently producing films and finding new channels for distribution. Over the last several years, the Kendrick brothers succeeded in cracking the Hollywood monopoly with an independent film production company based in a Georgia church. Their Christian-themed films have grossed over $100 million, including both box office receipts and DVD sales.[13]

While it is true that there is more decadence and nihilism in the mass media today than there was in the 1970s and 1980s, the monopoly of the media machine is fracturing. Moreover, the media produced in the 2010s contains a much broader range of thought and production value than what existed in the 1970s. Decentralization is inevitable, and this will provide exciting opportunities for hundreds of thousands of Christians who want to form new cultural trajectories and build new social systems. Within another twenty years, the centralized system will no doubt lose control of the flow of information and media. The collapse is inevitable. It is just a question of when.

For the last ten years I have built an online radio audience, reaching tens of thousands of people around the world. I take market share from the NBC, CBS, and ABC networks. This was not possible in the 1970s. For $1,000, anybody can start their own program and take more of the share that used to be controlled by a few select AM and FM frequencies in metro areas. A radio or television station like this used to cost millions, if not tens of millions of dollars to purchase.

THE EDUCATION JUGGERNAUT

Without addressing the education juggernaut, there is no winning the battles in this worldview war. These are the temples of the humanist philosophers. This is where Dewey's prophets teach, and this is where

---

13. Billy Hallowell, "How the Church Behind 'Courageous' Is Making Hollywood Blockbusters & Impacting a Generation," *The Blaze*, Oct. 9, 2001, <http://www.theblaze.com/stories/how-the-church-behind-courageous-is-making-hollywood-blockbusters-impacting-a-generation/> accessed on Mar. 29, 2013

man worships. . . himself. Should Christians and conservatives neglect to address this juggernaut, all other political and social battles will be a waste of time.

First of all, if you don't like the ideas expressed by the philosophers of the age, you don't have to follow them. You can opt out! *You don't have to play.* You can unplug yourself and your family from the matrix. To put it in a vernacular all Americans understand, you do not have to send young people from the red states into blue city colleges to be educated as blue state voters. Moreover, home education is the ultimate decentralized form of education and it is growing. According to my calculations, the homeschool population will expand to 15 million children in the United States within another decade or two.

Any worthwhile reformational program must include a rejection of the humanist form in both content and methodology. Having spent most of my adult life working in public, private, and home education, I offer a few general pointers concerning the reformation of education. My assumption is that the reader is a Christian, or sympathetic to a Christian worldview.

1. We must obliterate the dualist distinction between sacred knowledge and philosophical knowledge, once and for all. To pretend that there can be religious neutrality in education is disingenuous at best, and can only ever be treacherous to the Christian faith.

2. We must teach the fear of God as the beginning of knowledge and wisdom in every classroom and in every textbook (whether public, private, or home school).

3. We must introduce a strong understanding of the antithesis into education—especially in the literature and liberal arts classes.

4. We must prioritize the "thesis:" God's revelation (the Bible), and literature written by committed, orthodox Christians. This is the material that must be taught first, because it is primary and basic to the education of children.

5. We must avoid setting our children at the feet of unbelieving authors and philosophers until they are matured in their understanding

of a biblical worldview. When we teach non-Christian literary works, we must set the thesis against the antithesis in sharp contrast. This author is preparing a high school and college curriculum for the liberal arts student that will do just this.[14] As Western civilization crumbles, succeeding generations must understand the forces that contributed to its demise, as well as the ideas that will rebuild new cultures in the years to come.

6. We must move education towards a discipleship model that stresses the importance of nurturing faith, character, the fear of God, and life integration. Education is more than stuffing facts into the head of a student. Without a dramatic shift in *the way we educate*, there will be no hope in salvaging any other aspects of Christian civilization. It is time for Christian leaders to engage in long and hard conversations on the form of education.[15]

The present educational systems are less-and-less capable of nurturing character, inculcating reverence for God in the chemistry classroom, and equipping students to apply knowledge to real life. Rising college costs have exceeded the Consumer Price Index by a factor of four since 1985,[16] and the unemployment rate for graduates is soaring. Over half of college graduates from the last five years are unemployed or under-employed.[17] Hundreds of articles coming by way of the mainstream media protest the unwieldy college system. The liberal college monopoly is cracking, and alternative, non-traditional degree programs are practically ubiquitous. Within another ten years, the old brick and mortar colleges will be a thing of the past.

I have personally worked in the area of mentorship for over seven years, and I have found it to be a terrific way to apply knowledge and prepare young men for work in the macro economy. There are many ways that students may now take care of their book work using cost-effective, online programs. They find mentors, network into the economy, and

14. The material will be made available in textbook and workbook form as curriculum for home and school use, in the fall of 2013. Reference www.apologia.com and www.generationswithvision.com.

15. I have produced a book on the biblical philosophy of education, titled *Upgrade, the Ten Secrets to the Best Education for Your Child*, in the hopes that this will be the beginning of a new conversation on primary, secondary, and higher education.

16. Steve Odland, "College Costs out of Control," *Forbes.com*, Mar. 24, 2012 <http://www.forbes.com/sites/steveodland/2012/03/24/college-costs-are-soaring/> accessed on Mar. 29, 2013

17. Jordan Weissmann, "53% of Recent College Grads are Jobless or Underemployed—How?" *The Atlantic*, Apr. 23, 2012, <http://www.theatlantic.com/business/archive/2012/04/53-of-recent-college-grads-are-jobless-or-underemployed-how/256237/> accessed on Mar. 29, 2013

immediately apply the things they get out of the books, in real life and time. Will mentorship, family discipleship, family-based economies, homeschooling, shepherd centers, self-learning programs, and on-the-job training programs displace the humanist methods of institutionalized education that dominated the West for hundreds of years? How many times will Christians repeat the same errors of Cambridge, Harvard, Yale, and Princeton Universities? When will they learn that educational methods and content are the core of the battle in the war of the worldviews? The humanists have had their shot at it, and they have destroyed much of our world. They have done their damage. Now is the time for the Christian worldview to re-engage and to rebuild. This is our opportunity!

DESPERATE TIMES CALL FOR DESPERATE MEASURES

At the time of this writing, the American people retain total liabilities in excess of $60 trillion dollars.[18] The European economy is crumbling. Japan, the second largest economy in the world, is in long-term economic decline.[19] Assuming that John Maynard Keynes was wrong when he blew off the long term consequences of his debt-based economic theories, there will be no recovery from this economic catastrophe. If the economy will be salvaged, this nation must begin now to rebuild the entire system on sound money. However, basing these economies on sound money means the Western world will have to give up on the existentialist worldview that frames the way they think and live. And that probably won't happen anytime too soon.

The demographic conditions in the Western world portend even worse times ahead. Birth rates are imploding in almost every developed nation around the world, including the United States. Some time before 2050, it seems that the demographic implosions will ruin the economies of almost every first and second-world nation. Based on data collected from 1950 forwards, the ratio of retiree-to-worker is expected to fall from 12:1 to 1:1 by 2050 in countries like South Korea and Japan. In America,

---

18. Justin Menza, "US's $60 Trillion Debt Burden Rivals That of Greece: Gross," *CNBC*, Oct. 12, 2012 <http://www.cnbc.com/id/49258472/US039s_60_Trillion_Debt_Burden_Rivals_That_of_Greece_Gross> accessed on Mar. 29, 2013

19. Charles Riley, "Japan's Economy Slips into Recession," *CNN Money*, Dec. 10, 2012 <http://money.cnn.com/2012/12/10/news/economy/japan-gdp-recession/index.html> accessed on Mar. 29, 2013

the ratio is predicted to fall from 7:1 to 2:1 during the same time period.[20]

The year 2011 was a significant milestone in the collapse of the American empire. It was the year that the first of the baby boom generation reached retirement age; and for the first time since its inception, the Social Security fund paid out more than it received in taxes.[21] Not to forget, it was the baby boom generation that eliminated 80 million of their children by abortion and the abortifacient birth control pill since 1960. This is also the generation that has incurred 50% more debt per capita than the silent generation (upon retirement).[22] The average family today carries at least five times more household debt as a percentage of the Gross National Income as those who lived 100 years ago. Since the 1950s, the Western world has consumed the capital from previous generations, increased the debt load on future generations and created a demographic implosion. They've already maximized on the efficiency of technology, automation, and computerization as much as possible. It is a perfect storm.

With bankruptcy looming, the worker-to-retiree ratio cut significantly, and the government welfare burden growing, we hope that the character of the millennial generation is sufficient to meet the severe challenges ahead; but that, of course, is only a dream. Thanks to Jean-Paul Sartre's existentialism and Margaret Sanger's sexual revolution, the character of each successive generation is in far worse shape than previous generations. The fatherless ratio for the current generation is seven times worse than it was forty years ago. The shack-up rate (those living out of wedlock) is ten times what it was in the 1970s. According to a recent *Newsweek* article, 70% of young men are not "grown up" at 30 years of age (an increase from 30% in 1970).[23] They play their computer games while Rome burns. What happens to an economy when 80 million baby boomers are playing golf while the thirty-somethings are playing computer games? There comes a point at which the philosophies of nihilism, existentialism, and

20. Reference www.PopulationPyramid.net.

21. Stephen Dinan, "Social Security in the Red This Year," *Washington Times*, Aug. 5, 2010, <http://www.washingtontimes.com/news/2010/aug/5/social-security-red-first-time-ever/> accessed on Mar. 29, 2013

22. Eric D. Beinhocker, and Diana Farrell, and Ezra Greenberg, "Why Baby Boomers Will Need to Work Longer," *McKinsey Quarterly*, Nov. 2008, <http://www.mckinseyquarterly.com/Economic_Studies/Country_Reports/Why_baby_boomers_will_need_to_work_longer_2234> accessed on Mar. 29, 2013

23. "Why Young Men Delay Adulthood," *Newsweek Magazine*, August 30, 2008, <http://www.newsweek.com/id/156372> accessed on Mar. 29, 2013

pragmatism can no longer provide the motivation and the social energy to sustain a civilization, and young men are getting the message by osmosis.

For the time being, women will attempt to salvage the economic situation. According to some reports, women now make up a higher percentage of the work force than men.[24] Young women are almost twice as likely than men to earn a college degree by age 23.[25] But with the combined effect of birth implosions and the absence of manhood, these feeble attempts will do little to extend the life of our civilization.

This is what the end of Western civilization looks like. What started humanist turned Christian. What became Christian turned back to humanism, and now it is dying. The humanist worldview that precipitated the two major collapses in the Western world proves itself to be rotten at the core. If the foundations are rotted away, all of its institutions must be reworked from the bottom up. In addition to a serious reconstruction of education, we will need to reorder economies, culture, church life, and family life.

The solutions are simple, though not necessarily easy to implement. Above all, we will need fathers, men with a vision to disciple their children in the Word of God, as they sit in the house, as they walk by the way, as they rise up, and as they lie down (Deut. 6:7). We need men to mentor boys into men. Without older men investing themselves in the mentorship of young men, our future families, churches, and economies *will not survive*. This is not hyperbole or exaggeration. As a pastor, a mentor, an educator, a cultural analyst, and a national speaker who has worked in churches and schools for many years, I know this to be the case. Tens of thousands of mature men are needed to sacrifice their time to disciple young men. Where Sartre has killed our relationships, where cold institutions create isolation, where programs displace relational human connections, where Facebook and texting have displaced true friendship, it is time to salvage true community. The relational reformer will always take the opportunity to trade his resources for authentic relationships where self-sacrificing love can express itself.

We must also establish family-based economies, where there will be maximum opportunity for fathers to mentor their sons as they sit in the

24. Hanna Rosin, "The End of Men," *The Atlantic*, Jun. 8, 2010 <http://www.theatlantic.com/magazine/archive/2010/07/the-end-of-men/308135/> accessed on Mar. 29, 2013

25. "Women More Likely to Earn a College Degree by Age 23," *USA News*, Feb. 16, 2011 <http://www.usnews.com/opinion/articles/2011/02/16/women-more-likely-to-earn-a-college-degree-by-age-23> accessed on Mar. 29, 2013

house, as they walk by the way, as they plow the fields, and work their businesses.

For those who have wasted their lives seeking ultimate purpose in pleasure, money, man, humanist philosophies, and man-centered empires, they will need to find their meaning in God and His purposes. "Seek His kingdom first and His righteousness, and all these things will be added unto you." (Matt. 6:33). Worship God, not money. Get out of debt, and stop living beyond your means.

It is doubtful that Western socialism will last as long as the communists did. This economy is too unstable. The Keynesian, debt-ridden economies cannot sustain the demands of a character-less, welfare state. Whether Social Security and socialized medicine will survive for the next ten years, twenty years, or thirty years, those with the most foresight will give up on the socialist vision now. This may be happening already. Only 29% of Americans have confidence in the public schools, down from 58% in the 1970s.[26] John Dewey's messianic vision for American public education is fast losing ground. Visionary, forward-looking men and women are abandoning these humanist systems in favor of privatized, Christian education models.

God-honoring Christians are also working on charitable systems that are voluntary, local, relational, and accountable. Public welfare (including Social Security, food stamps, etc.) is pseudo-charity that corrupts family relationships, destroys fatherhood, erodes self-government and the character of the nation, and creates more illegitimacy with every generation. Already a number of biblical churches are working hard to rebuild meaningful charitable programs for widows and orphans, systems that are completely free from government funding and control. In the wake of socialist medicine, this is a good time to abandon the government-mandated insurance programs and public health programs in favor of Christian medical sharing ministries like Samaritan Ministries.[27] Thankfully, there are still legal options for those who oppose government rationing, forced abortions of Down syndrome babies, and euthanasia of the elderly.

26. Jeffrey M. Jones, "Confidence in US Public Schools at New Low," *Gallup Politics*, Jun. 20, 2012, <http://www.gallup.com/poll/155258/confidence-public-schools-new-low.aspx> accessed on Mar. 29, 2013
27. Kenneth Artz, "Christian Health Sharing Grows in Wake of Obamacare," *Heartland*, Mar. 8, 2012, <http://news.heartland.org/newspaper-article/2012/03/08/christian-health-sharing-grows-wake-obamacare> accessed on Mar. 29, 2013

Wherever Christians abandon the dystopian ideas of humanism and existentialism, we will find islands of freedom, relational community, voluntary charity, mentorship, and fruitful families and economies. There is hope for the future here. Instead of consuming their children's inheritance and driving their grandchildren into debt, these families are having babies, building their economies, and passing on a heritage of faith, hope, and character. There is a vision for the future among these families.

While the rest of the world is spending their great-grandchildren into debt, we are getting out of debt and saving an inheritance for our children.

While the rest of the world is trusting in government social security and the Federal Reserve System, we are trusting in God and preparing charitable systems to help widows and orphans ourselves.

While the rest of the world is euthanizing their elderly and spending their children's inheritance, our families are taking care of parents in their old age and passing an inheritance from one generation to the next.

While the rest of the world is aborting their children, we are adopting them.

While the rest of the world's birth rates are imploding to 0.8, we are averaging a birth rate of 4.0 because we have hope and vision for a future.

While the rest of the world is destroying the character of their youth with toxic cultural systems and teen peer groups, we are creating our own life-nurturing culture that conforms to God's laws.

While the rest of the world is processing their kids through John Dewey's massive educational institutions controlled by powerful governments, we are opening private discipleship centers and mentoring young men and women in faith and character.

While the rest of the world has abandoned all possibility for certainty, for hope, and for meaning in their Nietzschean wasteland, our children and grandchildren are full of faith, hope, and joy!

Time is the great arbiter. The bankruptcy of the ideas espoused by the great philosophers will be increasingly evident in the next forty years. Their ideas do not have what it takes to sustain society and life on earth. They cannot hold the weight of the empires built upon them. In the years to come, the fruits of the prophets will be evident to all. "For there is nothing covered that shall not be revealed; neither hid, that shall not be known" (Luke 12:2). If we train our children in knowledge that is rooted in the fear of God, and in the firm hope of the resurrection of Jesus Christ, then our children will be the ones motivated enough to rebuild our broken-down systems. Our children will plant gardens in the ashes of what used to be called "Western Civilization."

> "And they that shall be of thee shall build the old waste places: thou shalt raise up the foundations of many generations; and thou shalt be called, The repairer of the breach, The restorer of paths to dwell in" (Is. 58:12).

SELECT BIBLIOGRAPHY

BIOGRAPHICAL AND HISTORICAL WORKS

Arkinson, Charles Milner. *Jeremy Bentham: His Life and Work.*
London: Methuen, 1905.

Bergman, Jerry. *The Dark Side of Charles Darwin.*
Green Forest: Master Books, 2011.

Cohen-Salal, Annie. *Jean-Paul Sartre: A Life.*
New York: Random House, 1987.

Cranston, Maurice. *John Locke: A Biography.*
London: Longman, Green, 1959.

Deetz, James & Patricia Scott. *The Times of Their Lives, Life
and Love, and Death in Plymouth Colony.*
New York: Anchor Books, 2000.

Durant, Will and Ariel. *Rousseau and Revolution.*
New York: Simon & Schuster, 1967.

Hall, Michael G. *The Last American Puritan: The Life of Increase Mather.*
Middletown: Wesleyan University Press, 1985.

Honan, Park. *Christopher Marlow, Poet or Spy.*
New York: Oxford University Press, 2005.

Johnson, Paul. *Intellectuals.*
New York: Harper & Row, 1989.

Jones, E. Michael. *Dionysos Rising: The Birth of Cultural Revolution out of the Spirit of Music.*
San Francisco: Ignatius, 1994.

Leithart, Peter J. *Brightest Heaven of Invention: A Christian Guide to Six Shakespeare Plays.*
Moscow: Canon Press, 1996.

Mellow, James R. *Nathaniel Hawthorne in His Times.*
Boston: Houghton Mifflin, 1980.

—. *Hemingway: A Life Without Consequences.*
Boston: Houghton Mifflin, 1992.

Miller, Edward Haviland. *Salem is my Dwelling Place, A Life of Nathaniel Hawthorne.*
Iowa City: University of Iowa Press, 1991.

Murray, Iain. *The Undercover Revolution.*
Edinburgh: Banner of Truth, 2009.

Parini, Jay. *John Steinbeck: A Biography.*
New York: Henry Holt, 1995.

Porte, Joel. *Emerson in His Journals.*
Cambridge: Harvard University Press, 1982.

Powers, Ron. *Mark Twain: A Life.*
New York: Simon & Schuster, 2005.

Scott, Otto. *Robespierre: The Fool as Revolutionary.*
Windsor: The Reformer, 1995.

Shelden, Michael. *Mark Twain: Man in White.*
New York: Random House, 2010.

Smith, Christopher Murray Upham. *The Genius of Erasmus Darwin.*
Burlington: Ashgate Publishing, 2005.

Wiker, Benjamin. *Ten Books that Screwed up the World and Five that Didn't Help.*
New York: Regnery, 2008.

Wineapple, Brenda. *Hawthorne: A Life.*
New York: Alfred A. Knopf. 2003.

CHRISTIAN WORKS

Saint Augustine, *Confessions*.
  Translated by Albert C. Outler. Peabody: Hendrickson, 2004.
Pascal, Blaise. *Pensees*.
  Translated by A.J. Krailsheimer. New York: Penguin, 1995.
Pearcey, Nancy. *Saving Leonardo: A Call to Resist the Secular Assault on Minds, Morals, and Meaning*.
  Nashville: Broadman & Holman, 2010.
~~. *Total Truth: Liberating Christianity from its Cultural Captivity*.
  Wheaton: Crossway, 2005.
Rushdoony, Rousas John. *Revolt Against Maturity*.
  Vallecito: Ross House, 1978.
~~. *To Be As God: A Study of Modern Thought since the Marquis de Sade*.
  Vallecito: Ross House, 2003.
Schaeffer, Francis. *How Should We Then Live?: The Rise and Decline of Western Thought & Culture*.
  Wheaton: Crossway, 2005.